Facing the Khmer Rouge

Genocide, Political Violence, Human Rights Series

Edited by Alexander Laban Hinton, Stephen Eric Bronner,
Aldo Civico, and Nela Navarro

Facing the Khmer Rouge

A Cambodian Journey

RONNIE YIMSUT

FOREWORD BY DAVID P. CHANDLER, PH.D.

AFTERWORD BY DANIEL SAVIN, M.D.

RUTGERS UNIVERSITY PRESS

NEW BRUNSWICK, NEW JERSEY, AND LONDON

LIBRARY OF CONGRESS CATALOGING-IN-PUBLICATION DATA

Yimsut, Ronnie, 1961–
  Facing the Khmer Rouge : a Cambodian journey / Ronnie Yimsut ; foreword by
David Chandler ; conclusion by Daniel Savin.
    p. cm. — (Genocide, political violence, human rights series)
  Includes bibliographical references and index.
  ISBN 978-0-8135-5151-7 (hardcover : alk. paper) — ISBN 978-0-8135-5152-4
(pbk. : alk. paper)
    1. Yimsut, Ronnie, 1961– 2. Cambodian Americans—Biography. 3. Refugees—
United States—Biography. 4. Siemrĕab (Cambodia)—Biography. 5. Cambodia—
History—1975–1979—Biography. 6. Genocide—Cambodia—History—20th century.
7. Parti communiste du Kampuchea—History. 8. Cambodia—Politics and
government—1975–1979. I. Title.
  E184.K45Y56 2011
  959.604′2—dc22   2011001099

A British Cataloging-in-Publication record for this book is available
from the British Library.

Visit our Web site: http://rutgerspress.rutgers.edu

Manufactured in the United States of America

REMEMBERING THE LOST

This book I dedicate to my beloved family, including my parents and siblings who did not survive the three years, eight months, and twenty days of terror under the Khmer Rouge. I dedicate this book to the memory of my childhood friends, to my neighbors, and to the countless innocents who died between April 17, 1975, and January 7, 1979, under that bloodthirsty communist regime. Be at peace; I am your voice.

I dedicate this book to those who are so traumatized and who are still suffering to this day the burden of their pain and tragic memories. May you find peace, hope, and healing within. May you find compassion, understanding, and respect from those who have not had your pain. More importantly, may you find enough courage to go on.

Finally, I dedicate this book to the Khmer, my brave people. We have endured so much, individually and collectively.

I love you so dearly, still.

CONTENTS

FOREWORD

Ronnie Yimsut's absorbing and passionate memoir deals with his life before, during, and after the Khmer Rouge era (1975–1979). It fits neatly into a genre of survivor narratives that have emerged from Cambodian authors since the 1970s, but it surpasses many of them in terms of its breadth of focus, its depth of feeling, and the clarity of its prose.

Like many narratives in the genre, *Facing the Khmer Rouge: A Cambodian Journey* has an almost mythic three-part structure that might be labeled Idyll, Horror, and Recovery. Yimsut tells the story of a large, relatively prosperous, and happy Cambodian family that suffered horrendous losses under the Khmer Rouge. Several of them, including Yimsut's mother, were brutally put to death before Yimsut fled the scene, found refuge in the United States, and eventually had the time and encouragement to write this book.

Ronnie Yimsut was born in 1961 into Cambodia's small, predominantly urban middle class. His father was a provincial official and part-time school-teacher in the town of Siem Reap. Because people in the middle class were the major beneficiaries of prerevolutionary Khmer society, they were singled out for harsh treatment by the (recovering bourgeois) leaders of the Khmer Rouge.

Most other writers of Cambodian survival narratives were also members of the middle class. Almost all of them hailed from Phnom Penh. They were thrown off balance in April 1975 by their exile to rural areas, where they were spurned by local people and proved largely inept at agricultural tasks. Yimsut, on the other hand, was raised in Siem Reap, which in the 1960s was still a smallish town. His semirural boyhood gave him skills (such as fishing and plant recognition) that made it slightly easier for him to cope with life under the Khmer Rouge than it was for urban refugees.

Where his narrative differs from many others and what makes it in more compelling, I believe, is that by waiting until 2011 to publish it, Yimsut has been able to place the trauma of his Khmer Rouge experiences into the larger pattern of his life and also alongside patterns in Cambodian history before and since.

The chapters that deal with his family's ordeal are the most vivid, wrenching, and passionate in the book, but they are its centerpiece rather than its raison d'être. The book you're about to read, in other words, is as much about

Yimsut's own resilience, his keen observational skills, and his personal "journey into light" as it is about his sufferings and those of his family under the Khmer Rouge. I found the chapters about his breathtaking escape to Thailand in 1978, his months on the Thai-Cambodian border, and his rewarding absorption into life in the United States as perceptive and readable as any others in the book. The closing pages recount his frequent returns to Cambodia since 1992 and the work he continues to do to help his fellow Khmer.

The trajectory of the book, like Yimsut's life so far, feeds into a familiar, partly misleading narrative of Cambodian history since the 1960s. This narrative reflects the way in which many middle-class Cambodian survivors of the Khmer Rouge era have constructed their country's history to coincide and harmonize with their personal experiences, often conceived in the triadic pattern (idyll, horror, recovery) that I mentioned above.

This pleasing, exculpatory construction begs a range of questions. Beneficiaries of the Khmer Rouge period, for one thing, including Cambodia's premier, Hun Sen, and the former Khmer Rouge leaders now on trial in Phnom Penh, don't see the 1960s as idyllic or the Khmer Rouge period as impenetrably dark. What's more, for many survivors in Cambodia and overseas, wherever they stood, politically, in the 1970s, the "recovery" (aside from the welcome end of fighting in the late 1990s) has been uneven or nonexistent. Aside from Khieu Samphan, the former Khmer Rouge chief of state, now facing trial in Phnom Penh, no beneficiaries of the Khmer Rouge period have published memoirs of their lives. Were they to do so, the three-part pattern of their books might fall into sections labeled Injustice, Empowerment, and What Came Later. The readership for such books would probably be minimal, but if we are to get a balanced and accurate view of recent Cambodian history, we have to remember that it has many voices, including those of people who have chosen, perhaps prudently, to remain silent. None of these issues, to be sure, lessens the immense value of Yimsut's book.

Another aspect of survivor narratives interests me more than their understandably subjective view of national history. Reading these narratives, I'm struck by the fact that the authors are writing in linear, biographical terms that were unfamiliar to most Khmer before the 1970s. It could be argued, in fact, that the Khmer Rouge introduced Cambodians to the concepts and importance of historical and biographical thinking. Whether the process was accelerated by their insistence that people repeatedly compose autobiographies, or *pravat'rup*, or has sprung from the necessity of survivors telling a personal story is impossible to determine. In any case, autobiographies were almost nonexistent before the 1970s, when the Khmer Rouge regime made repeated biographical demands on people and force-fed them with historical narratives of a simplistic, dialectical sort. Khmer Rouge officials referred to a merciless "wheel of history" and filled their speeches with visions of linear progress. When a Khmer Rouge spokesman in 1975 stated that "2,000 years of history . . . had ended" he meant that Cambodian history would now be written in a new way, after prerevolutionary, "feudal" social relations and injustices had been swept aside.

To engage with the future toward which the Khmer Rouge were driving their fellow Cambodians, it was necessary for Khmer Rouge officials to talk about how and why Cambodia had reached a point where a new kind of history could be constructed, based on continuous struggle rather than, as previously, on consensus. The darkness the people had allegedly passed through in "feudal" times needed to be spelled out, and so did the ongoing illumination that the revolution could provide. For loyal revolutionaries, the first parts of Yimsut's book, Idyll and Horror, were reversed. A third stage had not yet come into view.

In September 1977, Pol Pot delivered a five-hour speech to the Khmer Rouge faithful. The speech was concerned almost exclusively with his reading of Cambodian history, which he saw in terms of past injustices and the "inevitable" Cambodian communist victory. It's hard to imagine Prince Sihanouk, who had been overthrown as Cambodia's chief of state in 1970, or his successor, General Lon Nol, overthrown in 1975 by the Khmer Rouge, staying "on message" for that long, or thinking that correct notions of history had any connection with the way in which they exercised power.

Instead, following the lead of his French mentors, Prince Sihanouk often spoke admiringly about Cambodia's medieval empire, known popularly today as Angkor, which he conceived of as a benevolent and peaceable kingdom, like his own. He spoke even more warmly about Cambodia after independence, since his own empowerment. He said almost nothing about the centuries that had intervened, and they were not dealt with in Cambodian schools. Lon Nol saw Khmer history as a cloudy struggle between the Cambodian "race" and the "infidel" Vietnamese, a theme revived by Pol Pot in the last year of the Khmer Rouge regime. When he writes about the Sihanouk era or the Lon Nol regime, Yimsut's narrative conveys some of these interpretations.

Hun Sen, for his part, seems indifferent to the importance of history. In 1998 he admonished people to "dig a hole and bury their past" as far as the Khmer Rouge period was concerned, and more generally he seems to believe that significant Cambodian history only began in 1979, in the wake of the Vietnamese invasion. Nonetheless, anecdotal evidence suggests that the Cambodian reading public in 2010 is more interested in Cambodia's past than Hun Sen appears to be. People are also beginning to see the Khmer Rouge years no longer as an inexplicable, "un-Cambodian" horror but as part of a longer, continuous national story that needs to be explored in order to be understood.

By covering half a century of his life, Ronnie Yimsut's appealing memoir takes a long view but makes no pretense of being a history of anything other than his own experiences. Nonetheless, as we travel with him from his idyllic childhood, through a stretch of horrific darkness, into a sunnier period of middle age, we participate at second hand in the unfolding and often tragic history of Cambodia as well as in the pleasing, admirable, and courageous story of a single life.

David P. Chandler
Professor Emeritus of History,
Monash University, Victoria, Australia

PREFACE: BETWEEN WORLDS

When Americans or Cambodians ask me, "Where are you from?" or "What nationality are you?" their insistent curiosity is demanding, like an interrogation, a test of loyalty. My answers are prefaced with hesitation perhaps because I want the best answer but I'm unsure what it is.

This book is an attempt at a complete answer. My truth is difficult. You see, I don't feel entirely Cambodian or completely American. Cambodia is my birthplace, with the Khmer culture always deep in my psyche, but America is my home and my life. How do I give a simple answer to these questions?

My children are luckier. As they go through daycare, schools, neighborhoods, friendships, and jobs, they'll hear those questions but they know they are Americans; they won't be stumped. Otherwise, I hope this book will help them or, at least, remind their generation that some things must not, should not, be forgotten.

I'm into my twenty-fourth year as a professional landscape architect for the USDA Forest Service. In 1988, the University of Oregon granted me a degree in landscape architecture focusing on environmental planning and design. I spent most of my career in Bend, Oregon. Today my family and I live in Greenfield, Wisconsin, in a two-story wooden house with a porch in front. Programmable water sprinklers water the little garden and the yard in front. The kitchen countertops are made of marble. The stainless steel sinks have hot and cold water and a switch chops up garbage. The living room is filled with compact discs, DVDs, and tapes, with a lazy couch and a huge flat-screen TV. The study has a computer with wireless access. Outside, my remote control opens and closes the garage, which has two late-model cars, tools, shoes, and boxes of stuff. Summer and winter clothes are packed tightly and neatly in several closets. There are bags and shoes, toys, bedspreads and towels, underwear and toiletries for each one of us. In short, we have just about everything that an average American household has, and a whole lot more.

Our days are consumed by routines and discoveries, by traffic and tire chains, by food and entertainment. It's such a good life in America that I can almost forget the swarms of flies on dead bodies or the boy soldiers who attempted to murder me near the shores of Tonle Sap Lake, when I was barely fifteen.

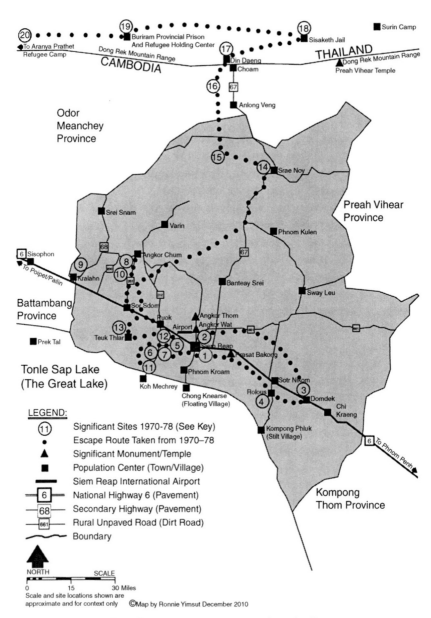

LEGEND:

- (11) Significant Sites 1970-78 (See Key)
- • Escape Route Taken from 1970–78
- ▲ Significant Monument/Temple
- ■ Population Center (Town/Village)
- ▬ Siem Reap International Airport
- 6 National Highway 6 (Pavement)
- 68 Secondary Highway (Pavement)
- 661 Rural Unpaved Road (Dirt Road)
- ～ Boundary

NORTH   SCALE
0   15   30 Miles
Scale and site locations shown are
approximate and for context only   ©Map by Ronnie Yimsut December 2010

Siem Reap Province, Kingdom of Cambodia

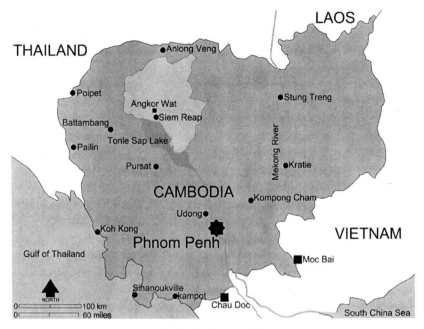

Cambodia Context Map

KEY: Significant Sites in Cambodia (1970 to 1978)

No.	Name
I	Wat Damnak
2	Sala Komrou
3	Domdek
4	Rolous
5	Krobey Riel
6	Keo Poeur
7	Kok Poh and Kork Putrea
8	Tapang
9	Kralahn
IO	Wat Yieng
II	Ta Source Hill
I2	Dorn Swar
I3	Prey Roniem
I4	Srae Noy
I5	Resin Mountain
I6	Deep Northern Jungle
I7	Din Daeng Village
I8	Sisaketh Jail
I9	Buriram Provincial Prison and Refugee Holding Center
20	Aranya Prathet Refugee Camp

For many years I denied my memories. In pursuit of the great American dream, I pushed away the haunting nightmares of the Khmer Rouge and I ignored those soft images of family now lost. Instead of examining my roots, I pressed ahead.

Eventually I invited the memories back in. My fear of the terrifying images was overridden by the drive to revisit my past, Cambodia's past. I decided that I must give voice to my intimate witness to the tragedies, to the genocidal images burned into my mind. Even harder, I had to go back and recall the sweet innocence of my family experiences before the war.

I remembered with fondness my childhood in Siem Reap, an agricultural town near the famous Angkor Wat temples and the Tonle Sap Lake. I learned to read and write at Wat Damnak, later going to Sala Komrou. I was only nine when war forced Siem Reap's citizens into the Angkor Wat temples for shelter.

Shortly after the Khmer Rouge's takeover of our town, I was in Krobey Riel, a few miles away. Angkar began to rule our lives. Over the years we were forced to relocate to the flood plains of Keo Poeur, the village of Kork Putrea, and the remote town known as Tapang. I worked on a massive canal at Ta Source Hill, not far from Tonle Sap Lake.

My escape at age fifteen took me from a haystack in Dorn Swar to the flooded forests of Prey Roniem; from huge trees on Resin Mountain to the deep northern jungle. My group and I finally ascended the Dong Rek Mountain Range to reach Thailand.

For being refugees, we were sent to Sisaket Provincial Jail, Buriram Provincial Prison, and then the holding center. Eventually we found our way to the Aranyaprathet Refugee Camp, from which I immigrated to the United States. I was not quite sixteen. I lived with my cousins in Washington, D.C., before moving to Seattle, Washington; Beaverton, Oregon; and then Eugene, Oregon. It was especially during this time that I excelled at blocking out my memories. You see, for fourteen years, I foolishly tried to ignore and hide from my past. I lived in tremendous physical pain and emotional suffering. Nightmares so tormented me that, at one time or another, I contemplated suicide as an easy way out. Fortunately, I could not muster enough courage.

Some people ask how I remembered so much detail. I started writing about my experiences in the refugee camp and I continued writing after I arrived in America. In revisiting my old recorded memories and writing this book, I ripped open old wounds that never really healed. It was terrible, so horrible of a torture to write out my memories. What kept me going was knowing that I had to express memories or die. Soon after I wrote the first paragraphs, the dam broke. I cried, reliving memories of good and bad times. For days, I couldn't sleep. I cried myself to sleep and woke up shivering, in tears. The anguish and pain were as real as the day they happened. Even as I write these words, that long-ago event feels like yesterday.

Over the next several years I found ways to cope. I faced issues that shaped me. I spoke out and wrote to people. The more I shared my pain, the better I felt. I encouraged others to confront their own pasts. I dared them.

I went to Cambodia where my tragic story began. I wanted the story to end there, where it all began . . . not so long ago. I refused to shut up and I also refused to give up.

The book you hold in your hands details memories forged at a time of great upheaval and crisis. My story is also a call for justice, and as such it is shaped and informed by the present situation in Cambodia. I have done my best to accurately capture the details of my experiences and confirm historical facts, and I am grateful to those who have helped me focus and occasionally correct my account. If errors exist they are mine and mine alone. I stand behind the truth of the events and memories. I hope that if I've made any mistakes, they will be forgiven.

Of course, everyone views events in unique ways, and I know that others will have their own tales to tell. Most of my family members perished during the Khmer Rouge era; my hope is that this story accounts for some of their lived sorrows and joys. Other Cambodians survived and migrated to America, each with his or her own stories to pass on. Surely these collective tales will add up to the truth of the Cambodian-American journey.

That is what I want.

This is who I am. This is a tale from a modern-day genocide survivor.

Ronnie Yimsut
Milwaukee, Wisconsin, February 2011

ACKNOWLEDGMENTS:
A BOOK IS BORN

This book was born out of the unrelated acts of people separated by different times and places. The first were my parents, who created laughter and unconditional love through our darkest, bitterest hours. Then came my siblings, who were there in good and in bad times. The memories they left are the foundations of this book.

Min Moeun, Peth Doeum, and Chea Sek rescued me, protected me, and helped me to escape Cambodia and thus death. This book is here because they existed and cared enough to give me a helping hand.

Out of the Thailand refugee camp to America, Cousin Ang Khen Chen and her husband Chun Chen supported me, opened their home to me, and became my foster parents. My time with them nurtured the rage and skills that created this book.

Friends touched my life in different ways. Brian T. Ellis, Bob Fonda, Phillipe Poulin, Brad and Mary Perkins, the late Dr. John Stephens and his wonderful family, the late Dr. and Mrs. Jan J. Muller, the late Mr. and Mrs. David Roach, the late David A. Linsdell, and so many others who had inspired me to finish this book were all part of the story.

I am particularly and extremely grateful to Pamela Denchfield and Jaime Cabrera, my two fabulous editors. They invested much of their time and energy to help shape and polish this book. Also, special appreciation goes to Dr. David P. Chandler, Dr. Craig Etcheson, Dr. Alex Hinton, Dr. Dan Savin, (the dearly departed) Dith Pran, Kim DePaul, Les Moscoso, Helen Maffei, Youk Chhang, Loung Ung, Reach Sambath, and countless extraordinary others who read the first drafts. Generous with time and knowledge, they helped much to ease this book's birth.

Above all, I am grateful to Thavy, my dear wife of twenty-five years, who gave me unconditional love and support, without which I would not have made it this far.

Oaur khun chran (thank you very much).

FAMILY TREE OF RANACHITH ("RONNIE") YIMSUT

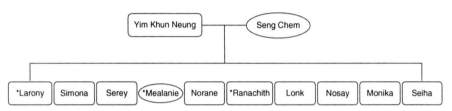

*The only known survivors of the Khmer Rouge genocide. (The rectangles indicate males and the ovals are females.)

CHRONOLOGY

Cambodia

1941 Prince Norodom Sihanouk is enthroned by Cambodia's French rulers.

1953 Prince Sihanouk succeeds in obtaining the country's independence from France.

1958 Sihanouk, who earlier abdicated his royal title to become politically active, forms a political party called Sangkum Reastr Niyum and wins office by a landslide. Sihanouk coins the term "Khmer Rouge" for the fringe Cambodian communist group, which takes to the forest for protection from state government persecution.

1963 In an effort to maintain neutrality as the war in Vietnam escalates, Sihanouk rejects American aid and severs ties with South Vietnam.

1965–70 Vietnamese communists set up sanctuaries inside Cambodia's borders.

1969 Sihanouk resumes diplomatic relations with the United States. America begins secret bombing of Vietnamese communist sanctuaries inside Cambodia.

1970 With CIA's backing, Lon Nol overthrows Sihanouk and establishes the Khmer Republic. Sihanouk issues appeals to Cambodians to join the Khmer Rouge and defeat Lon Nol. The rag-tag Khmer Rouge forces increase substantially and soon occupy half of Cambodia.

1975 The Khmer Rouge captures the capital city of Phnom Penh and all other populated areas of the country. They abolish money and prohibit religion and education. The cities' populations were soon forced to relocate to the hinterlands.

1977 The Khmer Rouge begins internal purges across the country.

1979 The Vietnamese army takes over Cambodia. Khmer Rouge defectors are in power; Hun Sen is appointed as foreign minister. The name of the country is changed to the People's Republic of Kampuchea. The Khmer Rouge continues its efforts to retake villages and towns; guerrilla fighting continues for ten years. By the end of the Khmer Rouge regime, 1.7 million have perished.

1989	The Cambodian government (headed by Hun Sen as prime minister) renounces communism. The last Vietnamese troops withdraw. The Khmer Rouge cadres continue to fight for power.
1991	The Paris Peace Agreements end the fighting among the state, Khmer Rouge, and other forces. The United Nations Transitional Authority of Cambodia (UNTAC) is established.
1993	Cambodia holds its first elections since the 1970s; Sihanouk's son Ranariddh wins the prime minister position but Hun Sen rejects the results. Under threat of renewed civil war, Ranariddh agrees to share power. The world's first co–prime ministers are created in Cambodia.
1997	Hun Sen's forces wrestle complete power from Ranariddh, killing many in opponents in the process.
1998	Discussing his role in leading the Khmer Rouge, known as one of humankind's most notorious regimes that killed millions, Pol Pot says, from his deathbed, "My conscience is clear." Pol Pot dies; his body is cremated without an autopsy.
2003–present	Hun Sen and his Cambodian People's Party rule Cambodia with impunity and with very little opposition.

Ranachith ("Ronnie") Yimsut

1961	Ranachith is born on an unknown date in the Year of the Ox, at the family's home by the Siem Reap River. He is his parents' sixth child.
1966	Ranachith begins kindergarten at Wat Damnak in Siem Reap.
1969	The family moves into their new home a few miles away, closer to Angkor Wat and to the forest. Ranachith attends classes at Sala Komrou in Siem Reap.
1970	The school principal is in trouble with the new regime of Lon Nol's Khmer Republic. Vietcong soldiers ask Ranachith's family and others to leave town. Eldest brother Larony is part of Lon Nol's special forces; Ranachith's father and two other brothers are conscripted by the town militia. Ranachith begins to experience life as a refugee, outside Siem Reap and even in his own neighborhood.
1971	A twelve-year-old school friend, Lan, is conscripted into Lon Nol's army. A relative is ambushed by Khmer Rouge soldiers just miles out of Siem Reap.
1973	The local market is shelled. Ranachith starts high school; one day he is pushed into a protest that becomes a looting of Siem Reap stores downtown. School operation is sporadic.
1974	The family hosts a wedding ceremony for Serey.

1975–77	The family receives news of Larony's hospitalization in Phnom Penh. The Khmer Rouge takes over Siem Reap; looting occurs. Ranachith joins Serey in Krobey Riel. Later he finds his town empty. The Khmer Rouge bans money; forced weddings are rumored. Eventually the Khmer Rouge forbids private cooking and restricts travel. Ranachith and others are ordered to dig canals, and to fish, tend to rice fields, or do other labor.
Dec. 1977	Ranachith finds long-lost family members on the march to certain death. He experiences a massacre at Ta Source Hill. Left for dead, he awakens hours later, only to see unspeakable horrors all around him.
Jan.–Feb. 1978	On a crutch, Ranachith leaves the shallow graves searching for food, water, and shelter from the Khmer Rouge executioners pursuing him. He travels through Kok Poh, Krobey Riel, Dorn Swar, and Prey Roniem. He joins rebels in plotting an escape from the country. The small group's fifteen-day journey takes them through Srae Noy, Resin Mountain, and the deep northern jungle to the foot of the Dong Rek Mountain Range bordering Thailand.
Feb.–Oct. 1978	Ranachith and his three friends are put in Thai jail but they eventually reach the Aranya Prathet Refugee Camp, where Ranachith is sponsored for U.S. immigration by a distant relative in the United States. Initially ambivalent because he seeks revenge against the Khmer Rouge, Ranachith eventually decides to emigrate.
1978–80	Ranachith is welcomed into Cousin Ang Khen's home in Arlington, Virginia, a suburb of Washington, D.C., where he attends Wakefield High School as "Ronnie" and immerses himself in American language and culture. However, traumatic memories continue to haunt him during his sleep.
1980	In a quest for solitude, Ranachith leaves his cousin's home and Washington, D.C. In Seattle he finds friends from the refugee camp. Soon he joins a friend in a trip to Beaverton, Oregon, where he stays for many years.
1982	Ranachith graduates from Beaverton High School.
1983	Ranachith and Thavy become engaged in a Khmer ceremony in Oregon.
1984	Letter is received from Larony, who is at a refugee camp in Thailand along with Mealanie and their respective families. A long struggle with Immigration and Naturalization Service (INS) paperwork and protocol ensues in an effort to bring them to safety.

1986	Ranachith and Thavy are married in an elaborate Khmer wedding ceremony in Beaverton, Oregon.
1988	Ranachith graduates from the University of Oregon with a landscape architecture degree. He begins a professional career with the USDA Forest Service.
1989	Larony, Mealanie, and their families arrive in Portland, Oregon, and reunite with Ranachith after more than fourteen years of separation.
1990	Daughter Samantha Rathanary Yimsut is born.
1992	Ranachith returns to Cambodia for the first time in the wake of the Paris Peace Agreements. He tours Phnom Penh and visits with relatives in Siem Reap. He becomes a staunch social and environmental activist in America.
1993–94	After another brush with death, Ranachith reevaluates his priorities. He takes a year of sabbatical leave so he can volunteer with an NGO to help rebuild Cambodia. During the course of teaching classes in Phnom Penh, he meets Prince Ranariddh and secures a generator for the school.
1995	Son Derrick Monorom Yimsut is born.
1999	With local and international reporters, Ranachith revisits Ta Source Hill, the site of the "Tonle Sap Lake Massacre." He joins reporters to face the Khmer Rouge in their Pailin stronghold.
2001	Ranachith becomes actively involved in writing letters, articles, technical papers, books, and produces film documentaries for local, national, and international media.
2006	Ranachith and family relocate to Milwaukee, Wisconsin, after twenty-five years of residing in Oregon.
2007	In conjunction with Project Enlighten, Ranachith formally founds and establishes the Bakong Technical College in his native hometown of Siem Reap. The college campus is located on his family's ancestral land, reacquired by Ranachith via multiple real estate transactions starting in 1993.
2010	Ranachith and other volunteers began Phase I construction work at Bakong Technical College campus as a special homage to generations of respected educators and administrators from his family.

Facing the Khmer Rouge

1

Childhood Idyll

Siem Reap

Early one September morning, I woke to the sound of dripping water. The first monsoon rains had come in the night. Outside my bedroom window, water rolled off the bright flowers and green leaves. The subtle aroma of dewy jasmine flowers enveloped me, and I imagined little jasmine buds in our garden, ready to unfold their petals. My three roosters—the pride of my collection—crowed their hearts out, the majestic Siem Reap River behind them.

I pulled the blanket around me. Norane and the others were already up; it was just me and my younger brothers, Nosay and Monika, who were still in bed. Nosay's slender legs fell almost off the bed while Monika's chubby frame took up the bulk of the rumpled covers. We were allowed to sleep late on Sundays so I didn't disturb them. I lay down again, enjoying the peace of an unrushed morning. Suddenly, I remembered my chores. We were all assigned tasks around the house, even though our live-in servant could have easily done all the work. With very few exceptions, we were assigned errands every day, including holidays. We cleaned the orchard, watered the vegetables and the flowers, swept out the front yard, or gathered eggs from our chickens. My siblings and I often complained to each other about our chores.

Today it was my turn to water the garden and the plants around the house. This task could take me all day so I decided to start while it was still cool.

I usually loved gardening, but this chore involved lugging gallons of water from the Siem Reap River, over and over. First I had to dip the tin buckets in, fill them with water, and hoist them up. Then began the long walk home, balancing the buckets on their bamboo stick. We lived just across the road from the river, but our house sat high on a landfill, and the distance felt much farther with all that weight, the angle much steeper. I watered the plants one by one, all around the house, heading back often to refill the cans. Fatigue threatened to overtake me before I got even halfway around the house. I pushed on, determined to finish quickly.

Near the last plant I heard chirping. It was a dying bird hidden by blades of grass. Its left wing bled. Feeling sorry for the little being, I took off my shirt and wrapped the bird inside it before running to show my mother. Maybe she would know how to help the bird get better, just like all those times she stayed with me through fevers and stomach aches, nursing me back to health.

I heard my mother in the front yard. She was talking about a new baby in the neighborhood. A short man stood next to Father's handwritten "Schoolteacher/Administrator" sign at the front gate, carrying a couple of bags on his shoulder. My mother's fair, moon-shaped face was open and cheerful. Her hair was short and she was a bit chubby, in a pretty way. But the most noticeable thing about her was her banter. I caught a grin on the man's face and guessed he was enjoying her loud but cheery chatter. He dropped some coins, *riels*, in my mother's hand. In his bags I saw custard apples and jasmine buds. They're from our garden, I thought to myself, proud that my help tending the plants had brought in some family income.

"Mae, can you help me?" I asked after the man walked away. Mae is the country word for "mother," and it was what my siblings and I called our mother.

"What is it? What do you want?"

"I found this bird—," I held out my swaddled treasure. "It's sick, Mae. How can I help it feel better?"

She smiled at me and patted my head. "These animals you bring home, they die. They are not well, Ah Ngouss," she said, using my nickname. "There is nothing we can do to help them. But go ahead; put it on the back porch."

She was right. The bird did not last through the night. In this way I learned about life, sickness, and death. But even as I learned these hard lessons again and again, I continued to believe that maybe I could help the next animal I saw.

My nickname, Ah Ngouss (pronounced ah-NGWAH), meant "Dummy." I was given that name because I was so quiet. At home, the Khmer (Cambodians) use nicknames instead of first names. This use of nicknames in Khmer families is very common. A nickname is a form of sharing affection with one another, specifically within a family circle. My parents never called me by my first name of Ranachith. They called me either or Ah Ngouss or Ah Nak, a shortening of my name.

My eldest brother Larony was called Ah Sangkom (Skinny), because he was the tallest and skinniest in the whole family, and my elder sister Mealanie was called Mae Moan (Mother Hen, pronounced mai MO-un), because, as the only daughter, she was expected to watch over the kids whenever our mother was not around. Mealanie even looked like our mother, so her nickname seemed doubly appropriate.

About my nickname I was secretly pleased when I heard my uncles and aunts calling my father Ah Ngouss as well. We were connected through that nickname, my father and I.

On an unknown date in the Year of the Ox, I was born in Siem Reap, an agricultural town of 25,000 located by the famous Angkor Wat temples and near the northwestern tip of a large freshwater lake called Tonle Sap. The Siem Reap River flowed through our neighborhood, just a few yards from my home. I grew up surrounded by majestic rain forests and temple ruins.

Most of the townspeople were well off, particularly the ethnic Chinese, who tended to excel in business. Farmers on the outskirts profited from miles of arable, fertile land. In the rice fields, children herded oxen and water buffalo. In the more populated areas, even the blind and the crippled participated in the local economy by playing instruments and singing folk songs on the street corners.

My family was typically large; I was the sixth of ten children. As I grew up, I couldn't imagine a life with only a few brothers and sisters to play and fight with. That must be so boring, I thought.

My eldest brother Larony was the crown prince of our family. Tall and light skinned, he was widely considered handsome. He knew karate and kung fu, and he spoke French fairly well. I looked up to him. His friends often came over on their motor bikes. Serey was skinny like Larony but of average height, maybe 5 feet 6 inches. He looked more like Father, who was dark skinned. In fact, Serey was the darkest one in our family. Mother used to say, "Serey must be someone else's kid."

For generations, my grandparents and great-grandparents had farmed, fished, and administered towns and districts in this part of Cambodia. My father came from the nearby Bakong district, and my mother was from Domdek, a small town about 20 miles from Siem Reap. They married in 1949 and my father taught in Bakong district before they moved to Siem Reap some years later. Through education, my father had accomplished the goal sought by so many Cambodians—an alternative to working in the fields. Yet, even with his success-ful work as a civil servant and teacher, my father wanted us kids to experience farming traditions, so he and my mother took us to the family farm in the Bakong district every planting and harvesting season.

My father was of average height and had a long, slender face and a narrow jaw. His skin was darker than my mother's. He wore his hair cropped back above respectful but minimal attire; no ties or jackets for him. His demeanor was quiet, low key, and observant.

Sowing seeds and gathering the harvest was a lot of work, but it went quickly with so many hands. Sometimes my father leased the land to farmers, but we still showed up at the beginning and the end of the season, and my brothers and I liked to help others in the countryside gather their rice, too.

We also enjoyed riding the ox carts and sitting on the buffaloes. Bonfires, festivals, and celebrations beckoned, but my favorite activity was the family picnics, which we had at every opportunity.

Our house in Siem Reap was built of solid hardwood felled from the nearby forest. The orange clay tiles on our roof were handmade by local artisans. When it was hot, my brothers and I played inside. The tile roof kept us cool despite the tropical sun. I was born here, and so were most of my siblings. For as long as I could remember, my parents had been building a new house on the outskirts of the city, but as far as I was concerned, this house by the river would always be home.

Large windows and French doors opened to the garden out front. Inside, there was plenty of room to run and many spaces in which to hide. The hallway alone was an endless stretch. We had a big dining area, a huge living room, and three bedrooms that were rarely used because we kids slept all together in the common room, on reed mats with our soft kapok pillows, preferring each other's company to time alone. Like many children in our town, we were also afraid of ghosts and goblins and felt safety in numbers. Besides, it was cooler in the common room.

The roomy, dark pantry held pots and pans as well as garlic, shallots, and the traditional smoked and dried salted fish. For our big family, we had to store a lot of food in a safe, cool, and dry place. A 50-pound bag of rice lasted a week, if that. One pantry door opened to the kitchen while the other went to the backyard. This room was the perfect place to escape my problems. With the kitchen door locked and the back door open to let the light in, I read my books and let my imagination roam wild. I took trips to some of the most exotic places in the world. In this way I nurtured the skill of hiding physically and emotionally.

Every morning, six days a week, my elder siblings walked to the school nearby, and my father drove to work on his motorcycle—the only motorcycle in the community. My father did administrative work in the city and sometimes taught for the school district. My mother stayed home to watch after us kids.

Dinner was planned in the morning. Sometimes I accompanied my mother to the market before I went to school. She bought fresh pork shoulder or mud fish, and she socialized with friends and neighbors. Often she picked up little snacks for me and my little brothers, as well.

In addition to our live-in servant, extended family, and tightly knit clan, visitors came and went all hours of the day, often to talk with my father. He was well known and respected in the community. My father was a quiet, shy man, but when he spoke, everyone stopped talking to hear what he had to say.

Once, my father invited me to go with him to a meeting at the temple. The group was planning an upcoming festival. A man suggested showing movies and the crowd grew excited.

"Let's get kung fu movies!" said a bearded man. "Everyone loves kung fu. Like *Mui-Thai* [kick-boxing]—." His mention of the popular TV show was interrupted.

"No," said a man wearing a tie. "We should get something educational."

I wanted kung fu. I silently appealed to Father but he remained still, listening.

"Remember, there's going to be different ages," said someone else. "Not just kids."

Father leaned forward and a hush fell over the crowd. "How about showing some movies from the archive, from during French rule? Then people can see what the village looked like before."

"Oh yes," said the bearded man, "that's a good idea."

"Right," said the man wearing a tie, "that makes a lot of sense."

Just like that, the movie discussion was settled.

My elder brothers sometimes attended father's classes, and they told me that he demonstrated the proper way to plant rice and sweet potatoes, and how to maintain the correct water levels in rice paddies. My brothers told me that Father encouraged the students and coached them. They were surprised to see anyone teach this way, and I agreed, thinking of my intimidating teacher at school. I wished I could go see my father teach, but I was too young. Father was kind and understanding. Unlike Mother, he rarely punished us. This was because we obeyed him more. I looked up to Father as if he were our Lord Buddha.

The kitchen was tucked way at the back of the house. Here, the servant or one of us children prepared meals under my mother's strict eye. I skinned and dressed chickens, careful in my selection to leave the better producers of double-yolked eggs in our flock. For generations, we'd kept this line of chickens going, enjoying their high-protein, duck-sized eggs. These hens were a family heirloom.

I also pounded paste for curry and chopped vegetables and fruits. If I slit the mango the wrong way, Mother would say, "No, you have to cut down to the seed." She would take the knife and show me. Mother loved to cook and encouraged us to practice cooking, which I enjoyed very much. I served up nothing fancy, just delicious traditional Khmer food. Helping Mother dish up three meals a day for ten people or so gave me lots of practice. It was like running a restaurant.

Meals were always eaten together, often with extended family and visitors in attendance. At lunchtime my elder siblings came home from school and Father came home from work. We set the courses on the mat or table. In the rainy season, we covered our food with screens to keep away the extra flies and mosquitoes that showed up with the monsoons.

Mother's relatives often stopped by to eat with us. I especially remember Uncle Rou, who was really my mother's cousin. They were very close. I could pick him out a mile away because his skin was so blotchy. "Pou Rou, Pou Rou!

[Uncle Rou!]" I would say, running to greet him. Uncle Rou was kind and easy-going, and unusually quiet and polite for being from the Chinese side of the family. He was my favorite "uncle," even though he was really my second cousin.

As we ate, elder family members talked about the French oppression, and about the way my great-grandfather had received his education from the colonizers. Many thought Sihanouk was a hero for gaining our country's independence in the 1950s, but Larony, my eldest brother who was in college, said Cambodia should end its god-king era and Khmer royalty. He said we needed to modernize our country. An uncle would respond that the current regime was not broken. Why fix it? So went the political arguments that split our tight-knit family apart. This scene became very common in Cambodian homes.

No one complained about the food I helped prepare, but I was teased so often that I was not only embarrassed, I was humiliated. Wives were the ones to rule kitchens and serve meals. Men were supposed to wait to be served at the table or dining mat. However, Mother's kitchen lessons intrigued me. She used to tell me that cooking was based on individual creativity. "You'll be thankful later in life, Ah Nak," she said, "because this skill is essential." Thus, I never gave up on the two things I loved to do most: gardening and cooking.

In the cool, shady backyard, I spent many hot afternoons napping on a hammock hanging between the sugar apple trees. I loved to climb the trees, too, and I found the sugar apple tree's flexibility an exciting challenge. Every tree in the yard was unique, and I scaled them all: jackfruit, banana, and mango. I was an expert climber, even daring to sneak mangoes at night, when it was too dark to see and the ants came out.[1] Under the moon, sightless, I ignored the ant bites as I felt my way to the heavily laden branches high off the ground, where I plucked a prize mango. I thought to myself, climbing a tree is like a journey through life. It has its challenges, difficulties, and dangers but it also has its goal in the end. I told myself I would still climb trees even when I grew old and heavy.

Sunday was break time from school, but part of the school program was helping to keep the town clean, so the kids in our district rotated the duties. "If the streets are dirty, the tourists won't come," our teachers would tell us. "Community growth is more important than individual convenience," Father told us. My siblings and I developed a strong civic pride early in childhood. On our Sundays, we met at the temple to start our joint street-cleaning efforts. We knew that strong communities made a strong nation, and all the kids took their jobs seriously. If one of the boys missed their Sunday (which happened rarely), then he was sure to be there the following Sunday.

I heard over and over that everyone should help the many travelers visiting Angkor Wat. We were in the service industry. "Hospitality is a virtue," said the local government official on the radio. "Showing kindness to visitors is an honor," said our teachers at school. "Help that lady across the street," said my mother when we were at the market.

Jacqueline Kennedy visited Siem Reap when I was six, and I never heard the end of it. "Remember to always treat visitors with kindness. Siem Reap is world renowned. Jacqueline Kennedy spent three nights here." Everywhere I looked, it seemed they were right. The hotels were full. I saw *barang* (foreigners) everywhere. It did not matter that the Vietnam War was escalating nearby. The tourists came anyway.

Some of the towns in the other provinces were downright hostile. We drove through on the way to our farmstead, or to visit distant relatives, and the locals just stared at us. If we stopped for a meal and wanted to know where the noodle shop was, the people on the street rushed by, too busy to help us. It was nothing like Siem Reap.

Our parents always taught us to look after each other. They told us to help the poor, feed the homeless, and take care of the disadvantaged. "It's your duty to give time to others," Mother told us. "If everyone pitches in, then everything goes well. And whatever you give, you get back tenfold." If we saw an older woman holding a large basket, we knew we should carry the load for her, and we did, automatically. "Take care of people, be strong," Father said. "A strong individual makes a strong family. A strong family makes a strong community. A strong community makes a strong nation. A strong nation makes a strong world."

Like many other local boys, my elder brother Norane attended school at Wat Damnak, a temple that also served as a school. The Buddhist monk teachers did not allow anyone younger than five years old to attend classes, but when I was four, I tagged along with Norane and stood outside his *M'they* classroom every day. (*M'they* is the Khmer word for kindergarten.) While Norane sat in his chair chanting the alphabet and singing math problems, I stood outside, watching the lips of the robe-clad monk as he led every verse. "Ga, Ka, Go, Ko, Ngo" was the first verse of the alphabet chant. The following year, when I reached the age of five and was allowed inside, I already knew my alphabet and my math. But rules were rules. Every kid had to start in M'they, so it wasn't till the next year that I could skip a grade and join Norane in his grade, Grade 11. (In Cambodia, grade levels start at 12 and end at 1.)

I enjoyed classes for both the learning and the social opportunities. It was in Grade 11 that I met my best childhood friend Lan. My favorite cousin Thie (pronounced "TEE") also went to Wat Damnak. Although quiet, Thie's constant grin made him highly approachable. Thie was always among the tallest in our age group. His house was nearby and we often visited each other. In Grade 10 (U.S. equivalent of third grade), Lan and I learned to read Khmer script using UNICEF booklets that defined the Universal Declaration of Human Rights. I read that "human beings are born free" and that we all have the right to an education.

Wat Damnak also was where we celebrated Buddhist holidays and festivals, gathered for prayers, and dropped in to hear the latest happenings in our town.

We read the latest notices posted about weddings and funerals, and then pitched in to help.

A funeral starts with mourning. After the head monk leads the three-day rite with family, friends, and the town in attendance, the body is cremated to help the soul know of its passing. Everyone gathers again for the seven-day rite, when the soul has already realized its death. The hundred-day rite is a good-bye memorial to send off the soul to a better reincarnation.

Some monks in the temple were young men following the tradition of temporary monk hood as a way to thank their parents for their sacrifices. I always expected to follow this tradition myself, but otherwise I did not think of the monks or of Buddhist concerns unless we happened to be visiting the temple for sacred rituals. My mother was pious, however. She practiced five of the eight precepts she learned from the monks, missing only the precepts to abstain from butchering fish or chicken, to abstain from touching the opposite sex, and to give up all your wealth.

Once a year, around June, the Siem Reap River flooded most of the city. My friends and I placed sticks in the ground to measure the water rising. My cousin Thie and best buddy Lan often joined me. All of us had home-made fishing poles and we held them in front of us there on the road, knees getting wet within the hour. Many times we watched the river rise, an inch at a time, until our road, our way to town, was covered with 4 feet of water.

Usually we could walk to school suffering nothing more than wet legs, dragging our backpacks and flip-flops on rafts behind us. (Rafts were easy to make from banana tree trunks.) But on those few days of the year when the water rose above our waists or heads, our neighbor took us to school on his boat, and my father might ride with us as far as the main road, which was higher than our road to town. To keep his motorcycle dry, my father always rolled it into the house before the monsoon rains came. The brown water covered roads, ditches, yards, and plants for weeks. Some places were so deep a dug-out canoe was needed as transport.

Our house was up on a landfill, but I was glad for the added height lent by the wooden stilts underneath. The stilts caught the breezes, made the house cool, and kept us away from whatever the monsoon floodwaters brought, such as scorpions and poisonous snakes flowing in with the current.

Despite classes and chores, fun came first when the much-awaited flood arrived. Some teachers were tolerant, but not the monks. Every time I cut class, the teacher monk made me sweep the temple grounds.

The monsoon floods were simply irresistible. The other kids and I would jump in with our banana tree rafts, float for a mile or two, and climb out of the river to walk back and do it all over again. Fish were plentiful during the flood season. We dangled fishing poles over the town's only concrete bridge, which we called the Spean Thmor.

How I loved to climb that tall bridge and dive into the river below. I also loved to jump from what seemed to be a 40-foot tree by the riverbank into the river, floating with my friends for miles downstream. We became swimmers and fishermen by the time we were three. If you didn't, then you were not likely to live past five.

It was easy to blame Lord Buddha for the annual deaths of the little ones. Every year, an unfortunate child or two floated from the depths of the river, along with drowned chickens, dogs, and cats. Few of us kids were discouraged for long by these tragedies. If anything, it made us smarter and more determined.

When my brothers and I were inevitably late for dinner, our mother lectured us. She was worried sick, she'd tell us. One of my parents' worst fears was to see us fished dead from the river. They believed in making us responsible for our actions, but only up to a point. Like the others, I pushed my limits. I challenged the raging river by diving from the tallest tree and bridge every flood season.

At night, I often joined the other kids walking to town, where we passed tree-lined boulevards and bought sweet egg-yolk desserts from the street vendors. I could always count on seeing the man with polio at his usual spot, playing his bamboo flute. Around the corner from him was the tall blind man with his group of kids, playing their hearts out. While the blind man strummed his two-string *tro*, a kind of Cambodian banjo made of coconut shells and wood, the kids tapped their sticks on tiny snakeskin drums. Barang dropped coins into the hat while men in khaki government uniforms ate noodle soup across the street.

Sometimes, instead of going to the market, we went to our wealthy neighbor's house to watch Thai kick boxing (Mui-Thai) or kung fu movies on their black-and-white TV, or we stayed outside and picked teams, arming ourselves with sticks. In our play fighting, we used "swords" to conquer whole armies, just like in the movies. Guns were rare in our neighborhood. My father had guns locked up in his room, but they were for hunting.

Father practiced conservation long before anyone in Cambodia appreciated the concept. He took only what he would use. His ethics extended to big game, which he hunted with his forestry official friends. He always returned home with four doves all dressed, ready for cooking. It was always exactly four birds, no more.

"Why just four birds, Pa?" I asked him each time he returned.

His answer was always the same. "These are male birds, Ah Nak. The female bird does not need too many males competing for her. And these guys make too much noise when they fight for a female or a territory. Also, I can't eat more than four birds, can I?"

Every time he returned from hunting, Father always told the story of the hunt, the lesson, and the need for conservation. We wanted to go hunting with him but he refused. "Children can distract a hunter's concentration and ruin everything," he said.

I was thrilled when, one day, Father decided to take me with him. Looking at the others, he said, "Ah Ngouss is the quietest of you all. He won't scare off the birds."

Father was a very patient hunter. He spent an eternity aiming before he took a single shot. He would steady his old bolt-action 22-caliber rifle on my shoulder. He took so much time to set up each shot that sometimes I fell asleep waiting.

For every shot he fired, there were at least ten he didn't.

But he was good. I watched him shoot four times, and four birds fell from the highest sugar palm trees, which were at least 500 feet away. I plugged my fingers in my ears during the ordeal. I hated loud noises.

When he aimed at a chicken, I turned to him, puzzled.

"Steady, will you?" he said to me, smiling. "How can I make a clean shot if you keep moving like that?"

"But that's a chicken! You can't shoot a chicken on the ground like that," I said.

"Why not? I have my four birds. Where's yours?"

"That's not our chicken. You can't shoot it."

"So you shoot it. For your dinner, right?" He placed the rifle on his shoulder for me to fire.

"No. I don't like guns. And I don't want to shoot the chicken."

"Why not?"

"That's not a dove. That's a chicken. We shoot only four doves, not chickens. And that's not our chicken!" I yelled.

Father laughed out loud and gathered his birds. "You're learning to be a real hunter, my boy. When you're old enough, I'll take you hunting big game." We never went. Many other things happened before I got old enough.

In the summer of 1968, Father took me with him on a bus trip to Phnom Penh. During the two days we sat on the bus, Father and I talked like equals. I was only a skinny seven-year-old boy but Father told me stories, and he asked me what I thought. We talked like buddies. It felt very good.

Off the bus, however, Father was his usual self again, his face a frozen mask, no more stories from his lips. I missed the man from the bus. Perhaps it had something to do with our culture, where children were expected to rank their parents up there with Lord Buddha and give them the utmost respect and absolute obedience—no ifs, ands, or buts. Perhaps I didn't know my father at all. Perhaps that was just the way he was with his children.

I always thought my father and I had similar natures except that he was much smarter than I would ever be. We both thought a lot about other people, and we were both shy and quiet.

I was often sick. Each time I was ill, my mother was there, nursing me back to health. She was a very kind lady who used every bit of her time on household chores and attending to us. She loved us unconditionally. As the educator and law enforcer in the house, she treated us fairly. My brothers Lonk, Nosay, Monika, and I deserved every spanking and whipping she gave us. Aside from my father, she was my biggest role model.

With us at school and Father at work, Mother loved having the whole house to herself. Mother had a helper, a loyal servant who lived with us all year-round. She most likely helped to prepare the meals, clean the house, and take care of my younger brothers. When we returned home, the house was always neat and clean. There was always delicious food ready for us to chow down.

As long as I could remember, we always had at least one servant who stayed with us all year long.[2] Sometimes we had a personal nanny and a housekeeper to boss around.

One day, to our great surprise, our loyal servant of many years decided to leave. We had always treated her well and paid her well for her services. We didn't quite understand why she wanted to leave. She said she was returning to her family. We had grown to love her. My little brothers Nosay and Monika had even called her "Mummy." The house felt empty when she left, and we realized how much we needed her. It was even harder for Mother. We tried new helpers, but they didn't last longer than a few days. Finally we gave up searching and helped Mother with the housework and cooking ourselves.

I never thought the new house would be done, but it was finished in 1969, when I turned eight years old. Mother's elder brother, Uncle Vin, and his family would live in our old house. We moved to the new place, outside of town in a different district, less than two miles south of the Angkor Wat temple.

It was nice enough with its new wood smells, but it just didn't feel like the old house by the river. The garden had its fruit trees and flowers, which my elder brothers had planted long before the house was built. We had more land out here so my family acquired hundreds of chickens in addition to the family heirloom chickens we brought with us for their prize egg production. But the house was a bit smaller, and it looked and felt different. And those roof tiles weren't very sturdy, as we found out during a storm when a tile narrowly missed Nosay's head. My elder brothers said they liked it, though. "It's roomier here," they said. I didn't get it. We lived far from our neighbors, and the people here didn't join in the street-cleaning on Sundays.

Around the house were massive, huge trees. I called it our "house by the forest." Instead of my usual fishing trips, I traveled the forest with my slingshot. The nearest swimming hole was three miles away—past the city. The city was only a mile or two away, but we hardly saw anyone from there. Our closest neighbors were just a few hundred feet away but they kept to themselves.

I missed my friends, the river, and the old neighborhood. I had to start anew. But my new friends and I became kings of the jungle, headquartered at Angkor Wat.

I didn't appreciate the majestic history of our playground until much later when I had grown up. The Angkor Wat is made of sandstone quarried from the Phnom Kulen plateau, a low mountain range some 25 miles away. The sandstone was transported by barges on the Siem Reap River. A vast army of slaves, builders, and craftsmen quarried, moved, hauled and put the stones into place during the Angkor Period from 802 to 1431.

However, long before and after that time locals continued to live there. When Angkor City was abandoned after a Thai invasion in 1431, natives used the temples for social and religious activities. After the decline of the Khmer Empire, the Angkor Wat was maintained as a Buddhist temple. Although poverty prevented its upkeep, the Angkor Wat was never forgotten. When the French explorer and naturalist Henri Mahout "discovered" the Angkor complex in 1858 and brought it to European attention, we were still using the Angkor Wat.

Wat Damnak stopped at Grade 9 (equivalent to the fourth grade in the U.S.), and I dreaded going to a different school. Being very shy, it was hard for me to find and establish new friendships—good new friendships, that is. If only I could overcome my shyness, I could do anything in the world, I thought.

Our six-week summer breaks from school started with the dry season in April and ended in the middle of May, when we returned to school for a few weeks to prepare for examinations to go to the next level. In June we were allowed to take a small break for planting, to prepare for the rainy season.

My new school was a few blocks north of Wat Damnak, but it couldn't have been more different. The school was called "Sala Komrou" (Model School), and the twenty-five staff people there held classes for 300 children—boys and girls—in Grades 8, 7, and 6. Being a government school, the state teachers wore modern uniforms instead of the monk robes used at the other school. Students were expected to comply with this dress code, as well. Males wore khaki pants and white shirts while females wore blue skirts with white blouses. The principal was a traditionally high-ranking civil servant, thought of as a fair but exacting person. Standards were high. The bell rang every morning at 7 A.M. for all the students to gather around the flag pole with the principal and sing the national anthem of the Kingdom of Cambodia.

> Heaven protects our King
> And gives him happiness and glory
> To reign over our souls and our destinies,
> The one being, heir of the Sovereign builders,
> Guiding the proud old Kingdom.
> Temples are asleep in the forest,
> Remembering the splendor of Moha Nokor.

Like a rock the Khmer race is eternal.
Let us trust in the fate of Kampuchea,
The empire which challenges the ages.
Songs rise up from the pagodas
To the glory of holy Buddhist faith.
Let us be faithful to our ancestors' belief.
Thus heaven will lavish its bounty
Towards the ancient Khmer country, the Moha Nokor.

The midday break was 10 A.M. to 2 P.M., and we finished our classes around 4 or 5 P.M., depending on our grades and course selections.

I had many new classmates, and I had the choice of sports or gardening. It was an easy decision because I was not at all good at sports—I was neither very competitive nor aggressive. I was one of the very few boys in a sea of girl gardeners. Because I was shy and quiet, the bigger students often picked on me or hit me. Some of the older or larger girls fought me with their long fingernails. Through those bullies I learned to deal with some of life's adversities by "rolling with the punches." I enjoyed growing vegetables and fruits, a skill that would later save my life.

In 1969 and 1970 we heard more about the Vietnam War. One of the theaters in town played John Wayne's movie *The Green Berets*. Our play fighting moved from swords to guns, and our old sticks served well in becoming the new weapon of choice.

I loved playing soldiers with my schoolmates and imagining the glory of being a Green Beret like John Wayne. Every recess time, whenever we could, we fought and died in battles. We often wished we were real soldiers with real guns. Everybody joined in except my best friend Lan, who didn't like guns. I thought him strange. At home I studied guns in magazines, and when I got the chance I liked to handle Father's pistols and rifles, though I never wanted to shoot real guns. They were too loud.

School was too far to walk so we had bicycles. On the way, I often stopped to help an old man feed his half-tame elephants. He told me how he and other villagers spent weeks in the deep jungles in the north to capture wild elephants to train for riding and for hauling logs. The man was very simple—he wore only a short wrap around his waist. He devoted his life to his animals. Before his friends passed away, they used to stay in the forest together. Now it was just him. I found his stories of jungle travel engrossing. He told me of being lost in the jungle. To find his way again, he looked for elephant trails. Broken branches pointed to field trails while unbroken branches went to sources of water. "To find water in the dry season," he told me, "go to the mountaintops. Look for the vines that absorb water." If he was lost for hours or days, he told me, he would chant to avoid going crazy. The man showed me how to track animals and which plants were edible. I remembered his survival tips and techniques. His stories would later help me get through the northern jungle.

Our little band of forest urchins vandalized the walls of Angkor Wat with mud and chalk graffiti. What's so special about this broken stone? I often thought to myself. Years later, in 1992, the temple that had served as our forest headquarters was pronounced "an excellent marriage of Khmer architecture and Hindu art" by UNESCO, and designated a World Heritage Site. The self-proclaimed god-king Suryavarman II had built it at the start of his reign in 1131 and it was completed after his death in 1150.

Lan, Thie, and I played around the five tower-shrines[3] and the three galleries. We held mock sword battles along the first gallery, through the bridge across the moat. We raced up the banks, past square pillars outside, past closed inside walls carved with dancing *apsara* (goddesses).

We horsed around the pillared windows of the inner wall, ignoring the nude apsara dancing with male figures and prancing animals. We hardly noticed the lotus rosettes on the ceilings between the pillars.

We made up stories of adventure, daring, and valor, not knowing that the carvings on the gallery walls make up the world's longest continuous bas-relief, telling a continuous narrative of real and mythical battles from Hindu mythology, or that the Western Wall showed epic scenes from the Mahabharata. The center of our headquarters was the third gallery, which enclosed the five tower-shrines on a raised terrace and interconnected the other galleries. We had fun tracing the snake's body that ended on the heads of the *garuda*, fierce lionlike creatures from Hindu mythology, along both sides of the staircase that rose to the long avenue that connected the first and second galleries.

Months went by like a summer breeze. I must have been a country boy deep inside. I decided that I liked the isolation and the forest. To me, the capital city of Phnom Penh was filthy and crowded. However, I changed my mind after my second visit in the summer of 1969, when I was eight. This time, instead of a bus, I rode in a Mercedes Benz limousine. The car belonged to my great-uncle Ang Khiev, my mother's brother in-law and the father of a famed radio personality who worked for Voice of America in Washington, D.C. Cousin Ang Khen is her name. Uncle Khiev was a very successful tour guide, one of the few who spoke at least four languages and drove his own car. I wanted to grow up wealthy and smart just like him. Uncle Khiev was my idol and he had an impact on my young life in so many ways.

It was my first limousine ride, and we were going to be in the car for four hours. In the back seat was a young French couple from Paris, returning home from their honeymoon in Siem Reap. My elder brother Larony, my sister Mealanie, and I sat in the middle seat facing them.

I had seen barang before, but never this close. The couple smooched like there was no tomorrow. They hugged and kissed as though we didn't exist.

I tried not to stare. Mealanie gave me stern looks but it was too interesting. I was a bit embarrassed but very curious. I watched them while pretending to look out of the window.

It was very frustrating not knowing French. My brother and sister were able to talk with the couple, but I had to depend on my brother and sister, sometimes on Uncle Khiev, to translate when the couple spoke to me. We talked about how Cambodia was a French colony for nearly a century, starting in the late 1860s when France ruled Cochin China, which is now part of Indochina. We talked about the French "rediscovering" the ruins of the Angkor complex and other temples.

Cambodia's social, political, economic, educational, and judicial systems were being changed to follow the French systems, and the French language was now required in all schools. It was to become my second language.

We talked about how the French experience brought joy and pain to the Khmer and why too few native Khmer were in government. The French imported Vietnamese administrators from French-controlled Annam (Vietnam's historical name) to help run Cambodia. My uncle tried to change the subject. I remembered conversations over meals at home, anger over French oppression. The conversation went on about many things. We forgot the long, often bumpy road.

That trip was my first chance to meet foreigners up close and to communicate with people from another culture and language. Also, I was able to see Uncle Khiev, whom I so much admired and respected. We spent two wonderful weeks with him, his wife Aunt Chan, and our cousins.

And this was the only trip I ever had with any of my siblings. Larony and Mealanie and I have wonderful memories of this trip, our first time away from our parents. We only had each other to rely on in the big city, a place so different from our hospitable, relatively small, Siem Reap.

Lastly, I had a brief chance to enjoy Phnom Penh's unique character, which would never again be the same. As an adult I learned that war-weary American GIs and war correspondents had grown to love this Phnom Penh of which I had a glimpse in 1969 and which changed in just a few years under a genocidal government.

These are some of my happiest memories as a little boy in Cambodia. My family loved one another dearly, I had my neighbors and my community to rely upon, and most importantly, I had a country to call my own.

Before I lost my childhood, I lost them all.

2

Bamboo in the Wind

Regime Change in Siem Reap

An early breeze that swayed the bamboos carried a gecko's morning cry. Droplets of dew shimmered on spider webs. The bell rang once again for us to hurry to the schoolyard and gather around the flag pole of the Sala Komrou.

The morning of March 18, 1970, began just like any other day, except for the furious whispering of the older students and the teachers talking quietly among themselves.

"Everybody line up!" a teacher called out. We arranged ourselves according to grades and genders. As usual, our school principal came out of the administration building. This time, however, he was flanked by soldiers who appeared to be gripping his arms as they walked toward us in a clipped manner. Their uniforms had foreign emblems. The one on the right had stripes on his uniform, and as he neared us I could see a vein on his forehead throbbing. The principal looked ill. Everyone fell silent.

I was excited. This was my first time to be near not one but four soldiers with full combat gear. Their guns weren't anything like the hunting rifles and pistols that Father had locked up in his room. But their weapons looked familiar. I had seen them in magazines. These were M-16 assault rifles from America!

I couldn't stop looking at the soldiers. Their abrupt walking style reminded me of Phnom Penh. Their eyes scanned the school grounds carefully. Their unsmiling faces frightened me a little.

The soldier with stripes on his uniform handed a piece of paper to our principal, whose hands shook. When the principal read the words out loud, his voice quavered so I didn't quite understand what he said, but his speech was in the tone of a confession. I wondered why the principal was in trouble. He was sweating in the chilly morning air. When the principal stopped reading, the soldier shoved him aside. He stumbled and two soldiers grabbed him.

The soldier with the stripes spoke loudly toward us, "My friends, teachers, and all good students of this fine institution, do you know why we are here today? There is a traitor among us." He pointed to our school principal. "Do you know that this man is trying to destroy our great culture and wonderful society?"

He said a lot of things but my attention was now on the principal. He looked very sick.

After the speech, the soldier ordered our principal to pull down the standard government-issue flag, the *Sangkum Reastr Niyum* flag of the Kingdom of Cambodia. One of the soldiers tossed it into their American-made military jeep, and another gave the principal a bundle of cloth, pointing to the flagpole with his chin. The principal attached the new flag and the soldiers saluted as it went up the flagpole. The new flag had the same colors as our old flag, but the white Angkor Wat symbol was on the upper left corner instead of in the center. I thought to myself, the soldiers must have made a mistake—that's the wrong flag.

The soldiers manhandled our principal into their jeep and ordered us all to return home. The jeep drove away in a trail of white dust. Some lady teachers wept quietly. A few minutes later, we heard automatic gunfire from the jeep's direction. The teachers started; some cried openly. The older students began asking one another questions; the teachers hushed them and urged everyone home immediately. A few of the kids stayed and played soccer in the schoolyard. I went to my school garden plot and weeded my sweet potato patch to soothe myself.

Later, at home, I told everyone what happened, but it seemed that no one quite believed or understood me.

Father took me to school the next day. Only the janitor was there, sweeping the yard. While they talked in hushed tones, I watered my sweet potatoes. Father was quiet on the way home. His forehead wrinkled and his eyebrows twisted together, as if he had a headache. I reminded him that he had doubted me yesterday but he stayed deep in thought. He must have known what was really going on after all.

Less than a week later, I was back in school.

The new flag was still on the flagpole. Most of the teachers were unfamiliar to us. The new principal had a short, choppy accent—Phnom Penh, we guessed. We were ordered to sing a new anthem as loud as we could. "The louder the better," said the new teachers. The song was about the world-famous and respected Khmer *sah-teeahronahtroth* [republic]. I had never heard the word "sah-teeahronahtroth" before. The song was a little more upbeat than the old national anthem, but the rhythm was different and the tone seemed flat. We had to sing it before and after school. Among ourselves, we thought it the most boring song ever. "We people of Cambodia are well known in the world. / We succeeded in building monuments. / Our glorious civilization and religion, our ancestors' heritage, have been kept on this earth. / Cambodians, stand up, stand up, fight and defend the Republic! / When enemies attack, we defend, we fight!"

School was no longer fun. It took us a few weeks just to learn the new rules. We had more to study. Recess periods became shorter and the gardening classes were discontinued. I was not allowed to care for my vegetable garden. Pop quizzes happened all the time. We hated the new routines. We disliked the new principal. He peeked through windows and doors, walked into classrooms, and corrected the teachers.

Many of our teachers disappeared. We wanted them back. I heard that many of our younger teachers had run to the woods. I couldn't understand what they did wrong. Did they break some law? Had they done something against the new regime? Were they attempting to avoid what our principal had gone through in his confession/speech? I hoped that my initial guess had been wrong and that our principal was alive and well. I waited for our principal to return but I never saw him again.

More new teachers came. They were young and aggressive, and they punished us for the slightest thing. Many students returned home with bruises. Although it was common practice for teachers to punish naughty students, I thought they were too harsh, and many of their punishments were unnecessary. As much as I could, I avoided the teachers. This fear of teachers stayed with me a long time.[1]

Despite my phobia, I didn't stop going to school. I had passed the examination and was now in Grade 7 (equivalent to 6th grade in the U.S.). However, some students skipped classes while others stopped going to school altogether. I saw a teacher complain loudly to a man who came with his son one morning.

"Your child did not come to school yesterday!" she said.

The man smiled. "Don't worry, I will take care of him myself at home."

But only a few parents punished their children. They understood that the new teachers were enacting regime change at school, and they tried to cope without rocking the boat. The parents knew what was really going on.

Neighbors who considered themselves "Khmer of Vietnamese descent" disappeared. We heard that Lon Nol's soldiers had herded them out of town.

Like everyone else in the community, my family ignored these things, hoping the unpleasantness would go away in due time. This was an easy mistake that later cost millions of lives.

The new Khmer Republic government under Lon Nol published warnings about the Vietcong (communists from southern Vietnam). "Beware the Vietnamese guerrillas. They will kidnap you." Cartoons depicted grim soldiers with black buckteeth, conical hats, and Ho Chi Minh rubber tire sandals, holding AK-47s. "Report them on sight!" the literature said. On the radio, the government officials told us to beware of the Vietcong. They said nothing of the Khmer Krahom (Khmer Rouge). "If they are hiding in the forest and fighting our military, then they must be Vietcong. Khmer don't kill Khmer."

My parents and elder siblings listened to the news and had long discussions about Cambodia's becoming a republic. To survive the regime change, my father followed the "bamboo in the wind" philosophy, as did most other civil servants like him. When ordered by the new Lon Nol regime to repeat propaganda in his classes, he complied in a halfhearted fashion. An old Asian story says that "the strongest trees might be uprooted by a powerful wind, but the bamboo, bending with the wind, remains standing." Father was like a reed of bamboo, solidly rooted but flexible. Whatever the rest of us thought, we followed his lead.

I didn't realize that the kingdom we had known was gone. The regime change was so quick that only a few were then aware of it. All I knew was that we had to be "republicans" or else be considered enemies of the state. I didn't know the meaning of "republic" ("sah-teeahronahtroth" in Khmer), but I called myself a republican, like everyone else did. At the age of nine, I learned how to be a bamboo in the wind.

Still, it was an exciting time for me, seeing so many soldiers in town and planes overhead. I saw T-38 fighters and bombers, single-propeller Cessnas, and sometimes even a Huey helicopter. It was almost like being in a John Wayne movie.

I knew Vietnam was near our eastern border, but it was only when a few hundred tons of B-52 bombs began to fall in the distance that I heard of the Vietnam War. Much later I learned the whole story, including how Prince Sihanouk had exposed America's secret bombing of Cambodia, which led to numerous deaths and much destruction.

President Richard Nixon's administration somehow kept the bombings from the American public until a planeload of B-52 bombs obliterated Nek Loeung, a small city less than 30 miles from Phnom Penh.

Thus, it was not surprising that Prince Norodom Sihanouk's "neutral stance" on the Vietnam War actually favored Vietnam. He allowed the North Vietnamese and their Vietcong allies to build part of the infamous Ho Chi Minh Trail on Cambodian territory, which he did not have control over to begin with. This supply route to the south was vital for the Vietcong in their fight against the Americans and the South Vietnamese.

From nearby bases in Thailand and as far away as Guam, American B-52 bombers dropped millions of tons of bombs on the trail each day. The bombing campaigns on Cambodia's countryside had intriguing names, such as "breakfast, lunch, and dinner." The 500- to 1,000-pound iron "dumb bombs" destroyed remote villages and killed untold numbers of civilians. According to historians and reporters, 250,000 to 500,000 Cambodian villagers were estimated to have been killed by these American bombing raids alone. Over 2.5 million tons of bombs were dropped over Cambodia, according to air force records—a tonnage surpassing bombs dropped on Japan during all of World War II. Later, historians would suggest that these bombings helped the Khmer Rouge gain a military and political foothold in Cambodia, if not directly bringing them to power.

Prince Sihanouk banned the American B-52s from Cambodian airspace, which greatly hampered America's fight against the North Vietnamese Army and the Vietcong. While U.S. officers fumed, the prince remained popular among his people—for the moment.

Before he entered politics, he was King Norodom Sihanouk of the Kingdom of Cambodia. After wrestling Cambodia's independence from France, he abdicated the throne to become a politician and to govern instead of rule.

His right-hand man, General Lon Nol, was the chief of staff of the poorly equipped Cambodian armed forces. Lon Nol was part of a small group who opposed Sihanouk's neutral stance because it brought civil war to Cambodia. As did many Cambodians, Lon Nol's group considered Vietnam a historical enemy of the Khmer.

Because the prince favored the communist countries of China, North Korea, North Vietnam, and the Soviet Union, the Americans—probably through the CIA—made Lon Nol's group an offer too good to refuse. The United States promised to support a new Cambodian government if it would be its ally. The group executed a coup d'état when the prince was on a state visit in Russia.

Lon Nol announced a state of emergency, declared martial law, and renamed the Kingdom of Cambodia as the Khmer Republic (Khmer Sahteeahronahtroth). He ordered a new flag, a new national anthem, and issued new currency notes. Those who resisted the changes were jailed or taken away, such as my school principal who, like many of the civil servants, was a staunch supporter of the prince. With that brazen act, 2,000 years of kingship, or so-called God-King royalty, in the Kingdom of Cambodia ended unceremoniously.

In 1970, on the radio, we heard from the former leader of our kingdom, Prince Sihanouk. Speaking from Beijing, China, Sihanouk told us that he was now leading the Khmer Rouge, his historical enemy whom he had banned when he was in office. "Join us, my sons and daughters," Sihanouk said. "We must crush the traitor Lon Nol at all costs!" My elders said the prince must know very well that when the Khmer Rouge were done using him, they would "spit him out like a cherry pit," to use Prince Sihanouk's own words. However, the prince and the Khmer Rouge had the same goal for the moment: to overthrow Lon Nol.

Communist China backed the Khmer Rouge from the beginning and gave Prince Sihanouk a palatial home in Beijing. When we heard about China's support on the radio, my elders described how China had first backed the Vietcong, then the North Vietnamese. "And now the Khmer Rouge and Prince Sihanouk," they said.

With the U.S. B-52 bombing raid intensifying in the countryside, Cambodian villagers everywhere sent rice, livestock, and even their sons and daughters to the Khmer Rouge's Kong Top Pakdevat (Revolution Army), now headed by Prince Sihanouk. It was an honor for many to leave jobs and families to become guerrillas, even without pay. After all, Prince Norodom Sihanouk himself had coined the communist movement's name "Khmer Rouge" (Red Cambodians).

By the mid-1970s, the once ragtag Khmer Rouge was a potent political and military organization. Volunteers fought alongside Vietcong comrades who offered military advisers, equipment, and training.

To fight the Khmer Rouge and its Vietcong allies, Lon Nol began a conscription program to increase his army. When the countryside ran out of men, his recruiters turned children into soldiers. The U.S. government supported him with several billion dollars' worth of combat advisers, military hardware, and special funds.

Lon Nol's soldiers came to my school not only to arrest teachers for conspiracy but also to conscript students into the Republican Armed Forces. Thousands fled to the jungles to escape the American bombings and Lon Nol's abuses. Throughout Siem Reap, I heard of teachers, principals, and students going into hiding. They joined the Khmer Rouge out of desperation. I feared for my father, a prominent teacher and administrator in the Siem Reap School District. I didn't want him to disappear like so many others.

Earnestly, I joined my family in being a bamboo in the wind.

3

An Uncivil War

Heavy Shelling in Siem Reap

From miles away, strong gusts of wind gathered the monsoon clouds into dark masses. The winds died and warm air rose to meet the cold front. Eardrums popped as air pressures dropped, rose, and fell again.

Flocks of birds scattered at the tremendous sound of thunder. Solid sheets of rain came down and flooded the streets. The monsoon floods had come to Siem Reap once again.

We shouldn't have been so surprised when the battle began that stormy night. A few weeks earlier, the town militia had conscripted my father and my elder brothers Simona and Serey, who were college students. (My eldest brother Larony had already signed up for full-time active military duty with Lon Nol's forces, over our parents' objections.) Larony took intensive courses on using new U.S. weapons, but Simona and Serey, calling themselves "commandos," spent just a few days in basic training, learning to operate World War II surplus American rifles.

While my father and brothers prepared to join the Vietnam War, at home we stored food and supplies. My only sister Mealanie was now the oldest child at home, and Mother was recently pregnant. On the radio, the new government broadcast orders for everyone to build bomb shelters for protection. We dug a trench in the backyard, piled sandbags around it, and roofed it with timber.

My mother held war drills so often it became both boring and tiring. "When you hear the whistle, you know what to do," she said.

We immediately had to go to the trench and do a head count. Mother, Mealanie, Norane, me, Lonk, Nosay, and Monika. And we never knew when the drill would happen—sometimes it occurred in the dead of night. We had to know how to get to the trench, even in the dark.

"Those who are prepared enough will survive," Father always said. But who can really prepare for war?

Our house by the forest was just outside the city's defensive line. Instead of moving us into the city, Father said it was safer for us to stay at home because the city would be heavily shelled. He was right.

At about ten o'clock that night, as we huddled together in our new trench, the loud whizzing screech of shells joined the sounds of the thunderstorm. The roof tiles rattled and the house shook. It was like fireworks, but louder, though you could still hear people yelling. Man-made tracers joined Mother Nature's lightning. Intense odors settled around us. The papery sulfur smell of gunpowder was joined by garlicky phosphorus. My mother held little Monika in her arms and screamed.

Lon Nol seemed to be in firm command of everything. My father and my brothers were in Siem Reap, defending the city against the well-armed and well-disciplined Khmer Rouge guerrillas and their allies, the battle-hardened Vietcong who, for years, had taken on America's finest.

The chaos repeated itself day in and day out. I missed my father and my brothers Larony, Simona, and Serey. Outside our trench, power blinked on and off, and our radio often emitted static. It was hard to know the status of the war, of our father and brothers. I imagined them in flooded trenches under the rain, ready to shoot. "Please, Preah [Lord Buddha], take good care of my family and I will do anything you want." I repeated my prayer so many times that I lost count.

We became so hungry that we'd routinely send one person up to cook outside while the rest huddled in the soggy trench. We ate and slept in the trench. At night, a kerosene lamp gave us some light and the smoke blackened our nostrils. Severe headaches dogged us. I longed for my warm bed. We all did. "When can we go back to the house?" we asked our mother.

"This trench is uncomfortable, dirty, and wet," Mother said, "but it's safe." Our house was built high on stilts to avoid floodwaters but not artillery fire. So we stayed in our crude trench waiting for the firing to begin, at the same time praying that the war would never come.

After more than two weeks in the awful trench, Mother caved in. "I've had enough of living like rats in a hole. I'd rather die from bullets than drown!"

I looked at Mother's black nostrils and laughed.

"What are you laughing at?" Mother said, irritated.

"We have black noses, ha, ha, ha!" I showed her my darkened nostrils.

Mother chuckled. Then she burst into laughter. Soon we were all laughing like lunatics. (Looking back now, I wonder if it was carbon monoxide poisoning.) It was so good to see Mother laugh again. We eagerly headed back into our home.

That night, the skies opened up and dumped tons of water on Siem Reap, possibly the heaviest monsoon rainstorm of the season. My warm bed was heaven. My brothers and I snuggled against each other. "I'll never take simple things, such as my warm, dry bed, for granted ever again!" I said to myself several times before I fell asleep.

I woke up to the flash of light and the sound of a 55-mm howitzer shell landing close by. For a moment, I thought it was either a nightmare or thunder and
lightning, but then I was certain it was not. I could identify the artillery sounds.
The house shook; tiles flew from the roof and broke on the ground.

I was on the floor in seconds but I wasn't the fastest. Mother, always a light
sleeper, woke at the first distant sounds of small-arms fire. She roused us as the
big explosion came.

"Go, go, go!" Mother yelled. "Move it! Let's go! Now!"

We scrambled even as lights and sounds terrified, as bullets streamed red,
and orange tracers cut across the darkness and rain. Some hit our wooden walls
and roof; others zipped by with a shirring noise. The shells and bullets came
from the city, perhaps from my own father and brothers.

The night was bright. Flares descended like the annual temple fireworks,
pretty but way too loud and intense. The cycle of darkness, explosions, lights,
sounds, and darkness went on and on. Helicopters and fixed-wing planes
sprayed the ground with light and heavy shells.[1] Sometimes parachuted flares lit
up the sky followed by multiple explosions. We stayed on the floor, praying.
When something landed on or bounced off our walls or furniture, everyone
screamed in terror. I cried. My ears rang from the explosions and screams.

Mother decided to return to the trench. We ran out into the furious monsoon rain, whirring bullets, and exploding shells. We forgot our war drills,
running through the backyard every which way. At the mouth of the trench,
I stopped at the sight of the waist-deep water.

"Ah pret! [Little Devil!]" Screamed my mother, "Get in! Now!"

"But Mae, there's—" and I went headfirst into the trench. I opened my
mouth to cry and instead swallowed muddy water. One and then two kids fell
onto my back underwater. I swallowed a lot before Mother pulled us all up. The
water was up to my brothers' chins.

I coughed out muddy water.

"I'm sorry, so sorry," Mother was terrified. "Let's go next door. They might
have a better shelter."

Smoke and steam was everywhere. Bullets whizzed by; artillery shells lit up
the skies and rocked the ground. Next door was hundreds of yards away—we
couldn't even see it from our house. We ran right behind Mother, keeping our
heads low and crying in terror. But our neighbors' trench was full of water and
in worse shape than ours.

"They must have evacuated," Mother said. "Let's go to their house. They
could still be inside."

Our neighbors' house was made of concrete, a fact that gained new signifi-
cance in the midst of the shelling. I had visited only a few times before. Like our
parents, Ah Chhay's father was a civil servant and his mother was a homemaker.
They had moved in just a few months ago. The five-year-old son was Ah Chhay.

We called his mother Mak Ah Chhay and his father Pa Ah Chhay. (*Mak* and *Pa* are the city words for "mother" and "father," respectively.)

We didn't know these neighbors very well. Still, we sought their hospitality at this terrifying time. We pounded on the door several times. Mother called out, identifying herself. We screamed out, too.

The door stayed closed. We felt abandoned. We had nowhere to go, no one to turn to for help. Mother wept. Then the door opened just a crack. A woman's voice whispered: "Who is it?"

"It's us, Bawng Srei [Elder Sister]," Mother said.

The door opened. "Oh, it's you. Come on in! You're all soaking wet," said a gentle voice. "Please come in!" Mak Ah Chhay's small, thin frame stepped aside.

It was warm and dry inside the concrete walls. I felt safe.

Mother was still crying. "We were nearly drowned in our trench. Can we please stay with you, just for a while?"

"Of course, of course. Stay as long as you like," said the small woman.

Mak Ah Chhay's husband was in the militia, just like my father and brothers Simona and Serey. She and her two small boys were as scared as we were, and they appeared just as pleased with the company.

Even though our family was drenched in mud, Mak Ah Chhay encouraged us to join her huddle for warmth. Once in a while, stray bullets rattled the walls, as if someone was throwing stones, but the concrete stayed solid. Mother sang a lullaby.

"*Kon euy kheng tuv* [Go to sleep, my children]," said Mother.

I leaned closer for comfort and warmth. I felt very sorry for her. I knew she was tired and scared too. Despite the loud noises outside, Mother's voice calmed us. I held on tight to her, as did my brothers. Soon, we were all asleep.

I woke early the next morning. It was quiet except for small-arms fire every now and then. I tried Mak Ah Chhay's radio but got static. The soldiers must have stopped fighting to eat, I thought. Against Mother's orders, I went out and looked at the walls of the house. Bullet holes and shrapnel scars were everywhere. If this house weren't made of concrete, we'd all be dead by now, I thought. I picked up a handful of twisted bullets. Inside, I couldn't resist showing off my find.

Mother was mad. "Get rid of those or I'll get rid of you," she said. I threw out my war booty fast.

About three hours later, the fighting resumed. My little brothers and I ran back into Mak Ah Chhay's house. My elder brother Norane was next door at our house to pick up a few essentials. He returned, breathless.

"Our house is still there," he said, "but there are many holes. The south wall has a hole as big as a car," he said.

Mother gripped Nosay and Monika tighter. No one said a word.

I thought, as soon as the soldiers stop for lunch or dinner, I'll go see for myself. However, the fighting went on for five days, most heavily during the night. The war didn't stop for meals. The explosions shook the house all hours of the day and night. Dust rained from the ceiling and I thought the walls would fall on us. We kept our heads as low as the concrete floor. I was scared by the machine-gun fire and explosions, *tat tat tat, boom boom boom*!

The days seemed long but the nights even more so. I cursed the airplanes that droned in the sky. I didn't care to identify them anymore. All I thought was that they could hit us. "On whose side are they?" I would say, screaming in frustration. "Why would anyone want to kill us?" Someone would yank me down to the floor as artillery rocked the house.

Every day we had rice gruel and watery soup with salted fish. As a picky eater, I began losing weight. Soon, we ran out of food. By the time the fighting slowed down, I was ravenous. My elder brother Norane and I went out in the rain, hungry, cold, and scared. We gathered anything we saw, including dead pigs and chickens. Oh, how I hated this war. How I really, really hated it!

The radio had been silent for days. We had no news from the city. I didn't know who was winning the damn war. We were caught between the bullets of our father and brothers and those of the communists. We worried that our father and brothers were hurt—or dead. Mother did her best to ease our anxiety and hide her tears. I, however, couldn't stop thinking.

"They're killing each other, for what? When will this end? When will all this stop?" I received no answers. I found myself believing that no one could help us, not even Lord Buddha. If he existed, he'd hear our prayers. He wouldn't let us suffer like this!

When Norane and I scavenged for food with our slingshots, I hid my fear—and I no longer cared about killing other people's chickens when I had to. We were often lucky to find dead animals and wild vegetables, but we really needed fever and pain medicine.

One morning, during a lull in the fighting when we'd managed to find a couple of chickens, we ran smack into a platoon of twelve soldiers that included four Khmer Rouge fighters. They all wore black cotton pajamas and the well-known rubber tire sandals.

They carried very little combat gear. Across their chests hung pouches with magazines and Chinese-made grenades, the kind with foot-long wooden handles. On their backs hung cloth tubes about four inches around, packed with uncooked rice. Their largest weapon was a small mortar and B-40 grenade launcher. These men were "the enemy." I wondered if my father and brothers had seen them in battles.

The men pointed new Soviet and Chinese-made AK-47 assault rifles at us.

I wet my pants. My hands went up and the guerrillas laughed.

Some had yellowish teeth but most had white teeth. I had expected blackened teeth like I saw in the frequent cartoons depicting the Vietcong. (The Vietcong were rumored to chew betel nuts, which discolored their teeth.) One lowered his rifle and smiled at me. I saw his crooked, black teeth. So the story of the Vietcong with blackened teeth was partly true.

A Khmer Rouge cadre in his early twenties asked politely: "Oan Pross [Little Brothers], where are you going?"

I didn't know what to say or think.

"Don't be scared, Oan Pross. We are your friends," he said.

"Food, food," I sobbed.

They lowered their weapons and spoke in Vietnamese. I stopped crying, but I was scared. One Khmer Rouge fighter said, "We have some rice to trade for your chicken," he said. "Will you trade?"

We had enough rice to last us a while, so I said, "Bawng [Elder Brother], do you have medicine for flu or fever? We really need it."

Norane kicked my butt to shut me up, handed the man my two dead chickens, and quickly stepped back. Scared shitless, I thought to myself. Some head of family you are. From that point on, I felt that I was "deputy" to the man of the house, Norane.

The older fighter said something, and one of his men produced some white pills. "Here's some aspirin. A fair trade for your chickens," he emphasized the last two words, *your chickens*. "Go home and don't say anything or I'll come and find you. Go. Now."

We grabbed the medicine and walked backward, our eyes on them. When the laughing guerrillas melted into the forest, we rocketed off until we collapsed at the front door where everyone was waiting. Mother was relieved to see us. Nobody asked where we got the aspirin, and we didn't say anything about meeting the Vietcong and the Khmer Rouge. It was quiet that night. The monsoon rain came and went. I snuggled into the warm blanket. No aircraft flew overheard and nothing fired or exploded. It had been only weeks since the first explosion. Surely Father and our brothers would come back home now.

Little did I know it was only the beginning.

Before the war would end, children and old people would suffer much. Land mines and weapons from foreign countries would threaten millions of homeless civilians. The civil war would kill or injure thousands of thousands. It would take five years before the Americans would stop supporting Lon Nol. The Khmer Republic would collapse in its own corruption, but not before more than a half million Khmer died senselessly.

4

Shocks and Surprises

Angkor Wat and Domdek

A massive rainstorm came and refreshed everything. Afterward, the sun returned with a heat so strong that rainwater evaporated into a thick fog blanket that covered Siem Reap. A humid breeze riffled the coconut and banana trees. Through the early morning haze, a rainbow glowed in the distance. Birds sang.

Surrounding me were the scents of war: gunpowder, cordite, and burned things. A coconut tree was blown in half. Branches were stripped off other trees. Shattered tree trunks littered the ground. Stillness pervaded the scene. Except for rooting piglets and sows, the road was deserted. I considered our next meal.

Even the thought of chasing pigs tired me out; I could stun a hen with my slingshot, but not a pig. Besides, I thought, chicken tastes better. It would have to be chicken today.

Norane and I had been out several times to forage, but the other children had been cooped up for almost three weeks. This morning it was quiet, like it had been yesterday. Although we hadn't heard a single shot in the past twenty-four hours, Mother refused to let my little brothers out, not even to the outhouse. After hearing much pleading and repeated promises to stay nearby and to run home at the first sound of gunfire, Mother very reluctantly agreed to let my brothers play outside. The boys rushed to climb the guava tree in the yard. I stepped out cautiously.

"Don't go too far. Take care of your brothers," Mother said, peering through the window. I waved in acknowledgment.

Framed by the window, my mother looked small. She's a lot thinner, I thought. Her once rounded face was now narrow and pale, her puffy eyes sunken, and her hair unkempt. I had seen her cry when she thought we were asleep.

I picked a guava fruit from a branch below my brother Nosay and bit into the crunchy sweetness. The fragrance reminded me of my home next door—the house we'd vacated. I thought of returning to get some of my things. Our home was only a short walk away. Still, I was afraid to go alone. Besides, Mother would be angry with me. Frustrated, I sat on a tree trunk and cried.

My brothers went back inside. I rose to go in behind them. Around the other side of the house I glimpsed men wearing black pajamas and holding guns. They were headed our way! I ran inside and locked the front door, giving Norane a silent head signal to get out of the house. He pulled our little brothers out through the back door. Everyone else tensed up.

"What's going on?" said Mealanie.

"Hide, they're here!" I said. "They're here, they're here!" I fought to catch my breath.

"Who's here?" Mother asked, walking to the front door.

I whispered: "Youn! Vietcong! Khmer Krahom!" She couldn't understand me. Trembling, I pulled her arm until she stepped back from the door. Outside, Norane and my little brothers hid in the banana grove. Everyone in the house was quiet.

As I motioned for them to follow me out through the back door, the front door shook from hard, pounding blows. Everyone froze. I shuddered as I recalled trading our chickens for aspirin. They've come to get me and Norane, I thought.

The loud pounding on the door shook the house. We huddled in a corner, afraid to move. I waited for them to kick the door down and rush in.

"Open up, now! We know you're in there!" a man called out in Khmer. Mak Ah Chhay's littlest kid began to whimper. I held my breath. She covered his mouth with her hand.

"We're friends," said another voice from the door. "We're here to help you. Please open up!" We huddled even closer together.

Then, from the banana grove, my brothers cried. I tried hard not to go in my pants again. The armed men entered through the back door casually.

"Good morning, folks. We didn't mean to scare you but we need to talk to you all," said the first man to enter, his rubber-tire Ho Chi Minh sandals tracking mud on the floor. He spoke slowly, clearly.

"Everyone in the area is being asked to move away from the fighting." He sounded almost polite with his loud, broken southeastern accent.[1] "We need you folks to move out as soon as you can, hopefully within the next thirty minutes. We don't have very much time so we need you out of here soon, please."

Mother and Mak Ah Chhay regained some color. "Why do we have to go?" Mother asked.

The man opened the front door. More Vietcong entered in a relaxed manner, holding their weapons loosely, looking around as though they had never seen the inside of a house before. Some faces were familiar. They had taken my dead chickens for medicine. I am the one who brought them here to terrorize our family, I thought.

"Please hurry. The cease-fire might not hold for long. Bring essentials only. You'll be allowed to return to your homes soon enough, three days at most," he said.

"Go to Angkor Wat," said the man who spoke without an accent. "Everyone in this area has been asked to shelter there. It's much safer and there'll be food for you. Looks like you folks could use some," he gave us a broad, crooked smile. He motioned to the other pajama-clad men to head out the door.

Mother barked out precise commands: gather food, sleeping mats, blankets, an ax, and a plastic tarp for the rain. Everyone scrambled.

Norane and I rode bikes to the old house to get supplies. I was stunned to see the roof tiles scattered on the ground and the bullet holes on the south wall of our beautiful, hand-built wooden home. There was the hole that Norane had reported—"big enough to drive a car through," he'd said. If the guerrillas had stopped here, they could have walked right in.

I paused at the bottom of the stairs and looked around. For two years, I thought, we had a happy and peaceful life in this house.[2] Norane yanked me up the stairs. We got an ax for firewood and packed our two bicycles with anything we could use. I looked down the street—a crowd of people made their way toward Angkor Wat as the guerrillas walked into another house. I exhaled. Maybe I hadn't brought the Vietcong to our family after all. They appeared to be knocking on doors everywhere.

Along the trail to Angkor Wat, we encountered small groups of Khmer Rouge and Vietcong who asked if we were hungry. "You can get food at a stockpile near the Angkor Wat," they said. "If you go together, you can get even bigger rations."

Starved for nearly three weeks, we didn't care where the food came from. We heard what we wanted to hear: that we could have food, shelter, and safety from the fighting. We wanted to go quickly, but the crowd was slow. The weak ones lay in the shade. Others sat anywhere they could. Some lay bleeding by the road. The wounded had dirty, blood-soaked bandages. Children walked around crying; some lay on the roadside. I remembered our house by the river, where I used to care for injured animals on the back porch. Now we had no porch, no house.

"Can we help them?" I asked my mother.

"Don't look at them, keep your eyes on the road," she said. "Watch your brothers or they'll become like those children."

The thought upset me. Lonk, Nosay, and Monika would surely die if they were separated from us. They were so curious. Once they picked up a live M-79 grenade the size of a fist. Luckily, it didn't explode.

"I'll make sure my brothers won't get lost." I said. I felt bad that I couldn't help the people by the side of the road, but my family needed me. Poor kids, I thought to myself. I hope they find their parents soon.

We met villagers from near and far. All had sad stories: relatives lost to stray bullets or shrapnel, burying loved ones under exploding artillery and heavy rain. All looked as though they had not slept, eaten, or bathed for weeks. I was also tired, hungry, and sick of thinking about what could happen to us. I was truly sick of this damned war!

We pushed our way through the crowd to find a decent place in the Angkor Wat. It felt right to seek refuge here at this time of trouble. The Angkor Wat, after all, was the symbol on our national flag during Sihanouk's rule and even now under the Khmer Republic. Also, the Angkor Wat temple was large enough to accommodate the entire town.

It was about three o'clock when we arrived at the edge of the southern moat. The trees here had branches, and they gave us a welcome shade. We rested. Although more people went by, many stopped to rest like us. Our mats, blankets, and other packed items made the 2-mile walk difficult. While others discarded their things on the side of the road, we chose to drag our belongings beside us. We'd need them sooner or later.

To follow the roundabout trail meant another 2-mile hike through the crowds. The shortest route was through the moat, only a few hundred feet's swim through waters infested with leeches and snakes. Alligators lived among the reeds and lotus plants.

The water isn't terribly deep, I thought. No problem crossing it by myself, but it would be a problem for my little brothers, my pregnant mother, and our belongings, too. I also needed to help our neighbor's two little boys. Mak Ah Chhay had been kind to us.

A feeling of panic crept over me. Which way should we go: through the nasty moat or on the crowded road? Oh, what to do?

Suddenly, a series of explosions rocked the ground. We dropped automatically. Smoke darkened the sky, flames glowed, and shrapnel sprayed tree chunks on our heads. People dove into the moat and cleared a muddy path to the temple walls. The decision was made for us.

Norane and I threw a log into the water. Children flew past. I looked up to see Mother tossing Nosay into the moat. My three brothers and Mak Ah Chhay's two boys floundered, coughing up water. I dove in and helped the boys to the log. The older ones could swim but being tossed into the water must have shocked them. Also, they knew of the alligators, snakes, and leeches.

Someone was missing. I could not see my littlest brother Monika! Panic again, and then I found him and helped him to the log. My three little brothers, Ah Chhay and his brother, all accounted for. I pushed the log with five clinging children. We waded through the mud and ran up the grassy slope with giant buffalo leeches dangling from almost every part of our bodies. Some leeches were as large as bananas. Finally we reached the 15-foot sandstone walls of the temple.

"Can't get any worse than this," I thought. Despite the waves of terrified humanity in front of us and behind us, I stopped to pull the leeches off the little ones, who cried as they clung to me.

Tears ran down my cheeks as I pulled leeches from necks, arms, legs, and even inside my pants. Mother, Norane, Mealanie, and Mak Ah Chhay had simply disappeared. I gave up. I closed my eyes and screamed: "I can't do this any longer. I just can't, goddamn it!"

When I opened my eyes, my brother Lonk, two years my junior, was just disappearing into the crowd. I scrambled after him, dragging the other children along. I cursed and cursed until I saw him with my mother and the rest of our group. Amid exploding artillery, a tremendous relief engulfed me. I fell on the grass. I never cried so hard.

It was sunset when Norane carried me into the outer walls of the Angkor Wat. We were both exhausted. We were hungry, but there was no sign of the promised stockpile of food. The Khmer Rouge had tricked us. Oh, how I hated them. Would we ever get to go home? Where was home, anyway? We couldn't stay in our bullet-ridden house.

For the next two or three days, I couldn't eat or sleep. Mother tried to cheer me up. I had a very high fever. I felt I was dying. "Why me?" I cried out in the dark. "Why us? Why Cambodia?"

Like other Cambodians, I believed that suffering was caused by lack of merit. I thought to myself, I'm suffering because I've done evil things in my past life and I'm paying for it now. I waited for the agent of death to claim my soul. This Buddhist belief helped me accept my fate, whatever it might be.

Mother gave me more and more of the aspirin that I had received from the Vietcong. The following week, my fever broke. So did my appetite. However, there was no food in the campsite at all. The communist guerrillas were very efficient and effective con men. They had massed us in the temple ruins to serve as human shields. Earlier, an artillery crossfire and air attacks had killed many civilians. A ground attack by the state militia would hit us first.

It was difficult to be positive. Many around me were in shock, and some killed themselves. Word came quickly when it happened, and everyone rushed out to look. People were alarmed when they heard of suicide, and stunned when they witnessed the dead body. But then it happened again and again. When we saw people gathering, we knew it was another suicide. After a while, it became routine. "Another one?" said someone when we heard of a woman jumping off the high wall. We became numb.

I hoped that we wouldn't have to make such a terrible choice, although the thought had crossed my mind. The tallest level in the temple complex was about 180 feet. Just close my eyes, jump, and all my problems would be gone—no more suffering. But I couldn't let my family down, particularly my mother. Her belly was growing. I had to be strong for their sakes. I had no choice but to be hopeful. I felt responsible for my family's well-being, even if I was only nine.

Khmer Rouge cadres often came by to eye Norane, who was eleven, and Mealanie, who was thirteen. Mother hid them. My sister was "old enough for bad men," she said. I wasn't sure what Mother meant but I knew the Khmer Rouge took anyone and anything they wanted.

As I was too young and too small to be of interest to the Khmer Rouge, much of the daily food search became my responsibility. I was no longer deputy; I was now head of two families. Frogs were hard to catch. First you had to find them, and then you had to be quicker than they were. Snails were an easy food source, but not plentiful enough. I forced myself to conquer my fear of snakes and to catch them in the moat. We ate snake soup with water hyacinth blossoms. We baked, boiled, steamed, stewed, and roasted snakes and snails. Sometimes we enjoyed a real treat: boiled rice with salt.

I thought I had learned the true meaning of starvation in the seven weeks we spent in Angkor Wat, living on snakes and snails from the moats. How naïve I was.

One day, I watched a man walk from group to group, searching. I had seen him before but I couldn't figure out who he was. He passed me by. His pale-white skin blotches clicked in my head. It had been a year since I'd seen him, but now I remembered who he was.

"Pou Rou, Pou Rou!" I screamed. It was my favorite uncle, Uncle Rou! I ran and clung to his neck like a baby orangutan.

"Who are you?" he said. He looked at me closer. "Oh," he said at last. "You're one of Bawng Chem's sons, aren't you?"

"Yes, yes! I'm Nachith," I said. "It's me, Ah Nak. Did you recognize me? I recognized you!"

"Yes, I remember you now, nephew. You're taller now," he smiled sadly, "and so skinny."

I nodded. I hugged him again to convince myself he was real. Seeing Uncle Rou was better than seeing Buddha. I was ecstatic. I held his hand tight, fearing he would disappear.

Did Lord Buddha send him? I thought to myself. Perhaps, but I couldn't believe that anymore, not after what happened. I pulled Uncle Rou past thousands looking at us. I was proud because he came to save us. He, not Lord Buddha, was my savior.

Like a mad water buffalo, Mother rushed through the staring people, bulging belly and all. For nearly twenty minutes, she wept on Uncle Rou's shoulder. None of us could stop our tears.

Father had learned where we were and sent Uncle Rou to fetch us. Uncle Rou came on his oxcart from behind enemy lines, across the heavy fighting area, which was completely controlled by the Khmer Rouge. He had come to take us to Domdek, my mother's home village, which was in the communist-liberated zone and controlled by Khmer Rouge guerrillas. Uncle Rou said we could live there in peace.

"How do we get past the Khmer Rouge guards?" I whispered to Mother.

"One step at a time," Mother said.

Uncle Rou had brought rice and salted, sun-dried fish. That afternoon, we feasted while others looked on. I shared my small fortune with the nearest kids who stood staring at me. They fought over the little I gave them. Mother gave the rest of the food to our neighbors. Trying not to draw attention, we quietly said "see you again" to Mak Ah Chhay and our other friends. (In our culture, you never say good-bye.) That evening, we loaded everything and left, keeping our eyes straight ahead. I wanted to see Mak Ah Chhay and her boys one last time, but I couldn't look back. I would feel responsible if I saw their pleading eyes as we left the temple. We had gotten to know many of those we were leaving behind, but we couldn't save them. That's what war does, I thought. War separates you from your friends.

Travel was slow going. The road was a muddy mess of clay, knee-deep in water. The oxen were often immobile. We pushed and pulled at the oxcart. My face landed in the mud frequently.

I was surprised to see people going in both directions. I couldn't understand why people were headed to the place we were escaping from. Some of the kids my age stared at us without comprehension. They probably thought we were nuts, heading toward the Khmer Rouge zone.

It was getting dark. I was afraid of walking around at night because I could not see a thing. I fell frequently. I was miserable, crying. Suddenly, there came the now-familiar screeching whistle, one volley after another and a series of explosions. *Kaphew! Dank, dank, dank!* Bodies and debris flew. Once more, my face landed on the thick mud.

When I looked up, the trees along the road were lit like a trillion candles. My ears rang and my head spun. Uncle Rou's oxcart was gone. My family was gone. Everyone was gone. I screamed! I heard Mother's distant shouts of horror. More shells exploded, but I ignored them and staggered toward Mother's voice.

I saw a small body moving in the mud. I crawled to its weeping sounds. It was my five-year-old brother Nosay. He must have been blown off the cart.

"Are you all right, Oan [Little] Nosay?" I asked. I felt his body. To my relief, he was not wounded. "Can you move? Can you walk?" I said, fearing the worst. He stood up and we followed the road.

A terrified Norane came looking for us. Cursing, he hoisted Nosay on his back. We sloughed through the mud until we caught up with the group. Incredibly, they were untouched. Nosay and I had apparently disappeared when the shelling began.

The oxen couldn't pull the cart through the thick sludge. All night, we walked in the mud half asleep, hanging on to the oxcart. Only our belongings and Monika rode. We never rested. When it was time to relieve ourselves, we did our business on the roadside in such a hurry that it was really very messy. Around us were hundreds of other homeless Khmer searching for safety and security. We were now refugees, displaced persons in our own country.

Mother had grown up in Domdek, leaving for the Bakong district when she married my father over twenty years ago. Her cousins, aunts, and her brother Uncle Vang and his family still lived there. I had heard that two of Uncle Vang's sons were high-level cadres in the Khmer Rouge, and those who weren't in the Khmer Rouge were at least sympathizers, including Uncle Rou. By choice or by force, we didn't know.

We arrived at Domdek in the morning. It was a small town some 18 miles west of Siem Reap, far enough from the shelling. We went to Uncle Rou's house.

People stared. "Go back where you came from," said some of the villagers. Some cursed us, calling us *pret* (devil), perhaps because we were so dirty. The pret are known to cover their bodies in mud to hide their true identities.

As Mother's pregnancy progressed, it was only Uncle Rou and his family who helped her with meals and supplies, with caring for the little ones. Uncle Rou told us to keep a low profile. So many of the townspeople were related to us in one way or another, but they either wanted to wipe us out or, at best case, pretend we weren't there. It wasn't surprising that very few looked kindly on us. Father and my three brothers were fighting on Lon Nol's side, so we were the enemy. War turns family against one another, I thought to myself.

In Domdek, there was no school. All the families had already sent their sons and daughters to fight Lon Nol's army—and they had suffered many casualties. The Khmer Rouge's ruling body Angkar (literally translated as "organization") made itself felt throughout the village. The secretive Angkar Leu (High Organization) reigned supreme. Those staying in town worked on the communal farm. The cadres told us we should all lend hands there. The leaders eyed Norane and Mealanie, hinting that they should join the troops on the front lines. It seemed we had to obey orders or die. The other option was to leave before the Khmer Rouge got a tighter grip on the town. We had to leave soon or end up fighting our father and brothers. We packed the few necessities we had, ready to dash at a moment's notice.

However, it was impossible to get out of Domdek. The battle lines shrunk and expanded each day. We never knew for sure which area belonged to which faction or group. Aside from that, travel was severely restricted. Those caught traveling without papers and identification were punished severely or shot like dogs on the street. Also, the communist cadres imposed frequent curfews, sometimes for twenty-four hours, and there was always the sense that people were spying on us. It seemed you couldn't cough without the comrades knowing.

This, however, didn't stop people from scavenging for food. The risk of being shot did not stop the roar of hunger. We waited for the right time.

Villagers sneaked off to the city to barter for supplies. From bits of overheard conversation when they returned, we pieced together rumors that Siem Reap was under Lon Nol's control again. The defensive lines had shifted away from the center of town. But then the next person said that the Khmer Rouge cadres were winning. We didn't know which way was up, but we thought whatever Siem Reap was like, it must be better than Domdek.

Rice was scarce. Money was worthless; everything was bartered or traded. Gold, diamonds, and rice were top commodities. People with food stocks wanted gold, diamonds, precious stones, and valuables. Price manipulation was merciless; kinship or friendship got you nothing.

My family had a small amount of gold, but with all the mouths to feed, it wouldn't last long. Mother decided to invest what was left in a food stall. We were going to make rice noodles and trade it for rice.

Making rice noodles was very simple but very hard work. First we soaked clean grains of rice for four hours. After removing the husk from the grains, we ground it to a watery liquid. For twelve hours, the liquid was drained off through a fine cotton cloth.

At four in the morning, we mixed rice flour to make dough by hand. We pounded the lumps into smooth dough, softened the dough with warm water and squeezed it through a noodle maker. After a couple of hours of arm-wrenching work, we blanched the fine noodle strands for a few seconds in boiling water, then drained and folded the noodles to size.

The entire process took a very exhausting twenty-four hours from start to finish. We all pitched in to keep busy, to keep our minds occupied, and to survive.

This was when I learned what being a *chun phearse khlourn* (refugee) really meant. We were refugees, seeking safety and fleeing from war. But who can really escape a war?

After three months in Domdek, we hated it so much that we were willing to risk our lives and head back to Siem Reap, to our old house by the river. My family's motto was "better dead than red." Mother would give birth soon, and we didn't want the new baby to arrive in such a hostile environment. We planned to leave just about everything behind when we left, so no one would suspect anything, particularly our relatives and nearest neighbors.

Two hours before our departure, Uncle Vin, Mother's elder brother, arrived from Siem Reap. He came east of the defense line on National Highway 6 with a group of firewood cutters. He knew we were in Domdek and came to get us out. What perfect timing.

We left town a few hours later than we planned, relying heavily on Uncle Vin's wisdom and on good omens.

Compared to Uncle Rou's oxcart journey, the trip to Siem Reap was a breeze. We sat in Uncle Vin's trailer, pulled by a 150-cc Honda motorcycle on the smooth asphalt of National Highway 6, a two-lane road. We stopped at a few Khmer Rouge checkpoints along the way. Some Marlboro cigarettes here and there got us through. I was pleasantly surprised by how easy it was to get through the Khmer Rouge line. "Uncle Vin knows what he's doing," I thought.

He said the government line would be more difficult. He was right. The Lon Nol soldiers didn't allow us through. The curfew was on; we had arrived too late. With some other families, we spent the night on a plain off the main road, right between the two fighting forces.

The night in the bush was uneventful. There was no real fighting, just an occasional guerrilla probe. Now and then a loud boom would wake us. "Land mine," I would hear. "Grazing cattle, or some unlucky person perhaps."

I got up the next morning, fresh and ready to go. Everyone was packing up. I was eager to return home, to see my father and brothers. Strangely, Uncle Vin told us it was too early. My usually gutsy uncle decided that it was wiser to wait. Like everyone else in our group, he feared land mines that might have been planted while we slept. Even the children were quiet.

After nearly three months of intense fighting, the defensive lines of both sides had been drawn. Now the plan was apparently to attack, counterattack, and plant land mines to expand areas of control. The land around us was sowed with thousands of antipersonnel land mines. We waited for someone to lead us through the mined area. By about nine in the morning, our group arrived at the government defensive line, safe but shaken. The soldiers accepted cash and anything valuable. Neither Mother nor Uncle Vin offered anything so they refused to allow us through.

While the Khmer Rouge guerrillas, who volunteered to fight without pay, were happy with a cigarette and some food, Lon Nol's paid soldiers extorted what they could. Finally, Uncle Vin pulled out a small stack of the new riel notes and gave it to the soldiers. The bills were different from the Sihanouk era banknotes. Wow, they even have their own money now, I thought to myself.

Our trailer stopped at the old house by the river, Father's familiar "Schoolteacher/Administrator" sign at the front gate. I could see a trench in the back. Uncle Vin's wife and children poured out of the house to greet us. I briefly hugged my little cousins but kept going past, running to the front room, looking for my father and elder brothers. The room was empty. Down the hallway, into the kitchen, even the old pantry I went, searching. No one was there. I ran outside and peeked in the trench. Nobody. Where is Pa? I thought. Where are Larony, Simona, and Serey? Mother said my question aloud.

"Have you heard from *Pa Vier* [the children's father]?" asked Mother. "How about Ah Kgnee [Larony]?"

"They're all fine," Uncle Vin said. "Don't worry."

We ate with Uncle Vin and his family. There wasn't much space to sit down. Uncle Vin suggested that we stay at Uncle Thongdy's vacant house nearby. Uncle Thongdy, Father's younger brother, was a district chief in a town far from Siem Reap. He and his family were also caught in a communist-controlled area and had lost touch with everyone here in Siem Reap. We were not too happy about our new living arrangement, but at least we would have a roof over our heads and enough space for all of us.

Uncle Thongdy's neighborhood looked much the same as the one we'd just left. Cratered buildings sat empty, but most of the houses seemed to have people in them, and the trenches were apparently reserved for night-time. Siem Reap was indeed in better shape than it had been when we'd left for Angkor Wat in May. I hoped that Lon Nol had things under control.

About two weeks later, Father received permission to come home from the front lines. My three brothers were fighting the Khmer Rouge north of the city. Father had to hurry back to his post.

In the short time Father was with us, my younger brothers and I tagged along, but he pushed us away. I felt so rejected. I didn't know if I would see him again. I cried after he left.

Later, Father and my three brothers were allowed to come home more often. Their visits soon became routine, but they never stayed very long.

Uncle Vin and his family found a new place to live just blocks away and we moved back to our old house by the river. A few weeks later, Mother gave birth to Seiha. He was the last to be born in my family. It was important to all of us that he was born in a free zone, not in a communist zone. For what it was worth, at least one of us was not a refugee, and he was born free.

5

A Time of Plenty

Back Home in Siem Reap

The relentless cold had dried up the small ponds and streams. As the waters receded, ducks, sand cranes, and other waterfowl feasted on freshwater fish, snails, crab, and shrimp. The ending months of 1970 were also a season filled with death and destruction.

Larony was sent to Bangkok, Thailand, for a year of Special Forces training. He wrote us often. Mona was permitted to stay home to help the family. Father and Serey came home from the front lines more often but never for long.

Our trench here was dry and roomy. Since our first attempt earlier this year, we'd learned how to waterproof the dugout, cover its entrance, and ventilate the sides. We kept snakes and pests out of the trench by throwing in lime rinds. Every time we heard a boom, we instinctively ran to the trench. This time we stayed dry, with plastic sheeting and warm bedding. Escaping the shelling became routine, and we always slept inside our trench instead of the house. When the shelling was heavier than usual, we figured that China had just sent fresh supplies to the Khmer Rouge. It was common knowledge by this time that the Chinese backed Sihanouk and the Khmer Rouge, and the United States backed Lon Nol.

The attacks came without warning. Shells exploded in the crowded streets or marketplace. The wounded and the dead lay untouched for hours.

Schoolchildren died, too. The schools closed for weeks, sometimes months. We held sporadic classes behind sandbags at odd hours.

The Lon Nol military forces controlled the city. Anyone with a military connection had access to Swiss bank accounts and trips abroad. To those with the right position or contacts, the war was a great business opportunity. Arms dealing was especially lucrative with U.S. military aid pouring into the country and the government encouraging citizens to arm themselves. Ammunition and grenades were cheap and widely available; it seemed that every house had weapons. On the black market, government soldiers sold pistols and small arms to anyone with cash, including Khmer Rouge cadres. Subtle corruption was practiced in one form or another by those who could, even in my own family, where Father used his associations to obtain medicine and, more importantly, to avoid conscription of any more of his children.

By 1971, many of my older classmates and school friends were in Lon Nol's Republican Army. I was ten, just old enough to be recruited into the military as my elder brothers (excepting Norane) had been before me. Father didn't hesitate to pull some strings.

One of our family friends, a general and commanding officer, helped so that the rest of my siblings and I were spared from conscription, which is certain death on the frontlines. I never found out how the officer prevented our recruitment. Others must have died in our places. This trading of lives shamed me, but we had to survive.

Those with neither money nor strings to pull found themselves at the frontlines after only a few days of weapons training. The youngest were usually assigned to the high-casualty Grenade Corps, a group of children whose sole mission was tossing grenades at the enemy. They were trained to follow orders well. Their commanding officers or squad leaders were often only in their very early teens.

One day I saw my best childhood friend Lan going off to the front lines. We had been classmates since Grade II at Wat Damnak (equivalent to the second grade in the U.S.). Lan was now about age twelve. Unlike the rest of us, he had never liked playing soldier or war games, and yet now he was joining a real-life battalion.

That morning, he wore brand-new green government-issue fatigues with rolled-up sleeves and pant legs. An old helmet with a finger-sized hole was too large for his head. One hand held the helmet while the other held an M-16 automatic rifle. "Made in America," he said, smiling wryly. That was my last memory of Lan, walking shoulder to shoulder with the other conscripts.

Back at home, my family and I heard the wailing well before we saw Aunt Thet. My mother and I ran out of the house to see Aunt Thet heading our way, sobbing, with uncontrollable grief on her face. My hero, Uncle Vin, my mother's eldest brother, who had helped us escape the Khmer Rouge–controlled town of Domdek, was the family's first known war casualty.

Someone had witnessed the gory scene, and now everyone knew the story, or most of it. Uncle Vin was riding his motorcycle on National Highway 6, towing a cart carrying two of his children. They were headed to Pouk, a friendly town about 10 miles west of Siem Reap, to get some rice. National Highway 6 was under government control, but the Khmer Rouge ambushed them in broad daylight. The guerrillas shot Uncle Vin in the thigh and left him bleeding. I cringed thinking about my cousins watching their father die.

My family exhausted every avenue before someone found the two kids in Battambang Province, some 125 miles west of the location where my uncle was shot. We pooled resources and hired mercenaries to bring them home. It took two months to find the children and recover Uncle Vin's remains for a proper funeral.

Uncle Vin had had seven children, mostly girls, with the youngest child being three months old. Lack of a provider, on top of the sufferings of war and the deprivations of poverty, made life most difficult for his widow, Aunt Thet. We all suffered along with her and did what we could for the family.

Mother lost another of her three brothers to a dose of bad medicine. Her remaining brother (my Uncle Vang) and his family were in Domdek under the Khmer Rouge.

Friends, colleagues, and neighbors around us died. We wearied of attending funerals, sometimes one after the other. We stopped counting.

By the time 1972 rolled around, almost all men and able teenagers were at the frontlines. Fighting had so intensified that even young women were required to serve in the militia as rear guards.

At home my elder relatives listened to the radio, especially when it was time for the Voice of America (VOA) to broadcast. The VOA was almost a religious institution in my family. A cousin, Ang Khen (daughter of Uncle Khiev in Phnom Penh), was the most famous radio personality in my hometown, perhaps in all of Cambodia. As we kept on the alert for news from the front lines, we would turn up the volume so the neighbors would hear our celebrity cousin. We were so proud of Cousin Ang Khen, even though we'd never met.[1]

Radio was one of the primary channels for propaganda, as well. The new Lon Nol government repeatedly warned us of the inhumanity of Vietnamese soldiers. Sihanouk, on the other hand, asked that every able-bodied man sign up for the fight against Lon Nol.

Larony returned from Thailand in a new military jeep. He was now a second lieutenant in the Special Forces. He was granted a month's leave, after which he was to go defend Phnom Penh.

Larony was the pride of the family. One rich family acquaintance offered him their only daughter in marriage. Being the eldest child, it was only right for him to marry first. However, things were changing; traditions were breaking up. Larony was going to war so marriage was out of the question.

One hot afternoon as we watched Larony leave, I heard the elders say we should not expect to recover his body for burial. I couldn't cry. I had no tears left.

Very few of those who died at the battlefront were found, and then the bodies took weeks to arrive home, often headless. Many families were unsure if they were cremating the right body, but no one complained about the missing heads. It was part of tradition, after all. After each kill, it was the custom to cut off the enemy's head and parade it across town. Although this made me sick, I raced with the other kids who tried to be first to see the latest head parade every time the government's platoon returned from patrol. Some soldiers were known to enjoy their kill's fresh liver with rice wine. This practice was known in both the state and communist forces.

By the middle of 1972, the city was taking in refugees every day, mostly farmers from outside the city's defense perimeter. Gambling of all kinds sprung up in just about every alley. Thai baht and U.S. dollars were often used instead of the new Lon Nol currency. Soldiers who ran out of money gambled with bullets and grenades, which sometimes exploded and maimed bystanders.

Early one morning in 1973, while Mother, Seiha, and I were at the local market, a shell exploded. We automatically went flat on the ground. Blood squirted, coating the ground red. The air was filled with screaming, moaning, and cries for help. In our prone positions, we were trampled by the panicked crowd.

"*Chuy phawng, chuy kgnum phawng*! [Help me, please help me!]," I heard the injured pleading. I heard more explosions from far away. After years of war, I was still scared. I clung to Mother, who was shaking, hugging my little brother to her chest. Bodies lay twisted everywhere. Some crawled, trailing blood behind them.

The shelling stopped, but the horrific screams went on. We found ourselves in an open sewer. Around us were bodies, rubber sandals, and overturned baskets of fish, fruits, vegetables, and broken eggs. Flies buzzed everywhere. I heard the frantic screech of whistles.

We climbed out of the sewage canal and ran for cover. Mother and Seiha were unhurt, but I had bruises on my rib cage that pained me as I ran. A patch of smoke cleared and I saw a man pick up a purse, look around, and stuff it into his shirt.

This memory still sickens me: the smells, the screams and yells, the police whistles, and the man who stole the purse. Since then, I have never been comfortable in crowded places. Whenever I find myself in a crowd, I always move to the edges as quickly as I can.

I continued to go to school with my bruised rib cage, which hurt for weeks. In May 1973, I passed the school examination and was admitted to Angkor High School. I was now three years away from graduating and getting my high school diploma.

During high-jump practice on my second week as a freshman, the seniors gathered all of us younger students together. "A protest! A demonstration," somebody said. The older students forced me to the front with the other freshmen. When the line surged forward, I was pushed by students who were probably being pushed by others behind them. In this way, we were marched toward the city center. I heard slogans being chanted.

After about a mile of marching and shouted slogans, I saw a roadblock. Row after row of government soldiers, military, and city police aimed their weapons at us. American-made M-113 armored personnel carriers with 50-caliber machine guns and cannons swung in my direction. I sweated. My legs buckled. So did the marching line. There was more pushing and shoving from behind. Slogans came from the back of the crowd, something about the economic disparity among the people.

Suddenly, just above my head, bullets streaked by with those unmistakable *whoosh* and *phiv* sounds. My instinct was to hug the ground but I had learned my lesson from the bombing at the market with Mother and Seiha. I didn't want to get trampled again, so I stayed up.

As the crowd pushed and shoved around me, I ducked away from the whips and rifle butts. I found myself being pushed right through the military line. Beyond the line of uniforms, I scrambled and found myself with a few others in the central business district, only a short distance away from the bridge where I had jumped off as a kid during the monsoon seasons. I wanted to dive into the river, but the water level was too low. I looked back to see policemen firing warning shots but there must have been thousands of students. Some didn't even look like students. The crowd broke through the security line and flowed into the central business district, and I saw people break windows and doors.

Students were ransacking the business district. I was stunned. They hauled items from shops, put them in a huge pile, and lit the whole stack. The smoke and flames spread and some buildings caught fire. I stood there watching, not believing my eyes. Some older students pressured me to join in.

Caught up in the moment, I grabbed and tossed things into the bonfire. Suddenly, a box of ammunition exploded and everyone scrambled for cover. I took the chance and ran away down the street. I'll have none of this, I thought, and ran toward home.

I slowed down in front of my favorite bookstore. Books littered the floor and spilled out into the street. I picked up an old fortune-telling book, hoping for a good omen. Sitting down and staring at the front cover, I made a wish before opening the book. The page I turned to told of hardships and struggles ahead. It described a long and difficult journey, and it said I would make it to the end, although I would be very lonely and independent. I tossed the book aside and stood up to head home. Fortune books all sound the same, I thought.

The soldiers had closed the bridge and people were crossing the shallow river with tables, chairs, furniture, and water jars. I felt sorry for the owners of the looted shops. They had worked hard to build their businesses.

I never found out what the protest was all about. Some said it was a Khmer Rouge plan to ruin the local economy, but I believed that it was an anti-Chinese rampage. The poorer Khmer towns people blamed the Chinese for ripping them off and manipulating the economy.

I found out later that the looting had not been a surprise to all of the business owners. Many well-connected Chinese businessmen were warned, and they had managed to save their inventories, although their shops were badly damaged. However, business never really recovered. The economy limped along badly. We carried our money in baskets, turning over handfuls of bills for essentials.

Siem Reap City, once host to thousands of tourists, now overflowed with refugees fleeing communist-controlled areas. There was never enough food. Getting a meal on the table became an entire day's struggle. Rice with salt was a decent dinner.

By late 1973, the double, triple, and then quadruple-digit inflation had rendered the new Lon Nol money almost worthless. Father worked in the state administration section and was home every night. However, his monthly salary could buy only 50 kilograms (110 pounds) of rice, which lasted our family of twelve about two weeks.

To help make ends meet, Mother began to sell general supplies, food, fabrics, and medicine. At first she sold wholesale but turned to selling retail for more profit. Mother worked hard and her business grew. She made a lot of money, perhaps much more than father ever made. What was Mother's secret?

It was very simple. She didn't sell in the city market, like the other vendors did. She sold goods at the fishing villages that dotted the northern edge of the Tonle Sap Lake south of Siem Reap.

She also started the unheard-of plan of buying-now, paying-later. Her customers got goods on credit at a markup. "What do you need?" she asked her customers. "If I can get it to you sooner, would you pay extra?" Business was brisk. Once I went with her to collect a past-due debt. She met the delinquent customers as they came into shore, their boat bulging with fish. "I'll take two kilos of that for the money you owe," she said. The fisherman gladly handed her the fish.

Mother cornered a big chunk of the market, which brought her new friends as well as enemies. She was locked up for collaborating with the Khmer Rouge. She didn't stay in jail very long, though. Mother bought her way out, a common practice that everyone considered indirect taxation.

Despite that setback, Mother's success continued. It was a cutthroat business, particularly for a woman, but her clients became so numerous we had to help. I got to know Tonle Sap Lake and the people of the floating villages very well. The lake and the fishing villages along the shore were my sanctuary from the savagery in the city. I hardly went to school, which was so sporadic it wasn't worth risking the almost daily shelling.

Near the end of 1973, school was closed indefinitely. I opted to work in Mother's business and soon became a very successful fisherman in the lakeside village of Koh Mechrey (Mechrey Island). So did my brother Serey, who fell for Sa-Oum, the daughter of a fairly wealthy and well-known fishing family there.

In June 1974, our family had its first wedding. I left the lake for Serey and Sa-Oum's celebration. For the first time in two years, Larony came home from the battlefield.

Mother ran around like a headless hen, exhausted and excited at the same time, making the wedding as special as possible. On the other hand, Father was calm, sitting near the hibiscus flower bed. Almost the entire neighborhood showed up at the wedding party, even the uninvited. What we lacked, we improvised. Even in the midst of war, traditions had to be honored.

One of the uninvited guests was Lim Voeun, a twenty-four-year-old man from across the river who had been eyeing my sixteen-year-old sister Mealanie. Mother told him that Mealanie was too young to marry. It was a polite way of saying "you're not good enough for my daughter." Lim Voeun smiled and joined in the celebration.

That evening, during the traditional big banquet, we had live music from a hired local rock band. Powered by a rented Yamaha generator, classic Santana tunes such as "Black Magic Woman" rang out in Khmer, drowning out sounds of gunfire and artillery.

Larony then left to fulfill his military duties and the war continued around us for many months. I went back to fishing at Mechrey Island and saving my money. I didn't allow myself to spend any of it.

On April 2, 1975, a messenger hurried to Father's office with a telegram from Uncle Khiev in Phnom Penh. "Dear brother and sister," said the telegram, "Larony was injured by a land mine blast yesterday. He hurts very badly and is now hospitalized in Phnom Penh. You must come soon. Ang Khiev."[2]

Father rushed home with the news, but it was Mother's wailing that told us. I had not seen Mother so distraught since the fighting began five years earlier. I could not bear seeing anyone in my family suffering, most particularly my mother.

So much crying and moaning went on in every corner of the house for days that I sometimes thought Larony was already gone. Conditions in the government hospital were notoriously bad; many had died there. The phone lines were down. The lack of information drove my parents nearly insane.

Travel was very dangerous. The Khmer Rouge had cut off all land and water routes to Phnom Penh, leaving the airport as the only way in. Later I would learn that the airport was the only lifeline for Phnom Penh's two million plus residents and the state government soldiers who were defending the city. Supplies were flown in but the international airport was now a primary Khmer Rouge target. Airplanes in the air or in the bombproof bunkers, including the CIA's *Air America*, were destroyed.

Within a few days of the telegram, Father found a seat in an old DC-10 transport plane bound for Phnom Penh. We tried to believe that Father would bring back good news about Larony. No one mentioned the possibility that Father might not come back. After seeing Father off, we sunk into an eternity of waiting for his safe return.

We were all relieved to see Father walk back into our house a week later. He reported that Larony was recovering from serious wounds and still alive.

Then Father told us about his trip to Phnom Penh. Shelling interrupted the DC-10's haphazard landing. He and the other passengers rushed for cover and rode into the city some 6 miles away. Some never made it out of the plane.

We had expected the worst, but Father had returned safely, and Larony was still among the living. While on patrol with his unit, he had stepped on a land mine. His right leg was shattered, blown off just below the knee, his body riddled with shrapnel. To save him, surgeons had to amputate above his knee, working in very cramped conditions.

Cousin Yim Tha used her high-ranking army husband's influence and wealth to help Larony recover.

Larony woke up to find Father beside his bed. Around him, relatives shooed away flies and insects from the bloody bandages on his half-naked body and on what was once his right leg.

Being an officer in the army's Special Forces probably helped, but without family and wealth, Larony would have died; if not on the battlefield, then in the hospital. Father left Larony in the care of our relatives in Phnom Penh, and for his return home he chose a water route.

By early 1975, General Lon Nol's army was bloated with corrupt, demoralized, and incompetent soldiers who refused to fight or counterattack. They had lost many battles and had very little ammunition left. Several commanding officers had left for unknown places, along with their families and wealth.

Backed by Chinese-made weapons, the Khmer Rouge's all-volunteer army attacked the city and government installations at will, often in broad daylight. No longer a ragtag group, the Khmer Rouge outnumbered General Lon Nol's forces almost two to one (not counting the "ghost soldiers" added by state military leaders for more money). The defense perimeter shrank ever closer to the city center.

Early in April 1975, around the time we received news of Larony's injury, we heard that Marshal Lon Nol and his family left for Hawaii.[3] We knew the war was about to end.

But when Cambodia fell to the Khmer Rouge, the victors cleared out the hospitals. Larony's bandaged leg was still bleeding when he escaped on Uncle Khiev's bike.

Similar stories were told and repeated by countless others during that torrid April of 1975. Life was forever altered for the millions who managed to survive this uncivil five-year-long war.

6

An Era Is Ended

Siem Reap under Siege

The mighty Siem Reap River turned into a trickle. Neither wind nor breeze came to relieve the deadening heat of April. It was only a tiny bit cooler in the shade. The temperatures remained high in the dry season of 1975.

The Khmer New Year was fast approaching, so the cease-fire was a welcome relief. Although there would be no more offensives, everyone was tense because the fighting could resume at any moment, for any reason.

Adding to the tension were the sounds of holiday gunfire, a new ritual for expressing pleasure. In the midst of constant food shortages, bullets were still plentiful. The problem was, no one could tell the difference between a happy burst and a rebel attack on the city.

Since the war started, the firing of an automatic weapon skyward expressed joy at just about anything: a lunar eclipse, a thunderstorm, a birth, and even a winning hand of cards. This practice resulted in many deaths from the falling bullets. What goes up must come down.

We still grieved Larony's misfortune but our parents encouraged us to go out and enjoy ourselves.

"Tradition is to be upheld as much as possible," said Mother, "even during bad times."

The New Year is the most important holiday in Khmer culture. It is a three-day celebration of gigantic proportions held every year from April 13 to 16.

My gang included ten kids between eight and fifteen years of age. We cruised the neighborhoods. Our motto was "We are lovers, not fighters." However, every now and then, we would have fistfights with rival gangs, kids protecting their turf. I was always first to run away from a fight but I fought very hard when cornered. When there was no choice, I fought to win.

I went to the city center to buy some snacks at the outdoor market. I was still wary of crowded places, so I stayed just long enough to see what was happening. Young men and women gathered there for late meals, for snacks, and, of course, to check each other out.

In Khmer culture, a guy may kiss a girl only after he marries her. Since marriages were usually arranged, love usually came only after the ceremony.

Dating was not acceptable. Some dared but society looked down on these couples. However, the Khmer New Year was a big window of opportunity for the amorous. During the three days of the New Year holiday, the elders were so tolerant that they seemed to expect dating to occur.

The young people primped during each of the three Sangkram (New Year) days, my elder brothers and sister included.

The dating ritual consisted of young men and women glancing at each other from afar, whispering among friends or conveying subtle messages to someone who could perhaps pass it on to the object of their affection. For the most daring, there was direct eye contact. This is how romance and marriage blossomed among the Khmer youth of Siem Reap.

At the time, I didn't understand all the fuss. In fact, I found it rather embarrassing. However, since I liked the snacks and desserts sold at the stalls, I went with my elder brothers and sister.

Small groups sang traditional songs or played folk games, punctuated by occasional cheers or sounds of excitement. At almost every roadside and street corner, business was brisk. Everywhere I went, I saw people gambling, selling, spending, laughing, cheering, arguing, and generally having fun.

Gamblers avoided sleep during the New Year celebrations because it was the season for legalized gambling. Street lamps lit up makeshift tents for the money tables. Other areas were lit by bright kerosene lamps or dim candles. Hawkers vied to lure people into their tents; the more gamblers, the more commissions they got.

Drinking was equally serious. Many walked around unsteadily, drunk from *teuk tnout chu* (sour palm juice). Many were sleeping it off on the roadside, the corners, anywhere actually. War and suffering were a world away.

When I returned home that night, my parents were on the front porch, the coolest part of the house during the early evenings of high summer. They smiled at me but I knew they were still talking about Larony. He was alive, but for how long? What kind of life would he have in a society that doesn't respect the handicapped, even if he was a war veteran?

"There are some leftovers for you in the kitchen," Mother said. Dinnertime was around seven o'clock. I was very late so it meant leftovers and washing my own dishes. I warmed up a bowl of sour freshwater shrimp soup—a favorite dish—and sat at the table alone, eating my soup with steamed rice, roasted tube fish, and an assortment of pickled vegetables.

At about 7:20 that evening, I tuned in to a local radio station, which was playing music. I was dressing up and getting ready to head out again when the music stopped.

Must be a power failure, I thought. Then the radio came back on with a repeating message, which always annoyed me. Propaganda again, I thought. It was an announcement from the Kong Top Pakdevat (Revolution Army), calling on all government soldiers to lay down their arms.

"The war is over," said the announcer, "and King Sihanouk will once again lead Cambodia to peace and prosperity."

I disliked these frequent political announcements, so I ignored it.

"Come on, Ah Nak, let's go!" My friends called from the gate. I turned off the radio and rushed out the door.

A New Year's dance party was to start at eight o'clock and no sane teenager would miss that. There would be snacks, some gambling, traditional folk games, and, of course, dancing. There would be girls to watch—or dance with, if one were so bold.

That night of the New Year was best of all. Everyone tried to make the festive feeling last as long as possible. The gambling, the partying, the dancing, and the drinking increased in intensity. My friends and I lost money in the children's gambling section. It didn't matter—we were enjoying ourselves. It surprised me that our celebration was rarely interrupted by the expected shots and explosions.

I didn't get home until way past midnight. All my younger siblings were sound asleep. I sneaked in through the back door, past the old dark pantry room where I'd often read to myself, alone. Not tonight—tonight I had celebrated the New Year with friends. I tiptoed, but the creaking noises gave me away.

"So you finally decided to come home, eh?" Mother said softly, without turning from the candle that flickered at the altar, an offering for New Year angels. She held some lighted incense. I suddenly remembered that Larony was suffering at the Phnom Penh Hospital while I . . . I was having fun.

Mother placed the smoldering incense on the altar, bowed momentarily in prayer, and then turned her full attention toward me. "Had enough enjoyment for the year? Hungry?"

"No, not hungry, just tired. Good night, Mae!"

"Not so fast, young man. Brush your teeth first," she said.

"Mae, I'm too tired," I protested.

"You may go to bed after you brush," she said, and headed to her room. I paused momentarily, wanting to talk to her, but then I forgot what I wanted to say.

After a few token brush strokes, I went to bed. I didn't get up until half past ten when Father gave me a good kick in the butt.

It was now April 16, 1975, the last day of the Khmer New Year festivities. Unlike my gangmates, I had no hangover, I was still a virgin, and I still had money in my pocket.

It was an ordinary day at home. There was no news or radio broadcast of any importance. There were no programs on the radio. People mostly rested, but some celebrated a bit more to top off the New Year celebrations.

It had been a long two days and two nights of festivities. After nearly ten hours of sleep, I was still dog tired but ready for more. Today was the last day when I was allowed to go "reasonably wild" without fear of punishment, and I wanted to make the most of it.

"After your chores, you may go," said Mother, the house dictator, when I asked her for additional New Year funds.

"Mae, my friends are waiting at the gate," I whined.

"So? Get them to help you and you all can go sooner."

"Come on!" yelled one of the boys. "Let's go! We're going with or without you."

"Your call, Ah Nak," Mother said.

"Please, Mae, they're waiting for me. May I do my chores later?"

"No chores, no cash," Mother said.

"How about an advance, Mae?"

"An advance? Get out of here, I'm no fool!"

I came home sooner than expected that evening. Without a healthy budget for New Year fun, there was no reason to stay out late. I had Mother's deliciously spicy *prahok tek kreung* (fermented fish paste with ground pork, bacon fat, tamarind, and herbs and spices). Mother made hers Siem Reap style, with plenty of coconut milk.

After a light dinner with my little brothers, I fell into bed and a deep slumber.

At about two in the morning, I woke to the sound of machine guns. Either somebody was really happy that it was the New Year, or . . . I did not want to imagine the alternative. If the enemies had penetrated our defensive lines, we would surely be captured or killed.

"Get everyone ready! Go, put those packs on the bikes!" Mother barked.

"Get out of the house now, prepare to leave!" Father said. My older brothers Mona and Serey quickly loaded everything they could think of on the bicycles and on Father's small motorcycle. We all headed out the door.

"Stay down near that flower bush," Father told us. "Wait for me. I'll go find out what's happening."

"I want to go with you," I said, following him.

Father looked as if he were about to scream at me, but then he gestured for me to join him. The gunfire continued, with the sounds coming closer. I was frightened as I followed Father next door, where the neighbors were scrambling about their front yard.

"Any idea what's going on, Bawng?" said Father. "I thought we had a cease-fire."

"I've no idea," said one of the men, stopping briefly. "We're getting ready to leave if the fighting comes any closer," he said, adding that under orders of the Angkar Leu, the Khmer Rouge soldiers were calling on everyone to greet them. "I think they're in town now. They're saying the war is over."

"The war is over?" people whispered.

Stunned, my father and I headed toward the city center.

Along the way, people emerged from their hiding places to face the Ho Chi Minh sandals and black pajamas of these soldiers who had shelled our city, the enemy we had been battling for five painful years. Here we were, face to face with the enemy, and they looked like us, except for their dark uniforms, Mao Zedong caps, rubber tire sandals, and weapons. They carried bullhorns, AK-47s, B-40 grenade launchers, and other implements of war.

In the early morning hour, we saw the strangest thing. Soldiers from opposing armies embraced each other, smiling. I saw people crying from happiness. I started to cry as well. The war was over? The war was over! The war was finally over, for real this time, and I was still alive!

Although there were many unanswered questions and the future looked uncertain, the moment was precious. Everyone was so happy and excited, so much so that tomorrow seemed irrelevant.

The machine guns from this morning had actually been shots of celebration. The war was truly over. Under the leadership of Angkar, the Khmer Rouge had broken through Lon Nol's city defense line practically unopposed.

As we neared the city center, the number of Khmer Rouge soldiers increased. They were most concentrated downtown. We watched the soldiers firing energetically into the sky. They were the victors of a last battle that didn't happen. We learned later that Lon Nol's army had surrendered, except for small pockets of resistance from the last remaining loyalists, which the Khmer Rouge soon annihilated.

A Khmer Rouge commander stood in front of a bullhorn and called on everyone in the city to turn over their weapons and surrender in the name of Prince Norodom Sihanouk and Angkar's Kong Top Romdoss (Liberation Army).

"We are here to liberate all of you," he said. "You're liberated from the puppet government and its American imperialist master. Let's end the killing now!"

The people cheered and the Khmer Rouge cadres shot more bullets into the air. More arrived to watch the celebrating Khmer Rouge cheering and shooting at the sky.

The government soldiers had neatly stacked their weapons and now stood watching nervously from a short distance away. They tried to smile but they looked miserable.

"Don't worry, *Mith* [comrades]," said the Khmer Rouge commander. "Angkar will take care of all of you." He smiled to the loud cheering. Most of the cheers came from Khmer Rouge cadres.

"Please unload your weapons here," said another cadre through a bullhorn. "Put your guns in a neat pile. You don't need them any longer." The weapons stacked up, pile after pile of guns, rifles, pistols.

I returned home with my father and our neighbors. Some people danced in the streets, big smiles on their faces. Others cried. I asked Father how he felt about everything that was happening. He stayed silent all the way home, his twisted eyebrows a sign of his worry.

Then I remembered the radio message that I'd heard two nights ago, alone in the house. "The war is over," they had said. A chill ran through my spine and my hair stood on end. I felt very stupid. I could have told everyone what I had heard, but I had chosen to ignore it.

At home, everyone was uncertain. I turned on the radio to liven up the atmosphere, but all we heard was the repeated refrain: "In the name of Prince Norodom Sihanouk and the Kong Top Romdoss, please drop your weapons and surrender."

The name of the prince caused everyone to stop and gather around the radio. Most Khmer saw Sihanouk as the "Father of Cambodia," much as Americans revere George Washington.

Over the years that Sihanouk was in exile, the people continued to respect and trust him. After all, he'd been the one to win our independence from France in the 1950s. Since the war had broken out, however, we had not heard from Sihanouk except for his radio broadcasts appealing for new recruits "to fight against the infidel Lon Nol."

And now Sihanouk was back, stronger than ever, head of state once more. Little did we know at the time that as the Khmer Rouge defeated the last free towns in Cambodia that day, Prince Sihanouk was under house arrest in Phnom Penh.

The morning of April 18 was hot. The dry season was on us with a vengeance. Mother served a traditional Khmer breakfast of *baw-baw* (rice porridge), and we all ate, staring at one another. I was not sure what to think. The radio repeated yesterday's message: "In the name of Prince Norodom Sihanouk and the Kong Top Romdoss, please drop your weapons and surrender." To this the announcer added, "The war is over. Angkar is asking you to stop fighting and killing each other."

Outside, people were hurrying toward the city center. Curious, I rushed along with the running children.

People were seriously looting the shops at the old town market. In fact, every store in the city was being looted. The Khmer Rouge soldiers even helped to break open a shop's steel door, using B-40 grenades that were designed to knock out 60-ton tanks. After the blast, people rushed in and fought over the goods in the shop.

The marketplace was overrun by Mith Chass (pronounced MITT cha), "old comrades" who had lived in Khmer Rouge–controlled areas during the war. The strangers took just about everything they saw and loaded it on their bicycles and oxcarts. I was stunned. Just yesterday these people had been begging from house to house for used clothes and leftover food.

Bodies lay on the street, many in government uniforms. I saw dead shop-keepers, riddled with bullets. Khmer Rouge soldiers stood by with AK-47 assault rifles slung lazily over their shoulders. I threw up my breakfast.

The Khmer Rouge soldiers laughed. One handed me his rifle. "Go ahead, *Oan Pross* [Little Brother], have some fun, they're already dead."

"I can't," I managed to say, shuddering.

"Oh come on, Mith, what are you afraid of? You'll get used to it eventually." He laughed out loud, and the other soldiers joined him.

I ran blindly until I found myself on a deserted street strewn with all kinds of candy. I would have taken a few bags, but I had lost my appetite. The laughter of the man with the rifle rang in my ears.

I walked confused among these people who were rushing about, looting and stealing. I tried to understand what I was seeing.

Numb and frightened, I crossed the Siem Reap River toward home, avoiding the bridge altogether. As I walked the streets I saw Khmer Rouge soldiers on either side, knocking on doors. I hurried home.

"What's going on out there, Ah Nak?" Mother asked nervously.

"You don't want to know, Mae. It's really nasty out there. Looting and shoot-ing and killing everywhere," I said, shivering.

"That is what I was afraid of. Preah [Buddha] will help us," Mother said. "Don't go out there anymore. Where are your elder brothers?" My elder brothers had left earlier, on their bikes.

"I don't know, Mae. I didn't see any of them."

Mother started to cry. Father was turning in his pistol and rifles, as required by the Khmer Rouge soldiers who came to collect the weapons.

"You want me to go look for them?" I asked Mother.

"No, stay here!" Mother said and went to the kitchen.

"I'll go play with Ah Monika and Ah Seiha," I said. My little brothers were seven and five years old, so they had no idea what was happening. Mealanie, who had been babysitting them, went to help Mother prepare food.

More Mith Chass in rags, dirty and thin, came to beg for food and supplies. These people looked much more desperate than the ones who had looted the shops. They could have been us, had we not escaped the Khmer Rouge zone in Domdek five years earlier.

Mother gave them some old clothes and politely sent them on their way. All day, more called from the gate, begging, but we didn't have much to spare. We later learned to ignore them altogether. There were just too many of them.[1]

My older brothers returned in the afternoon with more bad news. The Khmer Rouge soldiers had continued shooting more people, mostly Chinese storeowners and stall keepers who dared to protest the destruction. The soldiers claimed that the dead were enemies, or that the deaths were accidental.

When my brothers and I went out a couple of days later to get supplies, we visited the area south of town. I handed Lon Nol bills to a street vendor for her palm fruit.

She shook her head. "I don't take money any more," she said. "It's worthless."

It was April 20, three days after the fall of Cambodia. The Khmer Rouge had already abolished the national currency. We learned that it was illegal to keep Lon Nol bills or any other kinds of money, even if it was nothing more than inked paper now. This change was personally devastating for me. It had taken me years of summer fishing in the Tonle Sap to earn those funds. The only thing I had allowed myself to buy was a Seiko wristwatch. I had been saving up the rest for something special. Now I had to throw away all my hard work.

Tons of Lon Nol bills littered the streets. Some tried to pick up the paper money from the streets but the soldiers stopped them. Strangely, there were no U.S. dollar bills or Thai *baht* on the streets, although these were used widely.

People tossed stacks of denominations into the river. The surreal floating paper money simply mesmerized me. Imagine hundred-dollar bills flowing out to sea.

Within a week of the takeover, there was nothing to buy or trade. I wondered, What happens when the town completely runs out of food? The thought of cannibalism terrified me. I recalled stories of soldiers eating human livers.

Continuous looting and destruction turned the central market into a huge junkyard. Temples and places of worship were now heavily guarded pieces of property used as rice storage or even ammunition dumps.

The Khmer Rouge soldiers were in charge yet they were causing the quick deterioration of our town. Theft, robbery, and physical assault occurred, but we were given no direction except to "respect the curfew until further notice."

The Khmer Rouge had immediately closed down all the schools, government, and private facilities. No one had gone to work or school for over a week now. Our stocks and food supplies were dwindling rapidly.

Food soon had to be bartered for. Gold and jewelry became almost worthless. Currency, school, religion, and civil institutions were now gone. Normal life, if such a thing existed to begin with, ended when the Khmer Rouge conquered Siem Reap.

Everyone was frightened by the lawlessness. However, despite the confusion and uncertainty, people were more relaxed and seemed to feel safer now that the war was over. They were wrong to feel that way.

Before long came the first public condemnation and execution at the city center. Rumors spread like wildfire. People were being killed for no reason. They were simply shot point-blank and their bodies were left to rot where they fell.

Former government soldiers were being trucked off to the unknown. The Khmer Rouge assured us that the men would return safely. Truckloads after truckloads of former high-ranking civil servants were hauled off, allegedly to welcome the head of state, the returning Prince Norodom Sihanouk. So they were told. We would soon find out that it was a complete fabrication—a premeditated plan.

Khmer Rouge soldiers again knocked on doors, this time asking people to list each family member, age, sex, and occupation. Father listed my brothers Mona and Serey as students, himself simply a "high school teacher." Larony was not listed at all.

The soldiers collected, checked, and double-checked information, which went up the chain of command. Orders were soon given. Former state soldiers were the first to disappear, followed by highly positioned teachers and other professionals.

We feared for my father and brothers with their history of working for the government. They now kept a low profile. As we say, "the protruding nail gets the hammer."

7

An Empty Village

Krobey Riel and Siem Reap

A fierce April sun burned the sky. Dust devils chased dust clouds in the shimmering heat. At the peak of the tinder-dry season, Cambodia lay on the brink of anarchy, complete and total chaos.

Everyone waited to see what the new regime, the Khmer Rouge, would do next. One of the many wild rumors going around was that the new regime would order all single females to marry former Khmer Rouge soldiers, particularly those who were severely disabled by war injuries. Mother took special care to keep Mealanie in the house, and she told Mona to lay low. Mealanie had just turned seventeen; Mona was twenty-three.

I had been cooped up in the house for so long that I could no longer stand it.

As everyone else sweltered and prayed for things to become less uncertain, Serey decided to move his wife Sa-Oum to neutral ground. Sa-Oum's father and siblings were staying in a village called Krobey Riel (Wild Buffalo Roam), so named because most of its residents raised buffalo. The village had traded hands between the Khmer Rouge and Lon Nol forces during the war, but Serey heard that it was now outside the fighting zones. Serey thought he would avoid some of the chaos of Siem Reap and take this opportunity to try his hand at fishing and trading.

"We're heading west, Ah Nak," he told me. "Why don't you come with us until things settle down?"

"You mean, you'll take me with you?"

"Sure, why not?" he smiled. "If you give me any problems, I'll just send you back."

"Oh Mae, may I go with Bawng? Please?" I knew that if my mother agreed, Father would not object.

Mother wasn't so easily swayed. "Oh, I don't know," she said. "I'm not so sure it's a good idea right now. I think we should stay together. We don't know what's going to happen next."

"Mae, I'll be with Bawng Serey and Bawng Sa-Oum. I'll be fine. I'm dying a slow death here; I need to get out of the house!"

She sighed. After a long pause, she relented. "Well, you know where we are. Come back when you're ready."

I joined Serey in preparing to head for the countryside. I thought I'd tag along with them for a couple of weeks. I only wanted to get away from the city for a while. The things I'd seen had frightened me very much.

The rumors of forced marriage intensified as Serey, Sa-Oum, and I made our preparations to leave the city. Those who had been to the liberated zones swore that they had seen the Khmer Rouge order civilians to marry disabled cadres. Mother was so disturbed that she gave her only daughter away to Lim Voeun, the man across the river who'd had his eye on Mealanie for some time. Just as quickly, she married Mona off to one of our cousins. The whole city experienced a wave of quickly arranged weddings that summer.

On April 25, 1975, we left the city, traveling west for about 15 miles until we arrived at the house of Sa-Oum's father in Krobey Riel. The village was ringed by rice paddies. I thought it was beautiful—and peaceful, even if it wasn't exactly neutral. Angkar was here, but the village had not seen the looting we had in Siem Reap. The people here seemed more at ease.

I went around town to make friends. Soon I was playing a game of marbles with some country boys. Their "marbles" were softball-sized bombs and dismantled grenades. I thought it was very clever of them to turn something so deadly into something fun.

After a few short hours of marbles, I was deep in debt. It was easily paid. All I did was collect some of the money littering the roadside. I enjoyed the company of my new playmates.

One of the boys was especially friendly. His name was Laive. He was close to my age but a little bigger. He took me around and showed me how country folks did things. We shared whatever we had. We defended each other against other kids. We were inseparable.

Three weeks went by quickly, and it was time for me to return home. Laive said he'd go with me to make sure I got home safely. On the way, I told him what had happened in Siem Reap. I described the looting, the dead bodies, and the Khmer Rouge cadres.

Laive told me what he'd seen in his hometown Sisophon, a small trading city in Battambang Province. The government soldiers there had resisted the Khmer Rouge cadres to the end. Many soldiers died during the final battle. Those who survived surrendered—but were killed. Laive's father, an army officer, was one of the first to be executed.

Laive begged the Khmer Rouge to allow him to bury his father before they killed him too. When Laive said he wanted to share his father's grave, the cadres agreed. Laive took his time digging. With so many things to do, the Khmer Rouge left. After he finished burying his father, Laive found he was alone. He ran. He didn't stop running until he reached Krobey Riel, where a widow adopted him. Her husband, who had also been a government soldier, was killed in action.

"Remember, if you ever have to escape, never go back to the place you came from. We must do anything to survive, no matter what," Laive said to me, sounding so much older than his fifteen years.

"Yes," I said. "We should never give up." We spat in our palms and shook hands.

The walk to Siem Reap took almost three hours. Except for some military convoys, the city was quiet. Animals roamed around. Streets were littered with packages.

My home was deserted. There was the familiar sign on the front gate, "Schoolteacher/Administrator," in Father's own handwriting. Looking at the sign, I was struck with fear.

"Mae, Pa! Where are you? Where is everyone?" I yelled. Inside was the evidence of an interrupted meal: rice covered with gray-green fungi and rancid-smelling bowls of gray liquid. I felt a gut-wrenching loneliness and fear.

"Ah Nak, we will find your family. Please don't cry!" Laive was frightened but tried his best to calm me.

"Mae, Pa, everyone!" I screamed. "Where are you?" I opened door after door, but there was no one at all. The house was empty.

On the front steps, I wept. Laive told me to wait and see what tomorrow would bring. He could have left for Krobey Riel, but he chose to stay with me through the night.

At early dawn, the rumbling of a military truck woke us. We rushed to the road, wildly waving our arms. The monster truck hissed and slowed to a stop. The men stared at us. I ran to the driver. "Where is everyone? What happened here?"

Puffing on a home-made cigarette, he said, "Oh, everyone was relocated to work in the countryside a few days back. Angkar's orders." He shifted gears. The truck swayed on the potholed road. Black smoke puffed from the tailpipe as I stared helplessly, lost in this time of uncertainty.

I stood there, a statue with no strength, no will, and no thought. I felt empty. The idea of losing my family scared me so much I almost fainted. What is life without my parents and siblings?

I pinched myself. "This isn't happening," I said to no one. "It's only a nightmare." The soldiers in the back of the truck shook their heads.

Perhaps the old book of fortune that I'd seen in the 1973 riot had been right all along. I'll be alone from now on, I thought. The center of my life, my family, was no more. Gone! I decided I didn't care if I died right then.

Laive did his best to calm me. "Don't worry, I'll help you. We'll find them," Laive said. "Be strong, my friend. Be very strong. I've been there, remember? I made it. You will, too."

I stood up. Laive and I resolved to return to Krobey Riel. What else could we do? I had to tell Serey the bad news.

As we walked past the gate marked by Father's handwritten sign, I caught a movement out of the corner of my eye. Someone was in the house across the street! I ran closer to get a better look. It was our neighbor stuffing bags with rice and dried fish. Feeling hopeful and excited, I caught his attention.

"Have you seen my family, Pou?"

"Shhh! Come, quick!" He waved to me, eyes darting around. "What are you boys doing here? Why aren't you with your family?"

I felt very relieved now that I was talking with someone familiar. "I don't know where my family is, Pou. I've been staying with my brother Serey in Krobey Riel. Do you know where they went, Pou?"

He looked at Laive. "I don't know you. Who are you?"

"Laive is my good friend, Pou." I said.

The man went back to his bike, furiously stacking his bags.

"Do you know where my family is, Pou? Please talk to me."

"Your family must have gone east to Rolous or to Domdek. Everyone on this side of the river went that way."

"May I go with you?" I hoped he'd let me run behind his bike until I saw my family.

He paused. "No," he said, slowly. "I can't take you with me. You should go to your brother in Krobey Riel. It's not safe here. I had to sneak in to get my things. I hope you understand," he said. "Besides, I'm not sure that your family went east. I didn't see them. Really, I don't know where they are."

I felt great despair.

"Look, if I see them I'll tell them to fetch you. That's the best I can do. Now go, go before they find us and kill us!" He took off quickly.

I stood there till the man and his bicycle vanished in the dust.

Laive dragged me away. "Come on," he said. "It's still cool enough to travel. Let's go now before it gets hot."

I walked through the empty city as though in slow motion. Belongings were everywhere, perhaps discarded because they were too big or too heavy to carry. Fires smoldered. Abandoned vehicles testified to the chaotic evacuation of Siem Reap.

We reached the outskirts of the city. It was eerily quiet. The villagers were gone, too. Laive opened a ripe jackfruit and attacked the sweet-fleshy fruit. He gave me a large piece. It tasted like cardboard.

Now and then, Laive tried to talk of other things to keep my mind from too much worry. It was no use.

When I saw Serey that afternoon, I wept again. "They're gone!" I said. "I couldn't find them anywhere!"

A small crowd gathered. Laive and I described the discarded packages on the roadside, the empty homes, the eerie silence. No one believed us. After Laive left, I sat on a rocking chair on the front porch and stared into the simmering midday heat.

I had no appetite for dinner. I went to bed early and cried myself to sleep. The next morning, I was up first. I sat on the rocking chair, watching the sunrise.

I fetched a bucket of water for Serey's elderly father-in-law. When I handed him the bucket, he took it and stared at me, shaking his head. Perhaps he felt what I was going through.

Serey opened the door to let air and sunlight into the house. His eyes were puffy. "You have to stay with us until we know what happened," Serey said.

Weeks went by. Angkar issued a new curfew. No one could travel more than a mile from one's village or town, except with a travel permit, which was difficult to get.

We became restless. There was no news of our family. Serey and some relatives decided to risk a trip to Siem Reap. "There's a bike if you want to come along," Serey said. I quickly got on the bike.

To avoid checkpoints, we crossed through endless rice paddies with our bikes on our heads. Compared to being caught, it was a minor inconvenience.

At the outskirts of Siem Reap, a feeling of anticipation filled me so much that it was almost unbearable. I imagined that my family and all of the city's inhabitants had returned.

Everything was quiet. There were no other travelers on the road. As we entered the familiar streets, I saw that nothing had changed since I was last there. We heard voices in the distance and hurried on.

We walked through our gate together, passing Father's handwritten sign. Seeing our house empty, I was filled with horror once again. Nothing was changed inside. Household items were strewn everywhere. Serey took a long time gathering photos and mementos. I went to the chicken coop out back and returned with six of our prized hens. Serey left a note for our parents before we went out the door. "We could bring some tobacco back for my father-in-law," Serey said. "He enjoys a good smoke now and then." Serey gestured toward our neighbor's house. The Povs were major tobacco dealers.

Dishes with rotting food greeted us from the Povs' dining mat. Like our family, the Povs must have been evacuated from their home during a meal. I imagined Khmer Rouge cadres driving them out at gunpoint.

Serey found a bit of tobacco and stashed it in his pocket. As we were about to leave, I noticed a small opening—an access panel to the attic. We opened it and found the attic filled with bales of prime tobacco. We loaded two bulky bales on our bikes. No one was producing tobacco anymore, so these would eventually be worth their weight in gold. Again, Serey left a note.

We returned to Krobey Riel without incident, except once when we ran into a Khmer Rouge guard urinating in the bushes. The soldier was embarrassed and waved us away. We quickly left, thankful to get off so easily.

Back in Krobey Riel, no one knew for sure what really happened in the city. There were only rumors and more rumors, all frightening and impossible to believe. I never did get the whole story, just bits and pieces from people who survived the exodus of Siem Reap and the other large cities in Cambodia. Despite my burning desire to find out what happened, I never asked. I didn't really want to know. Not really.

The exodus of Siem Reap ended what remained of our civil society, and it ushered in Pol Pot's Khmer Rouge regime and its infamous and secretive "Angkar."

8

A Great Leap Backward

Keo Poeur, Kok Poh, and Kork Putrea

Toward the end of June 1975, cool air came down from the northern Dong Rek mountain range and began to blow the suffocating heat away. The bright blue of the sky turned into cooler shades of gray. Column after column of clouds rolled in and gathered above the Tonle Sap Lake until the sun was hidden away.

When lightning flashed so mightily, even the bravest flinched; the rest of us dove for cover. Thunder rumbled, rolled, and echoed and then the heavens broke open with the wild, rushing sound of a gigantic herd of water buffaloes. The monsoon rains had come again.

The Angkar began to tighten its grip on our lives. After the 10 P.M. curfew, we could not go anywhere without a permit. The Khmer Rouge cadres demanded that everyone turn in their watches, radios, and other electronics. I secretly held onto my Seiko wristwatch, the one thing I'd allowed myself to buy from my summer fishing wages during the war. Khmer Rouge cadres put up "processing centers" and began systematic interviews to determine who held what positions in the Lon Nol regime. Fear paralyzed our town as we realized that any truthful answer could doom an entire family.

The cadres were thorough. Bit by bit, each day, they squeezed out information from families, friends, and relatives. The truthful, honest ones died first. Blackmail became a minor industry.

The young executioners of the Khmer Rouge outdid each other in finding new ways of inflicting slow and agonizing torture. They lined us up and fired questions at us, one by one. Profession, home village, et cetera. The cadres took more time to interview men aged eighteen to thirty-five. After each interview they directed the person left or right. No one wanted to go to the right. That was the direction of the camps.[1]

Still, hundreds of *Mith Thmey* ("new comrades," people who'd lived in government-controlled areas during the war) survived the interviews. For them, the Khmer Rouge created camps. Widows and orphans of government soldiers were moved to these camps while soldiers who were still alive were moved to other camps farther away. It seemed that every day more people left. One of those people was my best buddy, Laive, who one day "disappeared" with his adoptive mother, a military wife. I did not think I would see Laive again.

After identifying government soldiers and their families and moving them out of Krobey Riel, the cadres interviewed those who had served in the Lon Nol regime in other roles: judges, lawyers, administrators, clergy, doctors, school-teachers, and college students. Then they, too, were moved to the camps. We tried to enjoy a normal life amid the hardships imposed by the new order. Travel was restricted, but fortunately for us, the village of Krobey Riel lay right in the center of the trading route between the fishing villages around the great lake and the large towns of Siem Reap and Sisophon. Villagers still traded in great numbers, carrying travel permits from Angkar.

Money and wages didn't exist anymore. Food and essentials were not plentiful, but life was comfortable enough for those who could barter. We were in the middle of planting season. The goal was to make it until the harvest in September. For rice, people often traded family heirlooms.

Sa-Oum's family had hidden a small battery-powered shortwave radio and we secretly listened to foreign broadcasts whenever we could. At 7 by 5 inches and just 3 inches thick, the radio was very small. The greenish black, Chinese-manufactured device had an antenna, a large tuner dial, and a smaller dial for volume. We listened to broadcasts from the United States, France, and other countries. Nobody seemed to know what was happening in Cambodia. But we knew very well.

There was still no news about our family, and Serey and I could not risk going out of town to find out. However, despite the formal travel restrictions, Angkar cadres still granted travel permits, so people still came and went. Private enterprise and trade thrived, albeit in the form of a black market. Through word of mouth, leftover goods from the old society could be bartered and traded secretly.

When word got out that we were sitting on two bales of quality tobacco product, people came to secretly trade their valuables. The village chief was a major tobacco addict. A little tobacco now and then kept him happy enough to look away.

We accumulated at least 5 pounds of assorted jewelry as well as plenty of rice, plus fresh and salted fish. All things considered, we lived quite well in the early days of the new regime. However, we knew of many others near and far who didn't fare as well. Some came to us empty-handed. We shared what we could.

The end of our early, easy days under Angkar came one morning. We were shocked to see the village chief, the same one who accepted our tobacco bribes, coming up to our house with two Angkar soldiers.

"All newcomers to Krobey Riel must relocate," said the village chief. He told us we were to move some miles to the south. Everyone in our house was new to Krobey Riel; Sa-Oum's father and siblings had come from Mechrey Island. We had two hours to pack up, and we could take only what we could carry. Anyone who refused would be "taken away." After the initial shock, we scrambled. Quickly we packed rice, pots and pans, clothing, and other essentials. Serey stashed the contraband radio underneath it all. We bound our hens' legs and carried them.

The soldiers marched us toward Mechrey Island, stopping at a flat, grassy area called Keo Poeur. The water was knee-deep when we arrived. Hundreds of Mith Thmey from villages along the edge of the lake milled around. Most of the men were fishermen or workers in fish processing or retail.

Everyone knew that this desolate place, 5 miles north of Tonle Sap Lake, was a flood zone. We guessed that Angkar wanted to develop the land for agriculture. With the silt deposit from the lake, this area was ideal for certain rice varieties.

We lived under a large tree during the first few weeks. Finally, we found a relatively dry spot to build a shelter. We exchanged our precious supply of food and tobacco for sugar-palm leaves, bamboo, and any building material that we could find. In less than four days, a tiny, one-room hut that could barely hold the seven of us stood on the flooded fields of Keo Poeur. Soon after, similar crude bamboo huts began to rise around us, a black market started, then food trading and bargaining followed. I packed my saved Lon Nol currency in a watertight package and buried it under our hut. I thought that maybe one day the new regime would reinstitute money.

The monsoon rains poured until our hut's floor was knee-deep in water. A hammock helped, but we were wet for weeks. Outside the hut, the water was even deeper, life even more miserable. We found it difficult to cook rice because the rain and wind kept putting out the fire. We learned to sleep wet, a spare shirt on our heads for warmth.

Life was strictly controlled. Eating, sleeping, work, dating, marriage, and even the bearing of children were regulated. To the Angkar, the Mith Thmey were enemies who must be taught. Part of the reeducation was integrating the Mith Thmey into labor groups.

The Angkar cadres said they had liberated us. "We are the People's Democratic Kampuchea," they said. "We are for the people." Through their rule they hoped to best Mao Zedong's "great leap forward." But the Mith Thmey grumbled to one another that Angkar policy was really about starvation and death. They pantomimed the leaders: "We'll starve you to sickness and work you to death. If you live, you'll die."

Some weeks later, the cadres ordered us to move several hundred feet away. Any timid protest was swiftly met with more work assignments, so we all moved our huts from one flooded area to another for no reason that we could see.

Over a couple of months, we were ordered to move eight times. Once, we moved the entire hut a few feet, just to make things look nicer to a ranking Angkar cadre. So this was communism, I thought. They tell you where to live, how to build your house, and what size it should be. I was disgusted by these senseless orders, but who would dare complain?

Everyone had to work for Angkar. The Mith Chass were free and lived in their own villages. We Mith Thmey were guarded closely at all times. While the Mith Chass plowed the fields, we Mith Thmey planted and harvested. The Angkar trucks hauled away the fruits of our hard labor.

Life under the "People's Democratic Kampuchea" was an unending chain of work, searching for food, then back to work. From dawn to dusk we worked. Our meals were small, so we searched for food whenever and wherever we could. The Angkar didn't seem to mind our food searches and private meals.

Then, early in 1976, a community kitchen was built in Keo Poeur. All pots and pans were confiscated. The Angkar decreed that private meals were illegal. We were not even allowed to keep our plates and bowls. A spoon each was all that was permitted. From then on, all meals had to be shared.

After work, we lined up at the community kitchen for our meager portions of rice gruel. Still, hunger drove many of us to search for food and cook in secret. Those who were caught suffered long periods without food, longer work hours, public condemnation, jail terms, and sometimes even execution.

I learned to cook with sunlight, mixing freshwater clams with herbs and spices and allowing them to dry, or dehydrating fermented daikon radishes in the sun. But sunlight cooking was too slow for me, so I reverted to fire. It's very difficult to conceal a cooking fire. It was a close shave many times but I was never caught. I'd pretend I was warming myself. However, to cook a meal was to risk my life. I was fourteen years old.

At the communal kitchen, the cooks struggled to feed their work groups. Each cell or work group of fifty had two cooks. Given about a quarter pound of rice for the entire cell, the two had to be very creative. They searched for edible plants and boiled these with a cup of rice in a 50-gallon iron pot, resulting in a gruel that looked and smelled disgusting. This is what we children and adults had twice a day, every day. There wasn't even a pinch of salt to go with it.

After dinner, we had to go to the lectures, which were followed by criticism sessions. The cadres said the very harsh criticism was meant to help improve our work performance.

The lecture-criticism sessions were held seven nights a week. We had to sit and listen to cadres preaching communist ideology or pontificating on how great Angkar was for everyone.

"Angkar is like your parents now," a top cadre would say. "You must obey Angkar without hesitation. Angkar will build a great society for you and your children. Your sacrifice will be rewarded."

I never wanted to go, but I did, night after night. There were those who didn't attend. In a day or so, we didn't see them anymore. It was whispered that they were sent away to the dreaded reeducation camps. Soon, we became immune to this, too. We learned to *dam doeum kor* (plant a kapok tree). This Khmer term uses word play to transpose *kor* (kapok) with *ko* (mute). "*Dam doeum kor.*" Plant a "mute" tree. We learned to look away. We learned to keep our lips sealed and eyes closed.

The presence of dear friends and families was a constant comfort. We still had remnants of our family ties and relationships, recalling the strong fabric of Khmer society. But Angkar found ways to weaken these links further, by assigning family members to different work groups for weeks at a time. It was in Keo Poeur that I first experienced Angkar's rigorous "purification" process. People were identified as tainted by imperialism simply by the cleanliness of their fingernails. The reasoning was that if your nails are clean, you must not be a farmer. These people began disappearing.

Sa-Oum's elderly father was allowed to work close to home. However, their demand that he create traps for fish devastated the old man. He strictly followed the ten Buddhist principles. He was more than ready for his next life, but the Angkar put an end to all the merits he had earned. By building contraptions to trap live fish, he sinned, violating one Buddhist tenet he had worked so hard to follow: not to take the life of any creature. There was no choice. The old man had to kill or starve to death.

Angkar completely controlled us now. Freedom of expression and movement disappeared. Angkar dictated what we did, what kind of clothes we wore, whom we would marry. There was no private property, thought, or opinion—not in the open, anyway.

My leg became infected because of the time I spent waist-deep in the water, looking for fish and water plants. Sa-Oum's father had some medical knowledge as a *kru* (shaman), and he applied many types of ointments, but I still had to crawl on my hands and knees to get around.

Through these months of suffering, I remained hopeful that I'd see my family again. In fact, I often dreamed about them.

One evening in late February or early March of 1976, a familiar figure came on a bike. It was Lim Voeun, who had married my sister Mealanie just before the evacuation of Siem Reap. When I made out Voeun's face, I was sure I'd see my parents and siblings again.

"So happy to see you all," Voeun said. "I had a hard time finding you. How have you been?" Everyone surrounded him, hoping for good news.

"Fine, fine. Doing just fine," this came from me, even though I could hardly get up or walk. I had been bedridden for weeks with the leg infection. "Where's our family?" I said right after the formalities.

"Mind your manners, Ah Nak!" Sa-Oum snapped. "Voeun just got here from a long trip." She and Voeun were distant relatives.

I ignored her. "Where are they?" I asked Voeun. "Have you come for me?"

"No," Voeun took a sip of water. "Everyone's all right. They're in the Kralahn District."

I'd never been to Kralahn, but it was only about 20 miles northwest of Siem Reap. I was glad my family was not too far away.

"Not in Rolous?"

"Who told you that? They're all in Kralahn."

"Please, Bawng, take me with you. I'd do anything you ask," I said.

"It's too far."

"Please. I'll run behind your bike all the way."

"You're better off here, Ah Nak," said Voeun. "There's more food here. We're starving there. That's why I'm here, to find food for us, don't you see?"

"I want to go with you!" I screamed. Voeun whispered to Serey, who shook his head. I crawled from my ragged sleeping mat but Serey grabbed me. Voeun quickly loaded his old bike with rice and dried fish and pedaled away.

I tried to go after Voeun but collapsed on the road. Serey dragged me back. I screamed and cursed at Voeun.

"We'll find them, I promise you," Serey said. In the dark, I heard his soft sobs. For a brief moment, our past had caught up with us. "We'll find everyone someday, I promise," Serey said.

Two months later, I was back in the fields on light duties, mostly collecting cow manure for fertilizer. I waited for a chance to head west, toward Kralahn.

We were ordered to move again, this time to Kok Poh, a well-established town 3 miles north of Keo Poeur. I wondered why we had to leave. We worked hard for Angkar. We hadn't done anything wrong.

At the new site we rushed to pick a place that would not flood too deeply. We built another little hut. Exactly three weeks later, we were ordered to move to Kork Putrea, just 600 feet away.

Some of our neighbors broke down and wept. A few refused to move and met the full fury of the young Angkar guards. I watched in horror as they kicked and dragged my neighbors across a rice paddy.

On the morning of May 10, 1976, I was again among a parade of Mith Thmey heading to an unknown destination. In a way, I was glad to move. We might meet my family.

As we marched past the fields of ripening rice that we had slaved over during the past months, I felt a pang of regret that I wouldn't see the harvest of the first rice crop that I had helped to plant and grow.

The long line of people numbered around 200. Every family carried what little possessions they had. Serey had buried our secret radio and its precious batteries under all our other belongings. I held two baskets, one hiding my pet yellow-brown hen. I'd remembered a trick from cockfights in Siem Reap—cover the hen's eyes with damp cloth and she'll be quiet. I put her in the back, "hidden in plain sight." A group of soldiers led us west, then northwest for several hours until we got to National Highway 6, which runs west from Siem Reap to Battambang Province.

We were ordered to stop at dusk. The communal cooks began their work while hungry children cried. The rest of us sat in the darkening hour, swatting at mosquitoes.

Long before the dinner call, people had queued up for a cup of rice gruel and *trakourn* (blackened water spinach). Sa-Oum slipped us a piece of cooked dried fish to go with the watery ration. After the meal, we were still very hungry but we didn't dare cook our cache of rice.

Hunger made me chew on the sour fruit of a tamarind tree. Curiosity led me to the temporary guard quarters. Empty bottles littered the ground, evidence of beer and soft drinks. It was too dark to see, but from what I could smell, I understood that the guards ate very well.

How unfair! The Angkar troops always had their own supplies and ate away from us. They controlled us not only through fear but also through hunger. They knew hunger could make a man do just about anything.

Mango smells wafted toward me. In the waning light I felt my way to a mango tree, climbed the trunk, and plucked some of the fruit, enduring the protests of the red ants. Fruit in the waist of my pants, I made my way back to Serey and lay down with everyone else for the night, sleeping in the cool rice paddy dikes on the side of National Highway 6.

The cadres woke us early the next morning, eager to show their superiors how tough they were. I wanted to sleep some more, but the march resumed. Herding us with long sticks were new Khmer Rouge recruits, as young as ten, as old as fifteen, with AK-47 rifles on their backs. Everyone was exhausted by noon, particularly the children. We had walked barefoot for at least 15 miles on hot asphalt. My soles had blisters. I was one of the first few who dared to walk on the softer ground. Soon the road was empty.

When the guards ordered a rest, I hit the ground and fell asleep. Serey woke me up to eat the crude food the communal cooks had concocted. We had no water. Half asleep, I drank from the drainage ditch that ran beside the highway.

As we continued the march, I ran to the bushes frequently. A strong dose of raw tamarind bark tea eased the diarrhea but the painful stomach cramps persisted.

It was cooler in the afternoon but the pains were so bad I could barely walk. Some children died and were left behind on the roadside. I was afraid Serey would also leave my body in a shallow grave by the highway, so I pushed myself to keep going until I passed out.

The sound of weeping made me open my eyes. Tears fell from Serey's eyes. From the stars, I could tell it was late and that we were heading north. I'd hoped to go west toward Kralahn, in case my family was there.

I was no longer marching with everyone else. I was actually tied onto a bike, like a pig taken to market. The bike was familiar. It had been Serey's bike before the Angkar nationalized it. Ironically, Serey had begged a soldier to lend him his own bike. For the privilege, he'd parted with about half an ounce of gold.

We lagged behind the line of marchers as Serey pushed and pulled the bike and me on a sandy dirt road. Every now and then, I could still hear the guards shout. "Move it! Keep moving!" A few stray kids screamed in pain as they were whipped. Everyone else tried to move faster.

"We're almost there!" said a cadre. "Just over that tree line there. Faster! Move it!"

It took us until dawn to reach the tree line.

The two days and nights of forced march to Tapang were eternity to me. I lost track of time and my sense of direction. I was disoriented and confused. We had no dinner on the last night, but my stomach didn't miss it.

Brunch was watery rice gruel again, with some kind of wild vegetables, mainly the *chrach*—a common water plant found in rice paddies. Those who had children got served first; the kids screamed with hunger. No pain is more severe, I came to believe, than the pain of hunger, especially among small children.

Serey brought me a bowl of the disgusting soup. "Eat, you need it," he whispered.

"No, thanks. I'm not hungry."

Serey left the bowl beside me and sat with Sa-Oum. He did not say another word. He must have been totally exhausted from dragging me on his old bike.

I rested under the tree. I took off my ragged shirt and saw my ribs and my swollen knees. It frightened me that I could see my own skeleton in only two days.

I closed my eyes and swallowed my tears, praying for a quick and painless death.

Memories of my wonderful childhood filled my mind. Oh, how I longed for my family!

I dreamed of my father, my mother, and all my siblings. As they began to disappear in a fog, I yelled, running after them. Two large teardrops on my cheeks woke me up. I was still alive in Tapang, my missing family in Kralahn or places unknown. I was still in hell and suffering severely. Death would be considered a blessing for me at that moment. I was still in Angkar's Year Zero.

9

The Death of Dogs

Tapang

Chilly air chased the monsoon clouds on the strong air currents that riffled the leaves. The weeping, high-pitched *kek-kek-kek* sounds of thousands of tadpoles echoed in the distance and sent chills up the spine. The beautiful Cambodian countryside hid a heart that was bleeding severely.

It was the sound of ridicule that woke me from my deep sleep. Some kids about my age looked me over and then laughed among themselves. Mith Chass teenagers surrounded me. These kids were "old comrades" who had supported the Khmer Rouge in the war and who now ruled. Their faces clearly reflected our low positions. We were the defeated *khmang* (enemies), prisoners of war to be used as "laborers," a polite euphemism for slaves. Among the jeering expressions full of hate was a familiar, kind face.

The face moved on. He didn't seem to recognize me. Perhaps my eyes had been playing tricks on me. That couldn't be Laive, my old buddy from Krobey Riel, I thought. Since that day long ago when Laive and his adoptive mother had disappeared from Krobey Riel, I'd thought my old buddy was dead.

"Welcome to Tapang!" said a group of town cadres in their black pajama uniforms, checkered *kroma* (scarves) on their necks, and Ho Chi Minh sandals on their feet. "We're happy you're here at last. We've been waiting for you all, Mith." They dropped the Thmey qualifier, calling us, simply, "comrades." Cheerfully, they invited us to the meeting hall for a formal welcome at ten o'clock in the morning.

At the entrance, a top cadre smiled. "Please join us! Welcome, welcome." I couldn't believe what I was seeing. Cadres were welcoming us? My brain must be really messed up, I thought.

Many waited for us inside the meeting hall, which was built on a high, man-made dirt mound.

Like me, my fellow marchers had to be aching and sore, but we sat quietly. Perhaps they were as stunned as I was by all the cheer.

As I listened to the *kamaphibarl* (high comrade, pronounced "kama-PEE-bar-l") giving his speech, my mind drifted to my trip with Laive over a year ago when we found Siem Reap an emptied city. Now everyone was under the new order. I saw why death was desired by many; time creeps by slowly while one is suffering.

I thought of my school and my lessons about the U.N. Charter on Human Rights. I became bitter, thinking about the control that Angkar exerted over us.

A light thump on my back woke me up. I turned to see Laive, who seemed not to see me. He pointed his nose at the kamaphibarl. I stilled my expression as I gazed ahead. It really was Laive, my best buddy!

I peeked at the note he put in my hand. "Meet me here tonight at ten. Don't forget. Come alone." I turned the note over. He had drawn a smiling face and wrote, "Good to see you again, *Ah Samlagne* [Good Buddy]!"

At noon, there was lunch for the Mith Thmey and the Mith Chass in the communal kitchen, our first. Very few Mith Chass touched the food, so we helped ourselves to double, triple helpings of the boiled rice and greens. The rice gruel had more rice flakes. Wow, there were bits of meat!

We ate as though we had not eaten for days (very nearly true), while the Mith Chass looked on in disgust. Laive told me later that they ate at home. Private meals were against the law, but the Mith Chass could do what they liked.

I ate as much as I could and vomited it right out. My stomach ached terribly. Laive sat a distance away, his dark-brown eyes on me.

After lunch, the town cadres returned—from their meals, I guess—and made more speeches.

Then came the order to build a house on a plot of land they had selected, again in the middle of a flooded rice paddy. I didn't care anymore.

After helping Serey and his in-laws pitch a temporary camp near the site that evening, I told my family that I had cramps (a frequent complaint) and I walked away toward the community center. I winced painfully as I climbed up the hill.

In a removed corner, I sat down and took out my Seiko wristwatch, a well-hidden remnant of the past. The minutes ticked by with no sign of Laive. At five past ten, Laive was still nowhere.

"Over here!" a whisper from a bush.

Slowly, I moved toward the bush. Laive grabbed my shirt collar and yanked me into his hiding place. With a finger on his lips, he peered around. There was only the sound of crickets and frogs.

"I thought you were dead, buddy!" Laive whispered. His bear hug hurt.

"Good to see you, too. Now let go . . ."

"Uh . . . sorry."

"That's okay." I got a good look at my friend. He looked older than he had in Krobey Riel, with more meat on his bones and well-defined muscles. "Hey,

I thought you died a long time ago. What happened? You disappeared so suddenly."

It took Laive almost an hour to tell me how he ended up in Tapang. After Krobey Riel, Laive and his adopted mother were relocated several times. He eventually found his real mother and two remaining siblings.

About four months earlier, they were relocated to Tapang with other Mith Thmey, mostly widows and children of executed Lon Nol soldiers. Laive and his family were registered as such.

"We've been working on different projects ever since. Life here in Tapang is miserable, ten times worse than it was in Krobey Riel. Many of those who arrived with us are gone," he said.

"What do you mean, 'gone'?" I waited for the gory details.

"They just disappear, simply gone!" he said in a booming whisper.

He stared at me. He was not the same Laive. He seemed more mature, much more so, than the Laive I had known in Krobey Riel.

"The old ones know the grave sites," he continued. "They bring back things to be distributed, mostly clothes and personal stuff, some with bloodstains."

I stared back at him. He was taller than I now, almost a full-grown man.

"Okay, I'll show you the open pits later. It's not too far from here," he said. "Our time will come eventually, I'm sure." His tone was matter-of-fact.

The thought of the grave sites terrified me, but curiosity made me nod. I wanted to see.

"Watch out for *chhlob* [spies]" he said. "The chhlob eavesdrop under the huts at night. They report even on their own families. Many innocent people have been killed because of them," he said. The chhlob (pronounced "chlope") were often from the Angkar Youth Corps. Loyal, well trained, and susceptible to brainwashing, the numerous chhlob were feared by all. "If you want to last long here, be careful and never give them any excuse to report you," said Laive, repeating himself several times.

"Okay, buddy. I hear you," I said. "I hear you."

"We'll meet here every two days."

"I'm glad to see you again."

"Be careful, Ah Samlagne [my friend]," Laive said, and disappeared in the darkness.

I took Laive's warning very seriously. Before I shared the warning with my family, I made sure there was no one around us. I could not sleep well that night.

Early the next morning, we were gathered for our first labor: house building. "Angkar will give you the basic necessities so you must provide the labor," said the cadres.

We did get some building materials. We built a small hut high on stilts. We were able to enjoy dry feet for a while. As soon as we completed our hut, Angkar ordered us to work.

Sa-Oum and her siblings were from a family of professional fishermen, and yet they were ordered to plant rice and potatoes instead. My brother and I, however, were ordered to fish in the Tonle Sap even though the cadres well knew that we weren't skilled fishermen. The Angkar liked the idea of "cross-training." Serey and I had to live near the lake. Learning to fish was tough, but under the cadres' watchful eyes, Serey and I met our quota, and more. We caught a lot of fish for Angkar over those three months.

When Serey and I were allowed to return home, I hid some of the fish for the walk. Our path took us past Kok Poh, where a distant relative lived. Aunt Samon was the younger sister of Aunt Thet, the widow of my Uncle Vin. Aunt Samon's family did not have much food. I gave Aunt Samon some of my hidden fish, which was really "Angkar property."

As it turned out, we had to move our hut four times during our stay in Tapang, sometimes only about 600 feet away, and always for no good reason. Each time we moved we had to rebuild the house. Angkar seemed to enjoy keeping us off-balance all the time. It must have been part of their strategy.

We learned not to waste any more time or energy than we had to. We built a shelter, simple enough to complete in two days, and sturdy enough to protect us from the elements. We remembered to *dam doeum kor* (plant a kapok tree, or be mute). Almost every day, more Mith Thmey quietly disappeared. This silence was echoed by the foreign broadcasts we infrequently heard on our radio, keeping our fingers on the dial and our eyes open for chhlob. To those outside our country, Cambodia was a curtained mystery.

Every night in Tapang, we praised Angkar and the cadres. We pretended not to see the chhlob under our hut. I even urinated through the gaps in the bamboo floor.

However, at the nightly criticism session, the teenaged spies humiliated and punished me. My crime was that I pissed under the hut. "It's unhealthy," they screamed. While they heaped abuse on my bowed head, I thought about going west to find my parents and siblings. I wasn't sure I'd survive Tapang.

Within a week, I was in a classroom of thirteen-year-olds. We spent much of our days listening to the revolutionary ideals, with some time in basic reading and writing. They didn't teach anything else.

I was so frustrated. I had completed primary school and had been attending a secondary school at the time of the Khmer Rouge takeover. I could run circles around these teachers in history, literature, geography, math, and science.

Very politely, I corrected the errors of the teachers when they taught us basic reading and writing. It was a big mistake.

I was immediately shipped out to a labor camp some 20 miles northeast of Tapang. There was nothing at the site but open fields, dense forest, and up to 20,000 people. I was now part of the infamous "Mobile Brigade," a work group of thousands of girls and boys between nine and fifteen years old.

We were ordered to build a water reservoir in three months. It was to be the mother of all reservoirs, to rival even the famous Western Baray of Angkor Wat.

Every day, we felled large trees and dug up deep tree roots until we cleared a huge square. We dug 60 feet into the soil until we reached the aquifer. We piled and packed the soil into a dike, a gigantic square 25 miles on each side.

All day and most of the night, for three absolutely miserable months, I lifted heavy loads of dirt and moved piles of rock.

I became very ill and the cadres took me to an Angkar hospital of sorts. Fearing that my death in their clinic would bring them bad luck, the camp nurse refused to take me in. The cadres were forced to return me to Tapang. They picked me up like furniture and loaded me in the back of an oxcart. I remember bouncing on its hard floor.

Only Serey's elderly father was at home. Serey showed up a few days later. I was delirious for weeks, unable to move or eat what little food there was.

"Don't go, please don't go," my brother kept saying. I heard him and his in-laws worrying about the lack of firewood for my cremation, and agreeing to bury my body instead. "He will no longer suffer," said someone. Buddhist chants filled the hut. Everyone kept saying good-bye to me, but I couldn't respond.

I dreamed of my family again. Mother urged me closer. I could not reach her no matter how I tried. Then my family faded away slowly. I saw myself lying on the floor of our hut. I screamed, but no sound came out.

A spoonful of liquefied brown sugar made its way down my throat. Serey had traded his handmade water bucket for sticky palm sugar from a Mith Chass. Slowly, on nothing but unrefined sugar, I recovered.

"You were unconscious most of the time," said Serey. "I didn't think you'd make it. I'm glad you decided to stay with us. I'd have been lost without you. You're all I have, Oan Pross."

I couldn't stop my own tears.

In the meantime, couples were rumored to be missing at the reservoir. Angkar strictly forbade sex out of wedlock. For this and various other crimes, many workers had been publicly humiliated, executed, or both. A greater number had died from accidents or illnesses.

There were no more Khmer civil engineers. They were either dead or kept quiet. The advisers from China did not like to spend time here because of the heat, humidity, and malarial mosquitoes. The Khmer Rouge cadres were left in charge. Most knew little besides fear mongering.

When I recovered, the reservoir work was complete, and all Mith Thmey had been ordered to work up to fourteen hours a day on other projects. Now they had to dig more irrigation canals, and harvesting rice planted by others before us, most probably those whose bodies were rotting in the open pits.

Even the old ones and the kids worked. Dinner was still a few grains of rice and some greens boiled in a cauldron of water. Sometimes Serey and I would smuggle in a little salt, sometimes a lizard, a water bug, a field crab, or a small fish. The rare egg from our yellow-brown hen gave us much needed protein.

However, day in and day out, it was the same: three hundred people shared a giant pot of boiled water with a few cups of rice and handfuls of wild plants. After each meal, most of us experienced dysentery and severe diarrhea.

Young Angkar "nurses" prescribed herbal remedies, mostly concoctions from wild plants, which made some people even sicker. I had heard that these "treatments" eventually killed the patients. "An honest mistake," the young nurses told grieving families.

I did my best to minimize my time with the Angkar health care system—no more than twenty minutes. When I saw the dirty syringes and dubious medicine, I made plans for my speedy exit. The nurses force-fed me pills that looked like rabbit droppings; I struggled. The chhlob and the nurses whipped me but I crawled on my elbows and knees to get away. I wanted to live, not die here in this crude, primitive place they called a hospital.

On the plus side, some of the nurse's tablets helped, particularly those made from rice powder and palm sugar. When I could get them, I ate them as food.

At home, I could hardly get anything to eat. My treasured Seiko watch got me only two tin cans of rice. If not for Serey, I would have starved to death. When he was away working for weeks, Sa-Oum's elder siblings beat me and kept me from the family's secret meals. This behavior worsened as food became scarce.

I accepted the physical and emotional abuse as my fate. Like a good victim, I swallowed my tears and took their abuse. However, I depended on Serey and, to some extent, Sa-Oum to help shield me from such abuse. Serey tried his best to shield me from the cruelty of my adopted family. Once, just before he departed for another long trip, he took a portion of the uncooked rice and gave it to me to hide. He fought his in-laws, sometimes even his own wife. I felt guilty for creating such trouble within the family. One day, I even threatened to report everyone to Angkar. If I did, the entire family would die, including myself. Even so, I was sorely tempted.

I had some peace for a while. When the abuse resumed, I threatened them again. This bantering went on until they realized that I didn't have the guts to go through with it. By then, it didn't matter. We were all starving to near death. Besides, no one stayed home long enough to torment me. One worked on a farm, another on a water reservoir, and so on. I was away for months at a time on yet another Mobile Brigade.

My troubles within our hut were nothing compared to what awaited outside.

Very few Tapang natives were friendly. My blood boiled when they made fun of us. Being "enemies," we endured everything quietly. Their animals received better treatment. Pigs had actual rice grains in their diet and cattle were well groomed. My value to Angkar seemed comparable to that of a chicken.

The Mith Chass children were spoiled. They would beat us for fun. During criticism sessions at the meeting hall, the well-fed Mith Chass teenagers attacked me, even though I could hardly walk.

The boys and girls ran around the work area as though it were their private playground. Some laughed at me for moving so slowly. I ignored them. Many of them were chhlob. One was the son of the town mayor. They could have killed me as easily as peeling a banana. I looked at the ground, hoping they would leave me alone, but they grabbed my arms, and I dared not resist. They spun me around and around. They laughed when I fell in the mud, and did it again. And again, and again until I fell unconscious. I woke up alone, muddy and cold.

With practice I learned to hide my humiliation. I will survive this, I said to myself.

I was so tired at the end of the day. There were always new work orders, long hours on the plantations and irrigation canals. Hunger almost drove me insane. I had to find something to eat so I could meet my work quota. However, even dogs and cats were now not to be found.

In the brief evening hour on the way home, I stayed alert for freshwater crabs, snails, rats, anything. I hate to admit it but I ate almost anything deemed edible. However, I would never eat human flesh. Many did, but I decided I'd rather starve to death than cross that line.

Arriving home at about six o'clock in the evening, I joined the rush to the forest where we searched for hours in the dark. We were forbidden to forage, but the Angkar guards often looked away. I rarely found something.

Serey always woke me up to eat. Our secret meals were always in darkness, on every night that we could manage it. Still, we were so thin we saw each other's ribs clearly. There was always someone in our hut who was sick.

In our rare spare time, we kept a small garden plot. We grew beans, corn, yams, and potatoes. We also raised chickens for meat and eggs. Even though it was common practice to nationalize any such private gardens in the fall, Serey was very upset when we were ordered to bring the vegetables and eggs to the communal kitchen. My kind and patient brother destroyed the crops instead. The chhlob and soldiers led him away.

When he returned, his soul was empty, his spirit robbed. He never spoke of his incarceration in Angkar's reeducation camp. He was never the same afterward. I ached for Serey, my beloved brother. I hugged him as he huddled with us inside our miserable hut.

Angkar dealt with violators swiftly and violently. Soldiers used their weapons on those who showed independent thinking or didn't agree with the system. Serey was used as an example. And they broke him completely, inside and out.

Those who professed belief in the system were rewarded with positions of power. Those who were uneducated, the simple villagers and farmers who lived so far from cities that they didn't know what a car or electricity was, were trusted the most by Angkar.

In my work, I continually pushed myself to the brink, but even so my cell leader would beat me up. When I was absent because of sickness or injury, the cadres increased my work quota and decreased my food ration. "After all, a sick person does not need much food," they often said.

The cadres threatened us. "To keep you or save you is no gain. To kill you is no loss," they said. I heard this refrain many times.

When the monsoon rains came, I was too tired to walk home. In fact, there was no point walking many miles in the rain, since the floods had swept away our hut.

After each day of exhausting work, I slept on the cold, wet ground. The rice fields were covered with up to 2 feet of water, and the best places to sleep had less than 6 inches of water. All dry spots were for Angkar's cadres, soldiers, and commanders.

After a while, so many children slept in the rice fields that a camp was built. Since we didn't have to go home, the cadres made us work longer. We didn't mind: we slept on a dry floor and received a bowl of rice gruel.

Three months later, the rains stopped and the rice stalks grew. The fields were beautifully green, stretching as far as the eye could see. For those of us who had survived the starvation and exhaustion, it was a long wait for the harvest. The Angkar now ordered us to build earthen water canals and weirs.

Planting rice was hard work, but building dikes and canals meant moving tons of soil, rock, and debris. More people in Tapang died from sickness, diseases, malnutrition, and executions. Some Mith Chass suffered, too, but not even remotely close to what we Mith Thmey were suffering.

One morning, the bell in the town's communal hall rang at about 5 A.M. I was surprised by the early bell. What's going on? I wondered.

My exhaustion made me want to return to bed, but my feet moved toward the meeting hall. By 5:30, a few were still missing so some cadres went to look for them. Soon, every single hut in town was emptied.

At about six o'clock the town mayor announced that some sweet potatoes were missing from the communal supply. Angrily, he demanded that the thieves give themselves up. He told us that the cadres knew who the culprit was; they only wanted to teach the town a lesson. "Don't ever try it! Come clean with Angkar now!"

Everyone was silent. Nobody twitched. When the mayor's angry eyes met mine, I remained still. I softly exhaled when his eyes moved on.

The mayor made a signal. Two armed guards struck a man on the head. The rifle butts hitting bone was extra loud in the silence. Blood gushed out of his head. His family wailed in fear.

It was Rom, a fellow Mith Thmey who lived next door to us. He had stolen the potatoes to feed his family. It turned out that their two little boys ate sweet potatoes in public. The parents did a good job of cooking it in secret, but failed to feed the kids in the house. The two kids knew where the potatoes were hidden and innocently ate outside their hut.

We all stayed very still and quiet while the soldiers took the father away. The family rushed after the mayor, pleading. It was no use. He was tortured for weeks. I secretly cried. When cadres were around, I showed them a happy face. I hid my feelings completely from the chhlob. Holding back was my survival strategy.

When Angkar searched Rom's hut, they didn't find any potatoes. When they dug up an old hole near our hut, they found potato peels buried there.

It was a relief that the cadres didn't search inside our hut or they might have found a bit of potato peel. I was worried because Rom's wife had given us some potatoes. We had suspected that they were stolen but had been grateful they were willing to share.

We went on working. It was useless to complain or try and change things. It was best to shut up. As long as we were alive, we held hope that things would change for the better. That we stayed hopeful in the most hopeless situation was another survival strategy.

I was so angry and hurt constantly that I sometimes wanted to commit suicide, but I wanted to see my family again, so I couldn't die. Many families killed themselves rather than endure the torture. They saved Angkar the trouble, I thought. And they no longer suffered.

Soon after the incident of the missing potatoes, the number of armed soldiers increased. We all became even more afraid as the rules worsened and the punishments became more severe. We could no longer go into the forest after work to forage for food. Except for work, travel was restricted to within a mile or two of the communal kitchen.

One day in September 1977, while I was working in the rice fields, I felt even more tired and hungry than usual. I had eaten leaves, earthworms, anything edible, but my hunger remained strong. I missed our secret nightly meals. We'd run out of food a while ago. We had no more gold to trade. Even my precious Seiko watch was gone, long ago bartered for rice.

I took a chance and filled my pocket with some early-ripening grains of rice. I didn't notice two boy chhlob come out from behind the trees, AK-47s slung on their backs. The pair dragged me for nearly two miles across town, then bound and gagged me and left me tied up under the commune chief's house. The mosquitoes feasted on me the whole night.

The next morning I saw a group of soldiers approaching. They stared at me under the house. The commander spat and uncocked his pistol. I closed my eyes.

Nothing happened. I opened my eyes ever so slowly to see the group walk up the bamboo steps. I breathed again. A commotion above me turned my relief into confusion.

"Please, Mith! Please! Don't! Please don't, Mith!" I heard our commune chief say in a strangled voice. The town mayor also pleaded and cried like a child. I was very puzzled. These two are the town's toughest men, I thought, responsible for thousands of deaths and suffering. Why are they crying?

The commander was the first to emerge from the house. The commune chief and the mayor followed, both gagged. Yellow nylon ropes pulled their elbows tight to their backs.

Payback time, I thought, quite pleased with what I saw. I almost smiled but their eyes met mine. Like them, I was also uncomfortable and bound. The commander walked toward me and yanked the gag off my mouth. I trembled but didn't wet my pants. I had already done that earlier.

"What did you do, Mith?" he asked, stern and tall over my frightened soul. I cleared my throat. I had had no water for more than twenty hours and I hurt all over. I gathered enough courage to reply to this mean-looking man.

"Nothing, Mith. I didn't do anything wrong, honest!" I was hoarse. "I only picked a few rice grains to chew on." The commander pulled out a knife. Again, I waited to die.

"Don't you ever do it again, you hear me?" He cut the rope from my sore and sleeping elbows, placed his knife back in its holster, pulled me up, and gave me a good kick in the buttocks, hitting mostly bone. "Get out of here!" He rubbed the toes poking out of his rubber tire sandal. I sprinted, glancing back to make sure they weren't going to kill me. They were too busy kicking the two town officials. Whatever they do to you, I thought, you deserve all that and more.

That day, new soldiers came and hauled away all the cadres, soldiers, militia, and chhlob from Tapang town. I didn't know it then, but I was witnessing part of a countrywide purge. Pol Pot rewarded the loyalty of his people, including my commune chief and mayor, with death. Entire families were wiped out by their now former comrades, their so-called Mith. Some Angkar men and women swiftly escaped to Vietnam.[1]

I slept well that night, knowing that the commune chief, the mayor, and his close associates were no longer a threat. Of the thousands who'd been in Tapang when we arrived, fewer than 100 Mith Thmey had survived long enough to hear of the death of these two killers.

They deserved to die like dogs. They deserved to go to hell.

The days passed in Tapang. We labored on the latest project of choice. The cadres only cared about the work quota. With their AK-47s, the cadres guarded us twenty-four hours a day while we worked or slept.

Serey's family—now my family—barely managed to stay together. Many of the Mith Thmey who had arrived in Tapang with us were dead; other families had only one or two survivors left.

It would not have been so bad if we had had some freedom to find a little food and earn a living to support ourselves. There was no money, no market or stores, so we traded. An ounce of pure gold got you half a pound of rice.

Everyone knew that trading was illegal. We traded in secret, knowing that to be caught was to be executed. The traders worked for Angkar; some were even Angkar soldiers or relatives. When they cheated us there was nothing we could do.

We again ran out of things to trade. My cheekbones protruded and my ribs showed. My skin turned yellow, my teeth and hair came loose. I thought of food, and more food, and about the day I'd die. Only the hope of seeing my parents and siblings continued to sustain me.

Food grew so scarce that no one would trade any more. Each grain of rice became very precious. "We can't eat gold or diamonds," the traders said. More people starved and died.

All of our family valuables were gone. There was nothing left to exchange. Our plates had gone to the communal kitchen so we used coconut shells for dishes. We could not cook because our hidden pots and pans had been traded for a little rice.

Rations at the communal kitchen worsened. More and more people died of starvation and sickness. Angkar severely punished those they caught having private meals.

We kept our small shortwave radio hidden in the roof of our hut. When the time for newscasts came, we would take the radio out of its hiding place, pop in the batteries, and listen to the news on the lowest possible volume. We heard about the Vietnamese incursion into Cambodia. The radio was our only link to the outside world.

Our two C-cell batteries lasted for a while as we used them less than five minutes a day, and only when we could. To lengthen battery life, we exposed them to sunlight, careful that no one ever saw them. Had any chhlob known we had a radio we would have been butchered immediately.

Ever so careful and secretive, we listened to the news in the familiar voice of Cousin Ang Khen from the faraway land of Washington, D.C. We strained to hear the Voice of America's Khmer Information Service until, finally, our batteries went completely dead. Our world became even smaller. We felt so hopeless; it was as if a black shroud had wrapped itself around us.

10

Miracle at the Temple

Wat Yieng

Very long before man had called this cold time of the year "winter," Himalayan currents blew a chill air over the Angkor plains. They did so once again, and so humans and their beasts stayed around warm fires in these early mornings.

In the daylight, the endless green of rice fields surrendered to the relentless brisk air and turned golden yellow. Where humans were too slow, birds by the thousands swarmed in and feasted. The rice was ready for harvest.

December 1977 was a time of long hours of back-breaking work to harvest the rice as fast as possible. The Angkar rewarded all completed work with time off and slightly larger rations—ironically from the very same rice we had planted and harvested. We still had the usual watery rice gruel but without any wild greenery thrown in. The pure, freshly boiled rice tasted mighty good.

What big changes had arrived! they were not like—night and day, but still far different from the days of cadres, soldiers, and chhlob. Now, Mith Thmey and Mith Chass suffered almost equally. Since the purge, execution was reserved for former cadres. Of the "new people," either illness or disease took the few who did not die. Best of all, everyone worked closer to home now. I spent more time in my hut than I ever had in the past two years.

I got permission to visit adjoining villages for salt and *prahok*, the famed Khmer fish paste present in many of our dishes. The rules against trading for food remained, but they were quietly ignored.

A Mith Chass named Phan gave me one of his extra sugar palm trees. He showed me how to work the tree for juice by hanging cylindrical bamboo containers to catch the drops from the tree's flower buds. When plugged with grass or palm leaves, a container could hold 1.5 gallons of liquid. The tree produced more sweet liquid than we needed for desserts, so I traded my surplus harvest for field crabs and fish. I lost two lower back teeth and many of the remaining ones became rotten, but I gained some weight. I still had a small scrap of life in me.

Sa-Oum's family decided to give up our dead radio, hoping that the new Khmer Rouge cadres might later do us a favor in return. The cadres praised our honesty and encouraged us always to "come clean" with Angkar. The small, greenish black radio, so long our secret worldly companion, was now communal property. The cadres could use it as they wished. I imagined them slipping a tape into its cassette player to broadcast revolutionary music.

The Angkar Leu "High organization" distributed vegetable oil, fabrics, salt, white sugar, and even kerosene to each family. I didn't know where these came from, but Chinese-made trucks brought them in, and left full of newly harvested rice.

It was too good to last. After a while the trucks began to arrive empty.

Soon, our communal food was watery rice gruel with wild vegetables again. Once more, people were suffering from malnutrition and hunger, even some of the Mith Chass.

More Mith Thmey died. Sa-Oum's older brother Tim died of severe malnutrition at the age of thirty-seven. His body could not be cremated due to lack of firewood. His remains were buried. The family was devastated.

After the harvest, Serey was permitted to return home. Sa-Oum was about to give birth to their first child. Laive came by our little hut.

"After tomorrow I don't know if I'll ever see a sunrise again," he said.

I looked at him in surprise. "What are you talking about?"

"They're going to take us away tomorrow," he said. "Please say good-bye to Phally for me, will you?" Phally was Laive's girlfriend.

Speechless, I stared at my buddy.

"Stay alive, my friend. Stay alive," Laive said. "Hope you'll find your family safe and sound. Take care. You be careful, you hear?" he hugged me tight and walked away.

Laive said something else but I didn't catch it. I was trying to keep my grief inside.

Laive had shown me the mass graveyard in the outskirts of Tapang. No matter how hard I tried to push the images out of my mind, I could not forget that place near National Highway 6.

There were wooden clubs, bent or broken, among bloodstained rags, rotting hair, and bones. There were scattered bodies, some still wearing their blindfolds, all arms tightly bound, often broken.

I had been to several graveyards. Some had twenty bodies; others had more than a hundred. Always, the bodies were half-buried, half out in the open. The graves were shallow.

In April 1975 cadres had called all servicemen, doctors, lawyers, teachers, and students to meet the Angkar leadership and receive Prince Sihanouk.

Hundreds of military trucks hauled them off to the meeting. With arms bound tightly behind them, they were killed, their bodies thrown in shallow ditches all across Cambodia. The Khmer Rouge didn't waste bullets on them. They smashed heads and necks with wooden clubs.

This method of killing was by now well known. Much later I would see Mith Chass, still in Tapang, who admitted to making wooden killing clubs for Angkar Leu, or who provided oxcarts to bring people to the trucks.

"My father is among these skeletons," Laive said.

"How do you know that?"

"I dug the grave. I told you when we were in Krobey Riel, remember? My father was a serviceman so he was invited to meet the Angkar Leu and the prince, along with all these people," he gestured at the half-buried bones, bleached after more than two years. Cows grazed nearby. "I went with him. I know who did the actual killing. I remember each of them." I was honored to share his bitterness and his grief at the gruesome site.

In the months that followed our trip to the graves, Laive had taught me much about life and survival in Tapang. Now he was about to be butchered and I couldn't do anything about it. How I grieved.

The next morning, we watched Laive's family as well as the Mith Thmey widows and children who had arrived with them walk away from the town.

When I saw that one of their guards was the man who killed the chief and the mayor a few months earlier, I prayed a quick and painless death for them all.

Three days later, I was stunned to hear that Laive had escaped. Cadres started a sweep search of the town's perimeter.

The whispers continued. Laive had returned to Tapang. Laive was hidden in the woods just outside town. Laive had slept on a bed of leaves in a thick bush. The search went on.

One morning more than a week later, the search team returned to town so cheerfully that I knew Laive's run for freedom had ended.

But, if only for a while, Laive had outsmarted and frustrated the dreaded, all-powerful Khmer Rouge executioners.

My best friend was gone, chased and butchered like a dog. He was a brave soul, my buddy Laive, and the only childhood friend I had under Angkar. Perhaps he had returned to see if I could have helped him. I would have, even if it meant risking my life. I wept alone, in secret.

A mere two weeks later, on December 22, 1977, the Angkar Leu ordered the remaining Mith Thmey in Tapang and nearby villages to leave within five hours.

"Do not try to take everything at once," the cadres shouted as we rushed to pack up. "All your things will be delivered to you at the destination." But they never said where we were going.

Others were at work, but the cadres assured us that we would all be together at the final location. No one was surprised that they wouldn't say where we were going. We knew our time had come. Only a few cried.

I was numb with fear. I remembered the half-joking words of an Angkar Leu cadre: "We will work and starve you to death, Mith Thmey. If you don't die, we'll just kill you."[1]

We, the last of the Mith Thmey in Tapang, were walking to our deaths, but my family worried that Sa-Oum would give birth on the road; as if there was anything we could do about it.

I knew it was best to bring as little as possible. With a *kroma* (scarf), I tied together sleeping mats and blankets. Now I had to find my hen. She had been with me from Siem Reap, on the bicycle to Tapang, on the marches. Sometimes I carried her, but most of the time she followed me. She was not only a family heirloom, but a true lifesaver with her double-yolked eggs that provided me with protein. Her chicks had been taken away at one time or another, but she had always remained with me.

Frantically, I searched for the yellow-brown hen, the only living memento of my life at home with my parents and siblings. She was the one thing I had that was never nationalized by Angkar.

We were ordered to gather along the main road just outside town. Because the soldiers would not say where we were going, the old folks believed that we'd be killed at Wat Yieng, an old Buddhist pagoda a few miles south. The Yieng temple was now the district's torture and execution center. There they had broken my brother Serey. There they had tortured my next-door neighbor Rom who stole sweet potatoes.

"If we walk past Wat Yieng, we'll be fine," the old ones whispered.

I still couldn't find my hen. As we marched out of Tapang under armed guard, I was very distraught, as though a sister had died. I kept looking out for a little hen with brown and yellow feathers. As we walked farther, my disappointment turned to despair. First my best friend, now my hen!

The march was hard on Sa-Oum. My sister-in-law had miscarried earlier and was hopeful that this baby would make it. Her father, who was in his mid-eighties, could hardly walk with his swollen knee joints. Serey helped his wife while I helped the old man. The families who dragged crying kids by their arms reminded me of our nightmarish march to Tapang just two years ago, but now, instead of over 200, we numbered just 85. The pavement burned the soles of our feet. Shoes were only a memory for us Mith Thmey.

When we arrived at Wat Yieng, the lead guard ordered us to stop and wait along the roadside. We collapsed in exhaustion while he went inside the temple.

"If we move on, we'll be okay," I heard the whispers. Everyone prayed. I was terrified. I'd never been much for praying, but I prayed really hard this time. I was scared to die.

Our escort returned with more cadres, armed soldiers, and about fifteen more Mith Thmey families. When they were about 60 feet away, I recognized some very familiar faces. My family! I kept my screams deep inside me.

They all look terrible, I thought, just skin and bones. I wanted to run and embrace them, to say how much I missed them all.

Mother and Father looked very, very old. They wore rags, like us. They walked slowly, their eyes on the ground. My not-so-little brothers trailed behind them. I counted them again and again. I wiped away my tears with the back of my hand. After all these years! There they were right in front of me!

Serey grabbed my arm. "Don't stare, Ah Nak," he breathed into my ear, using my nickname to emphasize that he meant it and I better obey.

"It's them, our family!" I whispered back.

"I know," he said. "Wait a while. Be patient." I saw his tears. He wanted to rush toward them as much as I did.

"All here except for Larony, Mona, and Mealanie," I said.

Elder brother Norane was seventeen now, one of the adults. Lonk and Nosay, thirteen and eleven, were two thin urchins with almost sunset-red hair, a sure sign of malnutrition.

Monika and Seiha were half-naked waifs. It took me a few seconds to recognize them. They had grown a little taller. Their rib bones showed and their starved bellies protruded. But they had survived, the poor things!

I stared at Lonk until we made eye contact. I smiled but he looked away, to my disappointment. Have I changed so much? I thought. I swept back my mangled hair. Or are they being cautious like we are?

After about an hour of rest the soldiers counted us and ordered us to our feet. We did feel better moving away from Wat Yieng, but we were still tense. However, I had found my family, so I didn't care. I was perhaps the happiest among that group of Mith Thmey. My long-lost loved ones were right behind us! Nothing matters now, I thought.

At National Highway Number 6, the soldiers ordered us to make camp for the night. They picked spots to put up their military hammocks. There was no food. People fell asleep in exhaustion. A few snored loudly even as children cried.

I took my small sack of cooked-dried rice and ate, nervous but walking very casually toward my parents and brothers and then past them.

Were they looking at what I was chewing in my mouth or were they looking at me?

When I returned, they were still looking at me. I swept back my long, tangled hair to show my face in the last rays of the sun.

"Mae, Pa, everyone. It is I, Nachith," I said softly. For a long time, they all looked at me.

"It is I, your son," I said. "Don't you remember me at all?"

Mother felt my face with her hands in the dim campfire light. Father was dazed. I had never seen them so thin, especially Mother, who I'd always remembered as a bit on the chubby side.

Mother looked as though she had seen a ghost. "Oh, my son. My son!"

Monika and Seiha had forgotten me completely. Lonk and Nosay vaguely remembered Serey and me. The four boys fell on my emergency rice. I would have given them my right arm.

We cried quietly. The soldiers were not too far away.

"Where's Serey and Sa-Oum?" Mother asked, wiping her eyes.

"I'll go get them," I said. "Don't go anywhere, I'll be right back!" I actually feared they'd be gone as soon as I turned away.

"We'll be right here," Father said.

My younger brothers followed me and my rice, not wanting to let me go. I grabbed two of them by their heads and kept them close to me as we walked. How I missed them!

We met Serey halfway. When I disappeared from the camp, he knew where I was. We went to fetch Sa-Oum.

"Where have you been?" Sa-Oum was on the offensive as soon as she saw me. "We were worried sick—you'll cause trouble for us all!"

"It's all right," Serey said, carrying our little brothers. "As I thought, he went to find them."

We didn't sleep much that night. We chatted quietly, sharing sweet and bitter memories. We were in tears most of the time.[2]

I had lost a hen, really a family heirloom. I'd lost my best friend, Laive. But in their place I found a miracle.

One united family, and the fabric of Khmer society was patched.

For a brief moment, I was my mother's little boy again.

11

Dead Weight

Ta Source Hill and the Massacre Site

The winds from the Himalayas in the north had died down enough for me to feel warm as my family and I huddled together that winter morning in early 1977. Mother clung to me at the crack of dawn when the soldiers started kicking us awake and barking orders.

"I have to join my group, Mae," I said. It was daylight. I was fifteen. I didn't want to be seen cuddled by my mother.

I helped Sa-Oum's father prepare for the next leg of the trip. I only had a few hours of rest and an empty stomach, but I was pleased that last night had not been a dream.

When the march resumed, my family followed, stayed close, and then joined us. Now we were a clan of sixteen people.

In less than two days of forced walking, we arrived at Ta Source Hill, about a mile south of Keo Poeur. Except for the twin dikes and a few other landmarks, the place looked so different from earlier that I hardly recognized anything.

At least 15,000 people worked on a very deep, scary-looking hole in the ground, a gigantic water canal. All over this hellhole the dead and the dying lay scattered as far as I could see. Every now and then, under the watchful eyes of armed guards, a group of emaciated laborers collected the dead bodies and hauled them away in makeshift carts.

Our escorts left us. "Find a place, make your camp, and stay together," the new guards said. We were hungry and exhausted but, except for Sa-Oum and the old man, we were put to work within the hour.

Like everyone else, we hauled dirt and gravel and dug until groundwater covered us. My family stayed together and said little. My little brothers clung weakly to me.

We worked all day and almost all night. There was very little food. Within five days, our group of Mith Thmey had been decimated: six children and two elderly men had died.

Serey somehow got permission to gather firewood to boil water for Sa-Oum's imminent delivery. He was nervous; the child would be his firstborn.[1]

The laborers became weaker and worked more slowly. The boy soldiers beat them, often to the point of death. Others were taken away in the night, never to be seen again.

Many more died of heat stroke, disease, fatigue, or starvation. Few bothered with proper burials or with emotion. "The dead suffer no more," I heard someone say. I prayed for Angkar to kill us so we wouldn't suffer anymore.

A sharp poke made me open my eyes. I looked up from the muddy bottom of the gigantic canal where I had fallen asleep.

The boy continued to jab me with the tip of his rifle, which looked too big for him. He was about three years younger than I, kind of chubby, and bursting with energy.

"Move it, Mith! Now!" he ordered. "Go, go, go!" I stared at him. I had only been in this watery hellhole for days, but I was ready for death. I pushed my mud-encased body up and walked to where my group was being herded together.

Five boy soldiers shouted at us to line up in four rows. Everyone knew what this meant. We were going to be moved away again, which was odd. Usually, weeks or months would pass at each site.

This could only mean one thing: they were going to kill us now. I could see the same thought run through the others' minds. I had been praying for death but now was already regretting it.

Phum, the eldest boy cadre, said: "Angkar Leu is moving you all to the Tonle Sap to catch fish. There will be plenty to eat there."

The group came alive. It was just what we wanted to hear, to get out of here, and to eat fresh fish. We doubted Phum a bit, but his words made sense because most of those in our group were Tonle Sap fishermen.

The lake was about 6 miles to the south. Five of the armed boys led us, some of them only ten years old. The previous year, I had walked this same path when I was assigned to work with a Mobile Brigade.

As I half-carried Sa-Oum's elderly father with me on the muddy track, everyone became more and more relaxed.

"Perhaps they're telling us the truth?"

"Could be. We're heading in the right direction."

"There are only five of them. If they planned to kill us, there'd be more of them."

A couple of miles into the hike, a child died. After some hesitation, the boy soldiers allowed the mother to bury her child, but cursed us onward. We left the woman and her friends to lay the dead baby to rest.

Halfway to the lake, the armed boys ordered us to stop. It was early evening. About half an hour later, the woman and her friends caught up with us.

"Up, all able men, young or old," the boy soldiers shouted. "Bring with you your tools, your knives and axes, and put them in this box." We complied immediately.

One of the boy soldiers prodded my shoulder blades, laughing: "This one's too skinny." He pushed me away. "Weak!" Mother's arms caught me. I must have been about four and half feet tall, no more than forty pounds of skin and bones.

Father was too old and crippled. He and Sa-Oum's eighty-five-year-old father could barely walk. Both were rejected.

"Take good care of our baby," Serey told Sa-Oum. Her silence said much.

"Don't you worry," I spoke up. "I'll take good care of her." Serey and my other older brother Norane joined the line of men and boys.

"Let's go," the armed boys shouted. "Before dark, you must finish a camp at the lakeside for the women and the children. Move!" Two boys with rifles led the group away.

Twilight became dark. One of Sa-Oum's older sisters gave me the last of our cooked rice. I threw a handful into my mouth and gave the rest to my little brothers. They fought as though it were their last meal.

It got darker, the wind chillier. The notorious Tonle Sap Lake mosquitoes came in swarms. Children cried.

About half an hour later, the two boy soldiers joined their comrades, talking among themselves. Someone overheard the soldier boys' whispers. The shocking news spread quickly. "A few got away," one of the boy soldiers had said.

This could only mean that they had intended to kill all our men. Amid the crying children, I heard the women weep, including Sa-Oum and Mother. I imagined how I might get away.

After some thought, I knew I couldn't leave my family and my pregnant sister-in-law. She was now a week overdue. Besides, where could I go? Eventually, I'd be caught and killed, like Laive. I decided to die with my loved ones.

The armed boys ordered us to move on. Despite everything I had seen and heard, they still looked like young Khmer boys to me. I had my doubts that they were cold-blooded murderers.

It was now about seven o'clock in the evening. I walked with Sa-Oum's arm over my right shoulder and a small bundle on my left. She wasn't sure if she was having stomach cramps or birth contractions, but her quiet weeping became stifled screams.

Mother whispered soothingly, "Sa-Oum, don't worry. I had ten and I made it. You will, too."

At this point, the soldier-boys ordered us to turn west, away from the lake. Everyone, even the children, knew that all of us were now going to die.

The soldiers pushed us forward on the muddy road. It was hard to move. People screamed, cried, and prayed. Sa-Oum's father walked alone, refusing any help. "Let me die with dignity," he said.

The soldiers kicked and beat those who slowed down on the muddy track. I kept Sa-Oum walking so the soldiers wouldn't beat us. At every step, I had to wrench my foot out of the sucking, oozing mud. I lost track of my family. It was very dark now. We had walked no more than 900 feet when the soldiers ordered us to stop.

I saw the silhouette of a very unusually contorted tree. It looked ghostly, shadowy, a good-sized tree for this place, which was flooded every rainy season. I fixed my gaze on the tree, thinking that it looked strong enough to shelter us, to hide us.

"Sit down, sit, now," the soldier boys yelled. "Stretch your legs to the edge of the ditch." I sat down quickly. I was so tired. The shallow ditch had a little water in it.

"Start digging! Make this ditch deeper," I heard kicking and cries of pain. "Use your hands. Now!" I jumped into the ditch and scooped mud.

The silhouettes of about fifty men with rifles, carbines, and wooden clubs emerged from the nearby forest and surrounded us. Those in the ditch began to plead.

"Be quiet, shut up," the soldiers shouted again and again. "Shut up, right now, all of you!" I heard wood crashing on solid bone and screams of agony.

"Please, Mith. Please. I beg you, don't hurt us. Don't harm my family, I beg you," said the elderly man named Rom. He was on his hands and knees. I recalled the torture Rom had endured for stealing sweet potatoes.

"Angkar Leu does not wish to harm you, Mith," the armed men still called us Mith. "Angkar Leu only wishes to ask a few questions, that's all. Don't make this any more difficult."

"Please, Mith, spare my family. We helped Angkar in the war. We gave food and medicine, we gave good information, spare us," Rom pleaded.

"When did you help Angkar? Where? Who's your contact?" the commander said.

I was surprised to learn that our longtime neighbor Rom was a Khmer Rouge sympathizer. Coward! I thought. You should die. You helped the monster come to power. I bit my lip to keep my rage inside.

"This is just an interrogation," the soldier said. "Angkar Leu suspects there are Vietnamese agents in this group."

What a stupid lie; we'd known each other for years. Perhaps there were Khmer Rouge supporters like Rom among us, but no Vietnamese.

A boy soldier came near. He smelled bad. He yanked away my checkered cotton kroma, tore it into strips and tied my arms behind me. I struggled in terror. This is the end, I thought. This is my end.

He hit my head. I screamed in agony. Another soldier joined him. They hit my head again and again and gagged me with some of the torn strips of my kroma. Blood flowed from my face to my chest.

Oh, the fear, the pain, the worst in my life, ever. This is what they did to anyone who resisted. But maybe I was not going to be killed? Maybe I was only being used as an example?

They tied the rest of the group quickly. Nobody resisted anymore.

I felt groggy. Blood got into my right eye. The chaos of sounds, pleas, and cries went on. When I heard the first systematic thuds, I was beyond horror. This is it, I thought. This is the end.

Sa-Oum's father was kneeling right next to me. I heard heavy blows and felt his body contract several times before he fell to his left, onto my body. His head lay on my lap, covering me, protecting me even in his death. Sa-Oum's father had been like a grandfather to me during the time of Angkar.

A small boy immediately in front of me—Phat was his name—stood up and called his mother. He was about six years old and, a son of Rom. I heard a swishing sound—the boy's voice stopped in mid-syllable. Something warm splashed my face and chest. Blood stung my eyes. My mouth was stuffed with a ragged cloth. I couldn't move my arms. Horrifying sounds filled my ears. We were all in hell.

Above the yelling guards and the cries for mercy, I heard the screams of my family. Their short, spluttering sounds froze me. Bodies fell near me. I heard their breathing stop. My brain wanted to shut down but couldn't.

This is not real. This is a dream, I thought to myself, or perhaps screamed it out loud. The surreal events around me occurred in slow motion. I became numb.

The first terrible blow came when I was face down on the ground, with dead weight partly covering me. I felt a whack just below my right shoulder blade, heard a popping sound, and then experienced total, excruciating pain. Every jolt of pain hit me to the fullest. I tried to scream and ease the pain but couldn't.

The next blow hit me on the right side of my head, just above my neck, making a cracking sound.

I passed out.

It must have been about four o'clock the next morning when the buzzing sound woke me up. I wondered why I could hear so many mosquitoes. I wondered why I couldn't move. I thought I was in my bed at home.

I didn't feel anything and my vision was too blurry to make anything out. A few minutes later, I began to see indistinct shapes. Finally I detected a bare foot.

"Whose foot could that be?"

As my sight cleared, I made out clouds of mosquitoes over me. I was in the mud, my elbows locked behind me.

And then the memories returned. I knew where I was. A blanket of fear covered me. I couldn't stop shaking. I broke into a sweat. I had never felt so cold in my life.

I must be dead, I thought, but my soul hasn't left my body yet. Then I felt the sharp-dull pains in my head, the painful remnants of the numerous blows all over my body.[2]

If I am dead, why do I feel so much pain?

I'm alive.

But I should be dead.

These are but some of the thoughts that ran through my mind. How can I write what I truly felt then? It's almost impossible. I was horrified, frustrated, confused. I was in pain, afraid and weak. These words aren't good enough.

The faint light of a new dawn broke through the clouds but it was dark and cold down there under the trees.

I pushed myself up on the muddy bodies to sit. My arms were riddled by painful tingles as circulation slowly returned. I worked on the cloth that bound me.

The light of the first day of January 1978 grew stronger. Birds sang. It took me a long time to free my arms. My right arm was dislocated and it dangled uselessly. My head hurt, oh how it hurt. It was difficult for me to move. An inch of movement was a pound of pain.

I couldn't stop shaking. I closed my eyes. Dizzy, I groped with my hands, clutching at anything so I wouldn't fall down. All I touched was cold flesh.

When I stood up in the ditch and looked around, within seconds, I wished I were blind again.

Bodies were everywhere, like firewood scattered by bad dogs at play. Their dead faces screamed in silence, their clothes were torn, some completely naked.

I searched for my family. Here was Sa-Oum and her unborn child. It was her bare foot I had seen when I'd first woken up. Her swollen belly was exposed to the chill air. Her father and her two sisters were on top of each other, all entangled. Here's my mother. There's my father. Here are my little brothers. I wished I had died with them.

I refused to look anymore. I closed my eyes and wept. I remembered the last sounds my family had made—their interrupted screams, their halted breaths—but all I heard now was my own weeping and the buzzing clouds of mosquitoes.

Voices broke into my sorrow. As the voices came closer, I began to panic. They're back to finish me off, I thought. They're coming to bury me alive.

Then I relaxed. They might as well. I had absolutely nothing to live for. The earlier terror subsided. I was resigned to my fate. An eerie calm descended over me in the light of the morning, even as the voices came closer, louder.

Suddenly, I felt the need to hide. Perhaps it was an instinct for self-preservation that made me move. I pushed myself up out of the canal and inched my way into some bushes twenty painful feet away.

I had a good view. The soldiers led a group of men and some women with arms bound behind at the elbows—with real rope this time. There's no way they can cut that rope, I thought.

The soldiers chatted as they whipped, kicked, and pushed the group, like cheerful boys herding cattle early in the morning. I heard a command. In minutes, they had clobbered, chopped, and hacked all the people to death. The bodies fell atop the dead bodies in the mud.

My hand was clamped over my mouth. I wanted to throw up, but nothing came out. I went through the ordeal of death and dying all over again.

"Do not, do not, do not make any sound," I chanted to myself. I was shaking. Again I passed out.

I faded in and out of consciousness. Hazy images of death taunted me in my restless sleep. I was awakened the following night, again by the sound of people coming. But this time I was no longer afraid. I was very, very angry. I decided to live for one simple reason, one purpose only—to avenge the death of my family, friends, and neighbors. This feeling saved my life as it became the rationale for my survival. It was all the more powerful for providing the motivation that I needed—revenge.

I was hungry, very weak, and very thirsty. My lips were split, my body coated with mud and blood, now cracked and flaking. I couldn't walk. I crawled on elbows and knees. Vengeance fired and fueled me. I wondered where to go. Laive had warned me never to return if I escaped. I wouldn't go back to Tapang.

I crawled west along the shallow ditch, bid my loved ones good-bye, and turned north to Kok Poh, where a distant relative lived.

In a short while, my elbows were badly bruised, my knees all cut up and raw. I kept going. I crawled until the dark chill of night covered me again.

I found myself trapped in a forest of thorny bushes. I went back and forth trying to find a way through. I ended up back where I had begun, near the pile of dead bodies. I felt my little strength diminishing.

After the fourth or fifth try, I was still lost in that thick, thorny bush. Utterly frustrated, I cried out loud. I was drained of all fear for the moment.

I must find a way out of this thick forest, I said to myself. I must find water soon or die of thirst.

I cried myself to sleep, but I got no rest. Instead I relived Phat calling his mother before he was silenced, then Sa-Oum's father falling, falling. . . . The tragic images popped in and out of my consciousness. The visions were relentless and brutally painful. My body shook and I sweated profusely.

Later that night, I woke up to hear movement within the forest. Perhaps I was not the only survivor. One of my family members or a neighbor or friend could be alive.

I didn't dare make a sound. I believed that I was the object of a manhunt. This must be how Laive had felt, I thought. I intended not to repeat Laive's mistakes. I decided to do all I could to survive—at all costs. Risking detection would be the last thing I'd do, and if they saw me I would draw blood on the first Khmer Rouge I came across.

The hours passed. All my circling and reversing must have confused the trackers. I was like a silent log of the forest.

That night, the nightmares didn't come.

12

Kill or Be Killed

Krobey Riel, Dorn Swar, and Prey Roniem

Up in the branches, a flock of long-tailed macaques screamed in the calm January morning. Light danced through the leaves to the wet floor of the Prey Roniem, the flooded forest of the north estuary of the Tonle Sap Lake.

I looked up as the monkeys screeched loudly. Did they want me out of their turf or were they warning each other of danger? Did they see a snake or my pursuers?

I sprang up only to fall in dizziness and throbbing pain. I stayed still, holding my breath, fighting the pain, keeping screams from bursting out of me. I hissed and puffed in my failed attempt to control the awful, throbbing pain radiating throughout my skinny body. Tears filled my eyes as raw nerves amplified the excruciating pain.

After I calmed down a bit, I heard a communist song coming from Ta Source Hill where I had last eaten a long two days ago. I thought to myself, they must be using the cassette player on the shortwave radio we had given up earlier to play that music. That radio must be the reason they butchered my family and friends.

We had hidden that precious radio for years, finally giving it to the new Khmer Rouge cadres in Tapang and hoping for some return favor. Instead, I reasoned, death met us for hiding contraband—a radio with no batteries. It was only much later when I realized that the radio had had nothing to do with the massacre; Angkar killed Mith Thmey as a matter of course.

With the help of a crude walking stick that I named "Caveman Club," I made my way on shaky feet out of the tangle of sharp thorns, cutting myself in many places. Using the sun and the distant music as guides, I moved away from the place of death in the forest.

In a few hours, I reached the edge of the forest by the flood plain of Viel Smeth. In the rainy season the *smeth* (wild rice) grew abundantly here. However,

Angkar had transformed Viel Smeth into a vast rice paddy to grow *srov vear*, a native rice variety unique to this region. This type of rice grows at an average rate of 12 to 18 inches per day, up to 15 feet in height, following the rapidly rising water from the lake. Indeed, srov vear grows as fast as the water rises in the rainy season.

Now it was the dry season; the lake had receded and this unique crop was ready for harvest. Unable to support its grains without the water, the rice lay down neatly, following the water's flow to the lake. Workers were in the field now, quickly harvesting the srov vear before the water rose again.

I rested against a tree and looked out across the open field between the dense forest and the northern villages of Kok Poh. To get to Aunt Samon's house, I would have to cross this vast rice field to its northern edge.

Only a few bushes here and there broke the field of srov vear. There was no place to hide. To calm myself, I washed my shirt several times. The bloodstains would not wash away so I buried the shirt in the mud. There were some things I wanted to forget quickly.

As I walked across the open field, I became dizzy from the heat. I needed food and water but I walked casually as though I were one of the farm workers.

In front of me were trees by ponds of cool water filled with fish, but the ponds were unreachable no matter how hard I tried. I soon realized that I was hallucinating. I found myself lying in the wet sludge, not knowing how I got there. I must have passed out a few times along the way. I scooped up some water to drink but I got mostly mud and leeches.

I washed myself to cool down, but the water dried and left a layer of mud on my skin. As it turned out, it was great protection against sunburn. I thought to myself, no wonder water buffaloes love to wallow in the mud so much.

Despite my fear and pain, I had a big smile for the workers. I must have looked awful to them: bruised black and blue, dried blood in my hair and wearing just a pair of torn shorts.

By late afternoon, I could hear children crying. A barking dog surprised me. I hadn't heard a dog since 1975. Kok Poh appeared nearly empty. Perhaps the villagers were at work.

From behind a bush, I watched the house of Aunt Samon, the younger sister of Aunt Thet, who had been married to my late Uncle Vin.

The last time I had seen Aunt Samon was about a year ago. Passing this way from a fishing assignment in the Tonle Sap, I had given her family some fish. For that I felt they owed me at least a meal. I wasn't sure if they'd help me or report me. People had been brainwashed to report even relatives, but I was desperate.

I must have dozed off. It was fairly dark when I woke up but people were still about. This must be a main thoroughfare, I thought, or Angkar is either working them late or moving them out.

To my pleasant surprise, the mosquitoes were kinder here, although other insects tormented me, including red ants. To top all that, a small dog sniffed me and barked at me.

How had this dog survived? Elsewhere, dogs, cats, and rats had been eaten. The dog continued to bark. It was a cute dog, but I didn't want to be discovered. I threw a pebble and the dog ran off with a yelp. I was hungry and thirsty. I could search for the village well or a pond but I really needed food so I waited for Aunt Samon.

When I saw Aunt Samon walk into her house, I moved quickly, afraid that someone would see me. I leaned on Caveman Club for support. My jerky motion pained my swollen neck, my back, and my legs. In tears, I fought the pain as I made my way to Aunt Samon's home.

Aunt Samon opened the door and immediately stepped back in shock, as though she had seen a ghost. Her eyes opened wide and her jaw dropped.

"Please, help me," I whispered. I painfully raised my hands into a *sampass*, the gesture for greeting or begging. "I beg you, I need help."

Aunt Samon took another step back. I must have looked like the walking dead. I was muddy and bleeding a little.

"Please help me, Aunt Samon!" I leaned on the door frame and fell.

She yanked me in and shut the door. I yelled to suppress the pain and my own yell at the same time.

Aunt Samon shook with fear. "Here, drink this."

My thirst slaked, I lay on the floor. The shocked family gathered around.

Aunt Samon offered me a little cooked rice and some salty dried fish, perhaps out of respect for my family. "Ah Nak, I know that Angkar took your family to the south, that's all I know."

I told them everything—the march to Ta Source Hill, the deaths of my family, my escape. Their looks told me what they dared not say out loud: a fugitive in their house endangered their lives.

After I ate the stale rice and fish, I left Aunt Samon's house. I was terribly hurt, afraid, and angry. The tears came again. It was too much for me to expect Aunt Samon to help me. I couldn't just put her and her family in a situation that might destroy them all. I wouldn't want someone from a graveyard in my home, either.

I was losing hope. I was ready to give up and die. In the dark I sat under a tree not far from Aunt Samon's home. That damn dog was still barking at me.

I didn't feel like giving it another pebble on the head. Such a tiny little rascal, I thought. The dog came closer.

At least this dog acknowledges me as a living person, I thought. "You'd want me to fight for my life, wouldn't you?" I asked him. The skinny little fellow actually cheered me up a bit. Now this little bag of bones was in my arms, snuggling on my bare chest, about to sleep. How could he trust a stranger so much?

No, I thought. I'd never trust a stranger as easily.

I stood up to go. The dog followed me for a while, its tail wagging. Was he blessing me with a safe journey? My staggering increased my pain. I lapsed in and out of consciousness. Thoughts came and went.

"I hope they won't report me, but if they were wise, they would."

"I must not depend on anybody except myself."

"Everyone for himself first, this is the rule for survival."

A herd of *krobey* (buffalo) feeding along the road drainage reminded me of Krobey Riel, and of Laive. Krobey Riel wasn't too far away. Honorable Brother Som lived there, being native to that village.

I had seen the former monk only three months previous when he became engaged to Sa-Oum's older sister. They were to be married in April, only four months away. Brother Som didn't know his fiancée was dead. The least I could do was tell him. Perhaps, in his Buddhist kindness, he would help me.

Feeling hopeful once more, I wiped away my tears and set out for Krobey Riel. I looked behind me for the dog. It was gone.

I asked for directions from an old man herding water buffalo on the road. He was a shadow in the dark; I could barely see him. Still, I sensed his careful gaze as he looked me up and down from head to toe. Finally, the man pointed and I nodded my thanks. I thought I saw the old man grin.

Leaning on Caveman Club, I walked eastward through the night, each step a pain. It was still dark the next morning when I reached Krobey Riel. People were still asleep. It took me a while to find Brother Som's home. After some hesitation, I banged on the door. The light of an oil lamp appeared through the cracks. Soon after, the door swung open with a slight screech.

"Yes? Who is it?" A familiar voice boomed. I collapsed against the door. Brother Som caught me instantly. "Who are you? What do you want?" he asked, until recognition dawned on his face.

Quickly, his father and siblings fetched water, washed me, and cleaned my wounds. They showed more generosity than my own relatives had.

It took Brother Som a while to absorb the shocking news that Angkar had killed his fiancée. He mumbled what sounded like a Buddhist prayer for the dead. He had been the head monk of a Buddhist temple in Mechrey Island when the Khmer Rouge came to power. Sa-Oum's father used to serve the monks at that temple.

I slept through the day and night. I woke up the next morning, a blanket covering me on the floor. The pain and the swelling had lessened. I saw food near me, and I gulped it down. I wanted more, but I vomited in pain.

Brother Som returned in the early afternoon with a fresh cucumber and a green watermelon.

"Stay where you are until I get back from work and figure out what to do with you," he said in his calm manner. "I'm going to try and ask permission for you to stay with us. I may have to lie a bit, something about you being a Buddhist monk, former or otherwise. I don't normally say false words, but these are difficult times," he said. Just before he left, he said, "Don't leave this house, not for any reason. I'll do my best to help you."

I slept some more. Two days passed. I felt better each day, but I expected Angkar trackers to capture me anytime. I nagged Brother Som about the official approval for me to stay in Krobey Riel. Each time, he said, "I don't know yet. Wait a little while."

The swelling went down and the pain was all but gone. Dark bruises were all over my thin body. The right side of my head hurt, and I recalled the second blow by the guard at Ta Source Hill. He'd left a dent on the lower right of my skull—nearly half an inch deep. The dent was very painful and soft to the touch. As the fracture began to heal, I had severe, paralyzing, one-sided headaches.[1]

On the evening of the third day, Brother Som returned with a grim face. I knew it was time to move on.

"Angkar won't allow you to stay with us," he said, referring to the town chief. "I'm so sorry. You must leave before we get into trouble." He gave me his ration of watery rice, a few grains of salt, and another small cucumber. "Please eat this, Nak," he said. I gulped them all down, wanting more.

What to do next? I looked to Brother Som's siblings for help, but they all avoided my eyes. I walked out the door and down the road, hopeless, on the verge of fainting. Brother Som soon caught up with me.

"I'm so sorry, Nak," he whispered. "I did my best."

"I understand, L'Bawng [Honorable Brother]," I said. "You tried and I appreciate that very much."

"You could go to Dorn Swar. Someone might be able to help you there," he said.[2]

I indeed had family friends in Dorn Swar, about five miles away. It was a good hike for an able body, but for me it would be an all-night walk. Still, it was hope.

Brother Som touched my head and said a Buddhist prayer. His act was punishable by instant death, but he went through his prayers on that open road without fear or hesitation.

I thanked him profusely and walked on. He followed close behind for a little while. When he turned around and left, he didn't have to say I'd never make it. It was in his eyes.[3]

Again, I was alone, on the road at night. I still feared the dark, which made me almost blind, but the darkness was my best cover. Brother Som's old shirt kept me warm and Caveman Club made my steps surer.

I walked west to Dorn Swar, determined to get there by morning. The coolness and the three days of rest made me feel stronger, but everything was still so uncertain. I slept briefly in a bush by the road. Passing oxcarts and voices woke me up from time to time. Nightmares of soldiers trying to kill me also woke me up. Sleep terrified me.

I started out before sunrise, feeling alone and lost. I thought to myself, this must be how all orphans of the world feel. But deep inside I knew my loved ones were with me. I prayed for the souls of my family to guide me. I walked on with new courage. Dorn Swar was just ahead. I'll get there, I thought, if it's the last thing I do.

In the early light a group of people walked toward me. They were being herded toward Ta Source Hill, doomed to digging a huge canal to Tonle Sap Lake. They'd be killed, just like my family and neighbors. I was the only one walking in the opposite direction. I felt very exposed.

"Ah La-Eth [Puny One]," said a boy soldier. "Where are you going?" He carried a rifle. "I . . . I'm looking for my buffalo, Mith," I was calm but it was very hard to control my fear.

"What's wrong with you? Speak up! You look all beat up!" The monster looked me up and down.

"Well, why do you think I'm looking for the lost buffalo? Mith Choeun beat me up really bad because I lost the damn buffalo I was watching!" I said, anger swelling.

"Get out of here, go!" He waved me off. As soon as he was out of sight, I changed course slightly, in case anyone tried to find me.

He bought it! I felt triumphant over my sworn enemy, the Khmer Rouge.

I arrived at Dorn Swar about noon and headed to a friend's house. No one was home except the friend's grandmother, who was watching the children. I knew her, too, but only by face. I knew the whole family but I didn't remember their names.

The grandmother put a finger to her lips and pointed to the back of the house. In a whisper, she told me that Wang (the widow of Tim, my brother's brother-in-law) was in the stack of hay.

Wang (pronounced WAHNG) almost choked me to death with her hug. She wept, at the same time trying to keep quiet. "I lost my baby, my husband, my younger sister," her tears wet my face and neck.

"We made it, Bawng. We made it," I said through my tears. I was so happy that I was not the only one to survive that massacre.

Wang nodded, unable to stop weeping. She described how her baby girl had died in her arms.

"Please, you needn't tell me. I was there, too." I didn't want to hear. I didn't want to relive the horror.

"I know, Nak, but I have to tell you just in case I don't make it," Wang's tears flowed with her words. Her dress was stained, like the shirt I had buried in the mud days ago. "Most of this blood," she said, "is from my baby."

The soldiers had hit her baby daughter's head until it shattered and then hit Wang. She woke to find the infant with very little of its skull left, its blood and brains all over her. Next to her were her sister and other relatives, all dead.

Wang had dark bruises on the face, arms, and legs but she had fewer injuries than I did. "I was lost in the forest for hours," she said. "I met three farmers when I crossed Viel Smeth. I told them what happened to me. They said, 'If you were a man, we might take you to the forest with us.' They gave me some food and asked me to move on."

For three days, the family friends in Dorn Swar had fed and cared for Wang. Now they hid both of us, giving us clean clothes, hats, and some dried rice. These were quite precious gifts in such time of severe shortage. They took a great risk for us. We knew we couldn't stay long. We were putting them in great danger the longer we hid there. Wang wanted to find those farmers. "They might take us in when they see you," she said. Wang remembered that the farm was called Tek Thlar (Clear Water).

We left the next evening and promptly got lost. Two farms had those words in their names: Tek Thlar Leu (Upper Clear Water), and Tek Thlar Krom (Lower Clear Water). Wang chose the latter for its proximity to the place where she had come out of the flooded forest.

We found the farmers late in the afternoon. The farmers gave us some food and sternly told us to go away. Distraught, we sat down and refused to budge.

"Go to Battambang and make your way to Thailand," they insisted. Reluctantly, we went west toward Battambang. We were no more than a mile away when we heard Moeun, one of the older men.

"Bawng Srei! Ah Khaoan, wait up," he called. "We had to make sure," he said, catching his breath. We looked at each other, puzzled.

"Come," he said. "We'll hide you in the forest with the rest."

There were people hiding in the forest? I dared not ask. It was enough that these strangers were willing to protect us.

As it turned out, the men were part of an underground resistance movement. They took us to the rebel group's hiding place in Prey Roniem, the flooded forests of Tonle Sap Lake.

To my surprise, there were at least thirty others there, mostly massacre survivors. The rest simply could not stand the abuses of Angkar anymore. Many were relatives of the three farmers.

"We thought you might be chhlob," they explained. "We had to test you, to make sure you were real victims. We had to send you away and see your reaction. I'm sure you understand."

Wang and I became part of what Angkar called *chau prey*, not even dignified as rebels or freedom fighters, only "forest bandits." It wasn't an organized group; it was only a bunch of desperate people on the run.

Over the next several days, my injuries began to heal with enough rest deep in the Prey Roniem. The cooked rice, roasted fish, and *krobey* meat helped me fill out, eventually adding twenty pounds to my small frame. More people joined us, either escaping from death or simply fed up with Angkar. Soon there were over a hundred of us, and then more than two hundred. At age fifteen, I was the only child.

The group was loosely organized into smaller groups led by the three "farmers," Min Moeun, Peth Doeum, and Chea Sek. Sek was a former military policeman; all had previously kept water buffalo and now they led us forest bandits.

We had assignments. We made bows and arrows for hunting, fishing, and for use as weapons. I was glad when Wang became one of the cooks; it kept her busy enough to lessen her sadness and depression.

I was a lookout, perched on the tallest trees at the edge of the forest. When I saw people coming I signaled the security detail below who were on the alert for chhlob. I longed to strike my revenge against Angkar. Caveman Club was with me even in the treetops.[4]

One cloudy afternoon I saw two men coming toward our hideout. They stayed on the sides of the trail, appearing alert and watchful. From the way they walked, I knew they were trouble. At my signal, they were nabbed.

Five people in our group knew one of the men well. He was a notorious chhlob, an Angkar spy since youth. They identified him as responsible for the deaths of their families and thousands of other men, women, and children. He denied everything. He was never an Angkar cadre, he said.

The other man was a local district chief who had ordered tens of thousands of people in the area to their deaths, perhaps including my family. He was fearless and felt invincible, being an important Angkar cadre. He and his right-hand man, the chhlob, each had a pistol. They had been caught by surprise. They were on an inspection tour of the area, which was under the district chief's jurisdiction.

The judgment from the People's Court was swift; the punishment took longer. The two men didn't look so tough anymore. They begged for mercy.

My reason to live had come. These men were high enough in the Angkar ranks to serve as my biggest stab at revenge. After exercising their power of life and death, they now looked pathetic. It was payback time.

The crowd closed in, beating, kicking, and clobbering them. My heart was a beast roiling with hatred and anger. The men were barely conscious when Caveman Club found them.

My first swing gouged one of their heads and it spurted red. The crowd cheered as I beat them. So this is what revenge feels like, I thought. It was a sweet rush, like nothing I'd ever felt before, nothing! "You're avenged!" I cried out in my passionate retribution for my dead family and friends.

Blood poured on the ground. The men wept, cried, begged for mercy with their hands. I heard the people cheer, urging me on. Now I had the power. "This one's for Laive!" I screamed, giving another blow.

They went limp and were dragged across the mud, deeper into the woods. My beating the two cadres didn't ease or end my ire. I had become a mad beast. I wanted to kill those two. I followed the chanting crowd.

Moeun stopped me. "That's enough, Ah Khaoan!"

I wanted more.

"That's enough. You've done enough, no more." He held me tight.

I cried. I never knew where they threw the two bodies.

The group in the forest swelled to over 250 men and women. We ran out of rice and fish, so we butchered Angkar's buffalo. We still had to get rice and build new shelter. The monsoon was coming. Soon the Tonle Sap's floodwaters would inundate the forest.

The three leaders, Moeun, Doeum, and Sek, made plans to raid the local Khmer Rouge garrisons at Ta Source Hill for food and weapons. We had bows, arrows, sticks, stones, a few knives, and two grenades.

"We have no choice," the leaders said. "We may die trying, but we have to try our best, for all our sakes. Are you with us?"

The forest bandits cheered. We knew what we had to do. We must fight or die, kill or be killed.

It was time to liberate the area. The night of January 27, 1978, some 250 men and women separated into three groups. I was in the command team with the three leaders and fifteen others. As back-up support, it was the safe group for weaker ones like me.

At about 2 A.M., we quietly marched toward Ta Source Hill where I had worked in a massive canal, where I had had my last meal before the massacre. The thought of returning there terrified me, but this time, I had a mission. It was a simple plan: kill or be killed. I was more than ready.

My heart was thumping. I was afraid, but I also wanted to give another blow for the death of my loved ones, my friends, and my neighbors.

Inching slowly forward and then hiding behind a low rice paddy dike, we waited for the attack signal. I had my trusty Caveman Club. Men in the lead group threw the two rusty grenades.

We waited. Two, three, and then ten agonizingly slow seconds went by. Nothing exploded. The element of surprise was gone.

Suddenly, the still moonlit night became chaos. It was a mad dash of our people screaming at the top of their lungs, rushing up the hill with my smaller group of misfits close behind.

The Khmer Rouge soldiers reacted. The large 50-caliber machine-gun fire erupted and bright red tracers arched toward us. The wounded screamed in pain. Bodies began to drop like scythed stalks of rice. Large explosions then rocked the ground all around us, kicking up dust and smoke. More of us fell even as we rushed almost blindly toward the bunkers.

Plumes of smoke and hot flashes burned up the sky. The night turned glowing red. The Khmer Rouge were using B-40 RPGs (rocket-propelled grenades), which were designed to knock out tanks at more than 3,000 feet away. The RPGs, mass-produced in China like the land mines, were the most feared weapons in the Vietnam War.[5] Through the hazy smoke I saw bodies fly sky high after an indirect hit. The reverberations from the blasts made my head spin.

I ran up the hill toward the Khmer Rouge's defensive line, scared, angry, and thinking of my dead father, mother, and brothers. That moonlit January night, I was a savage animal raging with a thirst for Khmer Rouge blood. Behind my fear, hatred burned and boiled, making me oblivious to the whizzing bullets, the explosions, and the dead and the dying around me.

The thirst for vengeance was powerful and addictive. I rushed up that hill, focused only on getting there and letting the first one have it. Life meant absolutely nothing to me at that moment. I was pure revenge on legs.

I was so close to the bunker that I saw the flashes from the machine-gun muzzles. An RPG whizzed by my head, trailing smoke and flames. I could feel the heat as it sped by. The ensuing explosions flattened me to the ground. I rose in a daze and rushed on.

"My loved ones, protect me!" I prayed. In a few steps, I reached the sandbags and looked into the bunker. There I glimpsed the face of my first victim.

We saw each other at the same moment. He was no older than I, perhaps a little smaller. His dark round face, his eyes under his Mao Zedong cap shone in the moonlight. He seemed to have just awakened from a deep, sound sleep. He could well be one of those who killed my group of nearly eighty unarmed people a few weeks ago. This boy soldier and I, bound by fate, were locked into a deadly showdown. It was kill or be killed. There was no avoiding it.

He hurried to lift and aim his oversized AK-47 assault rifle at me. I put my full fury into a swing and, in a split second, Caveman Club found the boy's right temple. Thwack! The Chinese-style military cap flew off his head. The soldier shuddered and fell limply on the ground, face down.

I raised Caveman Club and gave him another massive head blow. In a moment, just like that, I became the beast I so despised. It was easy to reason and act against my own kind. It was nothing at all. I felt no sense of remorse.

I reflected on Caveman Club's history. The first two, the district chief and his chhlob companion, had not been entirely my kills. They were pure vengeance, while this boy was self-defense. I wanted to kill more Khmer Rouge before my certain end. Death awaited me, I well knew at that moment. I was resigned to my fate.

I reached for the boy's rifle and heard a trigger click. I instinctively turned to see a dark figure behind me point his weapon at me, another Chinese-made

AK-47. He pulled his trigger yet again, and then again. Nothing was fired at me. The soldier looked at his jammed weapon with disgust.

In a mere split second, without even thinking about it, I swung my club at his head. He staggered and then fell to the ground. I finished him off with several more hard blows. A sense of satisfaction filled me completely. In my first hand-to-hand combat I had scored two kills in less than five minutes, with not a scratch on me. Adrenaline coursed through my veins.

I sought my next score. A woman from my group grabbed the boy's rifle and ran, firing at the other bunker. I followed close behind, almost pushing her slowness.

Amid the gunfire and explosion, I heard a loud snap. The woman fell on me with arms outstretched. We dropped onto our backs, her limp body on top of me. I could feel her warm body.

While I struggled under her dead weight, she jerked and shuddered as more bullets riddled her body. I was bleeding. Why did I feel no pain? It was only when my terror subsided that I found I was unhurt. Her warm blood had spilled all over my body. That woman was my guardian angel, whoever she was.

The fight raged on, now mostly hand-to-hand. Moeun and the others called for retreat. Tracer bullets lit up the early morning sky. Fear pushed me to run quickly back downhill, through the muck. The machine gunners continued to fire at us. I ran even faster when I saw that my group was far away. Foolishly, I had been the last to retreat.

The next morning, our forest bandits appeared a sorry lot. Many were badly wounded, many others missing. The Khmer Rouge was never known for observing the Geneva Conventions for prisoner-of-war treatment. We only hoped that our missing friends and fellow rebels died quickly.

We did get some pistols and rifles but we failed to get food, and we had not claimed the garrison. However, I had avenged my family and friends with only Caveman Club and my 4½-foot, 60-pound, fifteen-year-old body.

So, what next? We looked to Moeun, Doeum, and Sek, our humble leaders.

"We must post guards immediately," Moeun said. "Any volunteers?"

After a pause, some hands reluctantly went up.

"We must link up with the freedom fighters along the Thai-Cambodian border," said Doeum. "We have been in contact with them. We'll go to the border in small groups." He slipped a pistol into his pants waist.

"Let's get moving," said Sek, the former military policeman. "We're not safe here."

I stood near the three men.

As we prepared to leave, Wang said to me, "No matter what happens, stick with the three leaders. You'll be safe with them. They seem to care about you."

We all departed our hiding place and went west along the edge of the flooded forest. Ahead of us, Wang left with a group of women. The four of us, the three leaders and I, were the last to leave.

About an hour later, the sound of automatic rifles came from where we left our lookout sentries. "Don't worry," Moeun said, outwardly calm. Doeum melted into the forest. My survival instinct was urging me to bail out now but I couldn't. The three leaders were still leading.

A glance to my right, and I dove to the ground in horror. Uniforms and Mao Zedong caps were only a few hundred feet away. Mortar fire followed bursts of automatic rifle. The counterattack had come sooner than we expected. Quickly, I followed Doeum, Sek, and Moeun into the dense forests of Tonle Sap Lake.

Many of our group were killed or captured that morning. Our hideout in the woods was shelled for three days and nights. Hardly anything was left standing.

The shelling eased on the fourth day. We heard occasional shots and distant screams, which really bothered me. I knew those voices. I thought of Wang. For sure, she would be cruelly tortured before she died. For sure, I'd never see Wang again.[6]

We crawled on our bellies and slithered on our backs. For food we had just a little rice and cooked buffalo meat that I carried in an old army cooking pot. There was nothing to drink. We licked dew from leaves.

After three days of crawling on wet ground, we had no more food. I was so tired I didn't care if I died in my sleep.

I looked at Caveman Club one more time before I tossed it aside. It was battered, with blood dried in the splinters and dents. What I had done with this piece of wood sickened me. My parents and my Buddhist monk teachers taught me to revere life, but I had killed at the age of fifteen. What I did that terrible night would haunt me for the rest of my life.

I didn't know hate and vengeance would exact such a high cost. I would pay a heavy price for my deeds.

13

Barefoot Escape

Srae Noy, Resin Mountain, and the Deep Northern Jungle

A loud explosion awoke me to flying debris, scattering birds, and the sight of Moeun, Doeum, and Sek running through the burning forest. After a moment of panic, I gathered my stuff together and ran easily through the thickets. Safe in the moist, dense growth of trees and brush, I sat and waited for my larger companions. Moeun and the others had to crouch to get through. They found me and calmed down to an easy pace.

When we came to a field of tall grass, Sek, having been a military policeman, took the lead. We must have run about 2 miles when Sek stopped so suddenly that we fell into a pile on each other, breathing heavily. We were running for our lives.

We had come to the edge of an open clearing. It was mid-January; the moon sat low in the west. Exposed by the bright moonlight were jungle hammocks strung up between the trees. I trembled. If Sek hadn't stopped abruptly, we would have run into a Khmer Rouge patrol.

We backtracked quietly, and Sek led us as we slithered on our bellies and elbows. Every other minute, we stopped, peeked, listened, and crawled again. After about a mile, Sek said we could stand up and walk.

Our cautious walk soon became a speedy lope and then a full-speed sprint. When Moeun, the eldest in our group, couldn't keep up, we slowed down to a speedy walking pace.

When I found a buffalo waterhole, my companions drank with no hesitation. The stench was too much for me, and, after carefully swallowing some, I threw it all up. The rest of the day, I was thirsty and sorry that I hadn't been able to keep the disgusting water down.

Dawn was turning into daylight. Searching for a hiding place in the rice fields south of National Highway 6, we found a bush no more than 4 feet high.

We had to wait until dark to cross the well-used, well-guarded highway, which connected Siem Reap to the Battambang Province to the west.

By this time, our little group had come to a consensus. We couldn't hide in the forest forever. We would starve, die of thirst, or be killed. We had to find a place where we could be safe from the Khmer Rouge. Our quest for safety meant that, sooner or later, we had to leave Cambodia.

I woke up dizzy in the intense heat. We fanned ourselves and waited out the long hours until the sun set. At about two o'clock, some people started working in the fields and we feared someone would use our bush for a toilet. We stayed still, praying. I forgot thirst and hunger.

After about an hour, when the workers finally moved on, we agreed that we need to head for the Thai border.

We knew nothing of Thailand except that it was in the northwest. If anyone else from our forest group had survived, they probably also headed northwest to join up with the resistance fighters rumored to be there. We had no food, no supplies, and no choice but to follow the rumor.

I did what I could to help.

"I know where Thailand is, roughly, but I can't say how far it is or how much time it will take us to get there," I said, taking a stick to the dirt. "Tapang village is here, north and northwest of this highway."

The men grinned at each other and appointed me group leader. They didn't know the only landmark I needed was National Highway 6.

Because of my familiarity with the area and my love of geography, I more or less knew the places just ahead of us. At dusk, at about six in the evening, under clouds of swarming mosquitoes, I led the group on our journey toward the north.

Thus began our escape from Cambodia.

At 10 P.M. we were still on the narrow asphalt of National Highway 6. Distant headlights sent us scurrying down the embankment. Otherwise, we strode along confidently.

Suddenly, I ducked and stood still. The men fell to the ground, looking at me; there were no lights down the road.

I pointed to the glow of cigarettes up on the embankment, along the highway on both sides of us. Armed soldiers were spread out 300 feet apart—just far enough to see one another. We had found Angkar's secondary dragnet. Fortunately for us, the bastards were chain-smokers.

We retreated on elbows and bellies. For many hours, we remained quiet and still. At about two o'clock in the morning, Sek and Doeum quickly crossed the road.

Moeun and I waited. I was certain my rumbling stomach would give us away. I couldn't keep my knees from shaking. About five minutes later, Moeun and I followed, taking mere seconds to cross the highway. I dared not look left or right.

At the north embankment, we dove to the ground and lay there until Sek motioned us to crawl on. As quickly as we dared, we slithered through the foliage.

After about 3 miles of a fast hike—a slow jog, really—I again led the men on the familiar road east of Tapang. It seemed we'd made our way past Angkar's defensive line. The moon was low to the west. We slowed down a bit to catch our breath. Talking quietly, we came around a curve, and walked right into a group of men with long knives on their shoulders. The knives glinted in the moonlight.

The local militia group was apparently patrolling the outskirts of town. "Where are you going, Mith?" asked the leader. He spoke with a Mith Chass accent. None of the men wore the usual Khmer Rouge uniforms.

"Where are you from?" another demanded, pulling his knife and holding it at the ready. The others joined him. Seven knives stared at us.

"We're going to Tapang, Mith. We came from work at Viel Smeth down south," I was surprised at the confidence in my voice. My companions parroted me.

"Why are you traveling so late, Mith? Don't you know there's a curfew?" said the leader. He seized his knife with both hands.

I couldn't find a quick answer.

I knew Doeum's hand was on his rusty Colt-45 pistol. Only one bullet sat in the chamber. I was certain that the first man to swing his blade would get that bullet.

"A few hours ago Angkar Leu asked us to return home right away," Moeun said calmly. "We don't know why Angkar told us to stop working and return to Tapang."

The leader hissed and shouldered his long blade. The others did the same, looking at us each in turn, from head to toe. In the light of the pre-dawn moon, I felt their eyes seeking the lie behind our words.

When they waved us off and continued, we walked on nonchalantly. The moment their shadows disappeared, my three companions zoomed away and I was left temporarily alone, but eager to catch up with them. As always, it was every man for himself.

A burst of energy fueled by fear for our lives had propelled us. After a mile, I slowed down and veered northeast, away from the northbound main road, and there I found the three men, collapsed, just off the road. I was disturbed to see them lying under a thorny brush, asleep. I was even more concerned when I heard Doeum's loud snores.

I was tired, too, but my hunger and thirst were too severe to be ignored. As I often did, I felt around with my hands in the dark for food. Eventually I found a cucumber patch. I stuffed the succulents into my mouth and rolled more of them into my waist band.

I climbed a sugar palm tree, where I found more than enough juice to quench three days of thirst. I must have drunk a full bamboo container (1.5 gallons) of the sweet, refreshing liquid. A burst of energy engulfed me.

I awakened the men with cucumber and two bamboo containers of palm juice. They fought over it like little boys. "Any more, Ah Khaoan, any more?" Their voices held an accusatory tone.

"That's all there is," I said, yawning. Every man for himself, I told my not-so-guilty conscience.

I was ready for a nap, but dawn was approaching and we had to find a hiding place quickly. We made our way north and northeast to throw off any trackers. We followed an old oxcart trail through a forest. The three men had never been this far north, so I was point man once more.

After a while, we agreed to get some sleep, but red ants seemed to be in every bush we tried to use as a resting place. We finally found a spot with fewer red ants. I endured the stings and closed my eyes. When Moeun woke me up, Sek and Doeum were gone.

"Ah Doeum, Ah Sek!" Moeun yelled. "They left us," he said in a panicky voice.

We walked on in gloom, only to see the two walking by a herd of grazing cattle and, unbelievably, eating. Moeun cursed.

"Bawng, we found food! Here, have some," Doeum said excitedly.

"Where'd you get this?" Moeun asked, not waiting for the answer. We gobbled the freshly cooked white rice and the dried fish, licking our fingers and wanting more.

Hunger had driven Doeum and Sek to search for food. They met some boys herding cattle who pointed out their camp. It just so happened that Doeum knew the old men at the camp.

The men had heard of the rebellion and they were willing to help us. From them we learned that many of our fellow rebels had been captured. But a few had escaped and passed this way only yesterday.

They said all families of those involved in our rebellion were "relocated." Doeum's eyes swelled with tears. Moeun and Sek were silent for a long while, thinking of their families, now all gone, all of them killed by Angkar.

That evening, we shared rice and dried beef with the old men and boys at the camp. Doeum gave the men a silk kroma (scarf). They gave us rice, a cooking pot, a lighter, some salt, and two bamboo containers full of clear water.

"Angkar agents may be here soon," the old men said. "You must go quickly."

Doeum took off his trousers, tied up the leg bottoms and filled the pants with the precious rice grains.

As soon as darkness swallowed the trees around us, we took off for the northwest wilderness of Cambodia. Once again, I led. My stomach was full for the first time in weeks. We walked through the night. By early morning I was excited to see familiar landmarks.

"Not long ago, I was here with the Mobile Brigade building a water basin," I told my companions. "I was sent back to Tapang because I was seriously ill."

How could I forget: tens of thousands of Mith Thmey, toiling like beasts of burden with little food or rest.

"Now you will see one of the largest man-made reservoirs," I said, standing on the high dike like a conquering general. "For almost three months, I helped build this with my bare hands!"

However, instead of the clear water I expected to see, there was only mud. I recalled the absence of Khmer engineers. Hydrology and civil engineering had not been the cadres' strengths. Under their leadership, our efforts had been wasted. The reservoir was a failure.

I pointed out the palm tree that I used to work for its meager juice, mostly at night. We walked over to the slender tree and saw, to my surprise, some bamboo containers strung around the palm's flower buds. Someone still worked the tree for juice. I went up the bamboo ladder, hoping for some sweet reward from my old palm tree friend. Sure enough, each container was almost half full. I took a sip. Ah, the same familiar sweet taste from my old tree—only it was much, much sweeter this time of year.

"Bring us some juice or we'll go without you," Doeum yelled. I descended with the two bamboo containers. They took turns and drained every single drop. I should have drunk a lot more when I was up there, I thought. I won't make that mistake again.

The men dozed off under the tree. It was stupid for us to lie down in the open, but we were so tired. I was afraid that someone would come and find all the juice gone, but I joined them. I wasn't sure how long we slept there, but we woke in the early dawn and the sun was growing stronger in the east.

"I think we should head north again," Sek said. He led us into the forest until the trail disappeared altogether.

"Oh, no!" Doeum said.

"What?"

"I forgot the salt bag," Doeum said.

"Where?"

"At the sugar palm tree. I put it down when Ah Khaoan climbed up."

"How could you?" we screamed at Doeum. It was too far to return for the precious salt. We might not even find our way back again.

"I'm sorry," Doeum almost wept.

"Let's consider the salt as payment for the juice we took," Moeun said.

We went through the dense, large, tall trees. None of us had been here before. I heard eerie howling from the thick forest. "Timber wolves," the men said, grinning at my fear. I moved closer to Moeun.

At about five o'clock in the morning, we decided to take a short break. After a too-short nap, Sek got up. "Let's go," he said.

"I'll lead," I said.

"Ah Khaoan, you're no longer the expert here," said Sek. He and Moeun laughed. Doeum was still asleep.

"Hey, let's go," I tapped him on the shoulder.

"Yes, yes," Doeum said, but didn't get up.

Sek took the lead through the woods while I stayed close behind Moeun. A few hundred feet later, we heard Doeum's wailing reverberate through the trees.

"Where are you, guys? How could you leave me?" Doeum cried like a little boy. His screams must have scared the "timber wolves" into silence. We went back, yelling at him to be quiet.

"Even the most stupid tracker might find us now," Moeun said. Doeum didn't stop crying for a long time. To calm him I grabbed his arm and dragged him with me. A grown man crying. It seemed almost funny.

A few days later—I had lost count—we felt so confident we were far enough from any pursuers that we began to walk in broad daylight and sleep at night. Sek announced that we were now in Srae Noy.

"I've been here before to cut bamboo for Angkar," said Sek. He was more confident when we found the main dirt road.

I was now lagging behind. Every step I took was painful, but if I stopped walking, I was sure they'd leave me behind. No one would carry me, not even if they could. Every man for himself, I thought again. With great determination, I kept pace with the men on my blistered feet. I reached deep inside myself to find the last remaining ounce of will to follow the men under my own power.

On our northward trek, we met a convoy of oxcarts packed with bamboo going south. We must have looked terrible to the people in the convoy. Sek stepped forward.

"We're going to Srae Noy," said Sek. "Is this the right direction?" Of course, he didn't mention Thailand, our final destination.

"You're going the right way. Only a few miles more," a man said. After the convoy passed, we veered northwest instead.

We later learned the trackers were still hot on our trail. A Khmer Rouge search-and-destroy party was not far behind us. The people on the oxcart convoy apparently reported us.

Fortunately, while the soldiers were searching the Srae Noy hamlet, we were climbing a remote hill to the west.

Near a fenced area of growing crops, we encountered a middle-aged man who held a *phkak*, a razor-sharp long knife. He looked us up and down with keen eyes.

"Where are you going, Mith?" he demanded.

Doeum walked on with me close behind. Moeun and Sek gave him a barely audible reply as they passed by. We picked up speed.

The man followed us, screaming. "Stop, stop! I order you to stop, Mith Thmey! Stop now!"

We walked even faster, almost a run, but not quite. We were moving fast.

When the villager took off for the opposite direction, Doeum's pale soles left a trail of dust hanging in the air. We ran for our lives. I completely forgot pain, hunger, or exhaustion. I was surprised how fast we could go. Fear makes you forgetful.

A few miles later we slowed down to a fast walk. We were all breathing hard and trying to suck more air into our lungs. I was more exhausted than scared now. I had to jog to keep up with the adults' walking pace. I held my ground fairly well. I knew the rule of the road: Every man for himself.

Once again, on this dusty, desolate stretch of road, we ran into other people—this time a group of women and girls. Our sudden face-to-face meeting in the middle of nowhere must have surprised them. They slowed down and so did we. Soon, we met up in the middle of a road.

"Smile, people, just smile," Moeun hissed, but our best faces received no response.

They looked at us and we looked at them. To them, we must have just looked like a bunch of strange men with a scrawny boy. To us, local villagers simply meant more trouble as our location would surely be reported. As a courtesy, they moved to the side of the narrow road and we nodded our thanks politely.

"Are we heading in the right direction, to Srae Noy, that is?" Moeun asked politely. We were heading west at that time.

They just stood there stiffly. One of the women nodded. Suddenly, the others said, "No!" and, in unison, pointed north.

"Thank you all. Thank you kindly." We walked on westward nonetheless. We went off a small road by the time it was dark. As we were about to bed down, half a dozen military jeeps with armed soldiers passed by. We went west and then north again in our best attempt to confuse any tracker. We were convinced we'd been spotted and that we were in real danger.

For almost four days, with only forest, hills, and darkness for cover, our zigzag walk-and-run kept us just ahead of the search party. We slept hungry and made no fire. I soon got used to sleeping on an empty stomach. I wanted to sleep forever, but again and again, I woke up, hungry. I find words inadequate to describe how much I suffered during that blur of days and nights.

One afternoon, we found ourselves completely lost in a deep forest. We walked for hours until we found a footpath going up a tree-covered hill. We met a father and his son collecting resin from monstrous dipterocarp trees. They told us that the hill was called, quite appropriately, Resin Mountain. We asked for directions to Anlong Veng in the Odor Meanchey Province, a region that borders Thailand. The father didn't say a word, but the son pointed east, so we went that way. We had no idea where we were; we were really lost. The two must have known we were walking toward Srae Noy. No more than twenty minutes later, they came running.

"Don't go that way, Bawng. Angkar soldiers are there, waiting," they said, catching their breath. They knew about our rebellion and escape. "We heard that many Angkar were killed afterward." It seemed that we had become heroes of a sort.

"We applaud your courage from deep in our hearts," they said. "That you failed doesn't matter. At least you tried; no one else dared fight the Angkar before."

"Don't go that way, Bawng, they'll kill you," they said again. They called us brothers instead of Mith. It was a sure sign of their sincerity. "Some went that way before you. They were all killed after long torture and interrogation," the pair told us matter-of-factly. "Please let us help you." They gave us new directions to Anlong Veng, as well as a lighter, a very precious tool in the deep forest. The old man blessed us and taught us a chant: *Assak kombang batt* [May I be invincible to my enemy].[1] We had not said anything about Thailand but, to our great surprise, they mentioned that country.

"When you get to Srok Siam [Thailand], tell the world what's happening here. Tell them about the suffering of our country and our people." They waved good-bye and again urged us to pass on the news. "Don't forget, Bawng, don't forget."

Now it was imperative that we make it to Thailand. We had to tell the world what our people had suffered under the Angkar's Great Leap Forward, not only for us but also for these two good people as well as for those rebels who didn't make it.

We climbed more hills, hiked through dense forests, and crossed wide-open fields. Almost blindly, we went up and down steep, rocky places. We were desperate for water. A dry stream crossed our dusty track so we followed its sandy bottom until we had to stop for rest. Sek walked along the stream bed to find water.

We sat watching a group of long-tailed black monkeys on the tall trees. I stretched out my legs on the dry waterbed, thinking how life is like this stream fed by the monsoon rains. In the dry season, the water continues to trickle. It is only when the riverbed is arid, when we die, that our life journey comes to an end.

We can choose to enjoy and appreciate our journey. We can overcome obstacles and adversities or fall flat on our faces. The choice is clear as long as we breathe. The monkeys were getting increasingly agitated and aggressive. Doeum shooed them away but they continued to mock us. I grabbed Moeun's arm.

"Don't worry, Ah Khaoan," Moeun said. "We'll eat them if they come any closer." I relaxed a little.

At that moment, Sek came screaming: "Animal, big animal, run, quick!"

He scrambled up a tree, faster than the long-tailed monkeys. The three grown men were on the highest branches in no time at all. They yelled at me again and again: "Up, come on up," but, in the name of my frustrated soul, I couldn't even reach the tree's lowest branch.

After so many attempts, I ran to a small tree. The men shook their heads. I hung on to the tree, more a stunted shrub really, and waited for the big animal. I expected something like a wild elephant. I looked up, and the faces of the men in the big tree told me I was as good as dead.

I looked down and saw a fat sun bear waddle past. Sun bears stand about 4 feet tall, with an average weight of 100 pounds. They are near-blind, slovenly creatures that snack on roots, lizards, and insects. This one didn't even glance at me.

"Is that your big animal?" I said to Sek.

Sek came down sheepishly. Doeum and Moeun rained curses on Sek like two demented auctioneers as we backed away slowly. The wild sun bear stared at us. I felt ridiculous. I could only imagine what the bear was thinking. What were those fools doing up that tree?, it probably wondered. And what was that skinny boy doing on top of that shrub?

By about four o'clock in the afternoon, we came to a thick bamboo forest. There were signs of bamboo harvesting. Slashed debris made barefoot walking almost impossible. We rested in an old grass hut. There was nothing inside. Sek went out to explore. A minute later, several loud explosions shook the bamboo forest, sounding like an automatic gun, a new type that I'd never heard before.

"Get out, run, run!" Sek screamed just outside the hut, and dashed away. In a flash Doeum was gone, too. The old and the weak, Moeun and I, left the hut as fast as we could, which was at a snail's pace. We tiptoed to avoid the sharp thorns of the wild bamboo. Amid the loud popping sounds, we heard Sek scream in agony. I looked into Moeun's terrified eyes and we dove to the ground, onto sharp thorns. Our eyes watered in pain.

"Help me, help me," Sek cried. "Please help me, anyone!" I got up.

Moeun pushed me to the ground and motioned me to be very still. Instinctively, I wanted to rush out there and help Sek, but instead silently repeated my mantra: Every man for himself, every man for himself, every man for himself. Then I saw the cloud of thick smoke not too far from the loud popping and I remembered my brief physics class from years ago.

"That's not gunfire," I said. Moen looked at me. "Fire," I said. "It's fire that's causing the bamboo's airtight chambers to explode."

Cautiously, Moeun rose to a crouch. Sek's screams continued. We rushed to find Sek wounded, but not from any bullet. He had a large bamboo thorn lodged deep in the sole of his right foot. He held his leg, screaming as he bled.

Moeun called Doeum. "Come out, it's safe." But Doeum was gone. Moeun and I removed the large thorn from Sek's foot. The thorn came out along with a loud scream and a gush of blood. We had our first wounded companion, all due to stupidity, and we were nowhere near Thailand yet. We dressed Sek's wound and made him a walking crutch. Doeum arrived, limping. We didn't say a word. There was no need to talk of our foolishness.

We headed north by keeping the setting sun on our left. Huge animal droppings told us we were in wild elephant country. They were feeding on the bamboo. A few nights later, Sek stopped bleeding but he was weak and pale. His low fever worried us. His wound could be infected, I thought. We walked slowly, Sek limping with arms around Moeun and Doeum. We had to help each other if all four of us were to make it to the free world. We, three men and a scrawny boy lost in the wilderness, were now blood brothers. Slowly and surely, every man was no longer for himself. We had to help each other from now on in order to survive our trek for freedom. We all accepted this fact.

Although it was safer to travel at night, we decided to rest and start early the next morning. Sek was in bad shape. Besides, after all that excitement, we needed to rest. We were confident that no Khmer Rouge cadre was dumb enough to go through this mess of sharp bamboo stalks to look for us. We felt safe here.

We found a logging road that looked like it might lead to Thailand. Both sides of the road were cleared of large trees, but we did our best to find a good cover. After a light meal from our dwindling rice supply, we went to sleep just off the road. It was a mistake.

I woke up to the sound of what I thought was a charging elephant. I climbed a too-small tree and cried out to warn the men who were already running in different directions. Suddenly, a bright light broke through the night. A convoy of logging trucks passed by. Shaken, we decided to follow the logging trucks. It was another big mistake.

About 2 miles later, the open road became almost pitch black. Gigantic trees grew close on both sides of the double-lane dirt road. The three walked shoulder-to-shoulder on the road, while I lagged behind just a little. I heard a coughing noise behind me, just off to my left, as though someone were clearing his throat. I moved closer to Moeun.

"Did you hear that?" I whispered.

"Yes," Moeun said.

To my great horror, two snarling dogs rushed at us. Doeum took off, followed by Moeun and Sek. The dogs ignored them and headed straight for me.

As I tried to increase my speed on the sandy road, I noticed a commotion on my right. There were shadows around a small bonfire and people scrambling from jungle hammocks. Military jeeps with mounted machine guns and logging trucks were parked in a large clearing.

Shots rang out in the dark. The sound of AK-47s was nothing at all like exploding bamboo. I was not too concerned about the bright red tracers passing me; the damned dogs were closing in on me.

After all I had been through, was this how my life would end? I ran on in the dark, screaming at the top of my lungs, with two large dogs pursuing me. Dog bites are more painful than bullet bites, I thought to myself. I will not die of dog bites. Then I ran into a huge log totally blocking the dirt road.

The fallen log's diameter exceeded my height. I bounced off the log several times before the first dog's jaws closed on my leg. My pants ripped. I screamed in horror. The second dog rushed in. I turned my back against the log and gave the dog a kick to the head, a move that I had learned from my oldest brother Larony. The animal was momentarily stunned. It worked!

Then both dogs lunged at me, and I screamed. Suddenly I felt hands pulling me up. Who had come for me in the nick of time? It was Moeun. He threw me across the monstrous log to the other side, and I landed on the sandy road. Bursts of gunfire rang out. Red-hot tracers and bullets again slammed into the log. I ducked, got sand in my mouth, and ran for my life, still screaming.

I briefly looked for Moeun to see if he was all right. The two dogs came around one end of the log and thrashed through the thickets. I should have thought of doing that myself.

Moeun swung something at the dogs. He soon caught up with me and dragged me off the road. I realized that I was still screaming when he slapped me in the face to stop the noise.

We headed into the thick jungle, the gunfire far behind us, and lay down on the forest floor. Shaking, fearing the dogs would hear me, I held my breath until I almost passed out. Then we crawled away. I don't know how, but somehow we got away from those dogs and guns.

The next morning, the smell of roasted meat deep in the wilderness awakened me and Moeun. We hoped it was our companions cooking something to eat. On the other hand, we thought, only a fool would start a fire and cook meat after being chased and shot at.

Peering through the dense vegetation, we were surprised and pleased: Doeum and Sek were indeed there, chewing on roasted meat. "Come," Doeum called, so casually that we needed no second invitation.

Miracle after miracle: First, Doeum and Sek ran into each other in the forest. Then, that morning, they captured a sizable forest turtle. I had never been much of a turtle meat eater, but the many eggs in its belly were magnificent. Also, I still had two nearly full bamboo containers. Moeun had slammed the other two precious containers on the dogs; my water was now all we had.

That little water saved our lives as we trekked lost among wild beasts, herds of wild elephants, and black rhinos in the deep jungles of northern Cambodia.

After several days—I lost count after the fifth day—we ran out of water. Our rice supply was down to about two small tin cups. Wild fruits, leaves, and berries barely sustained us. We were reduced to skin and bones once again.

We searched for water and food while trekking in a north by northwest direction to Thailand. I ate just about anything that was edible. Memories of an old man and his elephants came back to me. All those years ago in Siem Reap, before the war, the simple man had shown me which plants were safe to eat and how to find elephant trails. Unbroken branches pointed to sources of water, he'd said. Unfortunately, the trails we found led us to muddy water holes where the water was dirty, smelly, and unfit to drink.

It seemed impossible to find our way out of this deep forest of majestic trees, with trunks 20 feet around. The forest was so thick the sunlight hardly reached us. Night was pitch-black darkness. We walked freely in the day without expecting to meet another person.

Our worst fears were wild beasts and large mountain pythons. The men were very afraid of the big snakes, though the shed python skins stretched to only a foot in diameter. I was told that these snakes could swallow a whole boy my size. You can imagine what those words did to me.

At waterholes we saw large paw prints, from tigers. At school I'd learned that tigers commonly weighed 200 to 300 pounds. The elephant tamer had warned me to limit my time at waterholes so I would avoid meeting a tiger. The men and I heeded that warning. With our weak states and my small size, safety from large animals was a constant concern. Occasionally, wild peacocks and pheasants would take off flying and scare us. We were probably the first humans they ever saw.

White gibbons hovered above us, howling and jumping up and down, swinging from tree to tree. I wished I had their skill and energy—and their knowledge of the terrain. I was so weak I couldn't even climb a tree to find a way out. The men encouraged me to do so, but the tree trunks were too wide and I was too frail.

On the morning of the twelfth day of our flight from Prey Roniem, we followed an elephant trail to a clearing where we found a gooseberry tree full of juicy yellow fruit. Doeum let go of everything he was carrying and rushed to the tree. We had eaten the last of our rice supply a couple of days earlier and we were all mad with hunger.

When I got to the small fruit tree, Doeum was already up, clawing away at the fruit. A large branch smacked my head as Doeum crashed to the ground with it. The impact knocked me out. I came to only to find Moeun laughing, rapidly fanning to revive me. I discovered a large bump on my head. I really hated Doeum from then on.

Doeum's trousers stored the wild fruit. This was to be our food until we reached Thailand, whenever that might be. As the smallest in our group, finding food or even getting a share was always tough for me. I did not expect Doeum to fairly distribute the yellow fruit. Without Moeun, I wouldn't have made it. He often shared his food with me, dragged me along, and watched out for me. To this day, I remain grateful to the gentle old man.

The open field gave way to brush and a shrubby plain dotted with some large trees. Herds of wild deer, antelope, and big game grazed on the dry, golden grass, some blackened by a recent fire.

Doeum was tempted to use his last bullet but he couldn't get close enough. The animals kept running away. After a while, he gave up and we moved on.

Under a large tree, we found *kokoss* nuts (pronounced "ko-COUGH"). We cracked and roasted them in an open flame. When the kokoss ran out, we found another kind of nut, the larger, almost palm-sized *unkogne* (pronounced "un-KO-un"). We were not sure if it was edible but it smelled like peanuts after roasting. Hunger prevailed over caution.

Ten minutes later, we paid the price. First came the severe headaches, then vomiting, and then severe diarrhea. I felt so sick and so stupid. After my incredible fight for survival, it appeared that I would die of eating the wrong nuts.

However, I was glad for these life-threatening conditions when they caused long worms to drop out of my body by the half dozen. The parasites had died and were evacuated from my system. No wonder I was so skinny; they had taken more than their fair share of what I ate. Now, if only I could find some food, I could keep all nutrients to myself.

The open plains became thick elephant grass country bisected by deep, dry riverbeds and canyons. We searched in vain for the Dong Rek mountain range that bordered Thailand. Our thought was that we had reached Anlong Veng in the northernmost province, Odor Meanchey. I tried to recall my geography. It was three more days of walking with no food and very little water before we saw the majestic Dong Rek mountain range, green in the distant northwest.

Finally, we were clear of the tall elephant grass and we found a road that led north. After a while, the road diverged. We took the northwest fork, away from the fresh tire tracks of army jeeps. Angkar soldiers? Surely. Looking for us? Most probably.

We got closer by the hour to the majestic green mountain range. The Thai border was on the other side of that green shadow in the sky. The men danced like drunkards. My spirit soared. With a renewed burst of energy, our pace quickened, but potential dangers sobered us. Surely Angkar's finest would be here, stopping people from crossing the border.

Again, Sek led. His wounded right foot had healed well enough. He moved from behind one tree trunk to another. We hopped tree trunks throughout the open area until we got to the forest near the foot of the mountain range. It was time consuming and very tiring, but Sek said it was vital to keep out of sight. "We have to stay hidden at all costs, now more than ever," he said.

Suddenly, we heard someone whistling. Sek signaled and we dropped to the ground. I stopped breathing.

The musical Khmer Rouge patrol came closer and closer. We hugged the ground as flat as we could. Only a few low shrubs covered me. Black pajamas and Ho Chi Minh rubber tire sandals passed a mere 5 feet from my eyeballs. I counted twelve soldiers with AK-47s and B-40 rocket-propelled grenades. I wished I had Caveman Club with me so I could take a few of the cadres with me to hell.

"Preah," I prayed to Lord Buddha, "help me out just this one time, and I shall ask no more. In return, I promise to be good and become a novice monk for a week."[2]

Quietly, I chanted the verse of the old man from Resin Mountain. I repeated the verse many times. "*Assak kombang batt. Assak kombang batt. Assak kombang batt* [May I be invincible to my enemy]."

The patrol passed by.

When the soldiers had completely disappeared we napped, right there by the roadside. Then Sek led us crawling on elbows and bellies into the forest. We followed his every move as quietly as we could. Sek motioned us to stop.

"Careful," Sek whispered. "Land mines."

I froze.

"See that trip wire?" Sek pointed to a thin, black line low on the ground, barely visible even in the daylight. "There are booby traps to our left and right."

I didn't want to move.

Moeun said, "Ah Khaoan, you follow us or you stay here, it's your choice."

So close to the border, and yet so far away.

We crawled and then walked about 60 feet apart, in case one of us would be blown up. I carefully fit my soles into Sek's exact footprints. I was last in the line. I'd never been this far away from any of them and I was terrified they'd abandon me. This was how I discovered that I'd rather brave a forest of land mines than be alone.

Doeum, too, feared that he would be left behind. Like me, he had to fight that fear on his own. However, he had real reason for alarm. He was putting all our lives in great danger. Over the past three days, Doeum's malarial shivers had become more frequent. He would tremble violently for an hour before the tremors subsided. His uncontrollable shaking and moaning in the mined and booby-trapped field scared us all. I felt sorry for him, but he was too noisy.

It took six terrifying hours to cross that forest of mines. Without Sek's military skills, we would have died there.

Dusk was falling when we reached the toe of the Dong Rek mountain range. Embers glowed in the distance. We froze and ducked for cover. From the edge of a 150-foot clearing, we saw guard stations every 300 feet or so. In each one was

a Khmer Rouge sentry with an AK-47 assault rifle. Again, their burning cigarettes had saved our lives.

Sek pulled his hair and banged his head on a tree. "What more punishment
are you raining on us, oh Preah?," he beseeched Lord Buddha.

"Ah Sek, we're all very tired," Moeun said cheerfully. "Let's wait for darkness
before we cross this clearing. I'll lead." Moeun's courage amazed me.

"What about the mine fields ahead?" Sek said, almost crying.

"We'll make it out." Moeun put his face close to Sek's face. "You and Ah
Doeum just take it easy and relax. Ah Khaoan and I will take care of it."

"Me?" I said. Wade through an area infested with land mines and traps.
I don't know anything, I thought.

"Oh, Preah," Sek said, turning his face away.

I knew Moeun was just as scared as I was, but someone had to lead. Doeum
and Sek were out. It was up to Moeun and me. "Preah, help us," I whispered.

We napped while Moeun took the first watch. He woke me up some hours
later. "Your turn. Wake us before sunset," he said, and he was soon fast asleep.

I watched Doeum fight his fever. Sometimes I thought he was dead, and
then he would shiver violently. I was glad he wasn't snoring now, or I'd kick him
myself. At sunset we inched closer to the clearing.

"When it's dark," said Moeun, "we'll cross one at a time."

In my fear and tension, I thought it would never get dark enough.
We ducked whenever the bright headlights of military trucks came into view.
Moeun looked left, then right, and went first. At his signal from the other side,
I ran, feeling very exposed during the 150-foot dash to the other side of the
clearing.

I never thought I could sprint so fast after more than thirteen days running
on severely bruised feet. I imagined that I must be breaking some world record.

At Moeun's signal, Sek made sure that Doeum got ready to go. Sek then
ran ahead, as quickly as he could. And then we waited, the tension thick and
unspoken. Finally Doeum staggered toward us like a drunkard heading home.

We listened for signs of pursuit but heard only the sounds of the forest.
With extreme caution, we moved up the steep hillside in front of us. A wildfire
raged on the hilltop. The fire crept, lighting our way. We had seen smoke during
the day but not the flames. We made our way to the top of the hill, only to be
greeted with an impassable wall of granite, sheer and white, thirty stories high.
How do we get over?, I wondered. We climbed, we crawled through and under
narrow ledges, went sideways and swung on vines like apes. Still, the sheer
white cliffs defeated us.

Exhausted, we hung on for our lives like trapped monkeys. After several
upward and then downward attempts, we found a very narrow pathway that led
us diagonally to the top. We clung to bamboo trees, which grew near the cliffs,
to make our way up. The fire continued to burn on the backbone of the Dong

Rek Mountain Range. Occasionally a gust of wind rained embers on us, a shower that burned. I thought, what worse punishment is waiting for me?

We reached the crest of the 5,000-foot range at about midnight, more than six hours after we'd started our ascent. The ground was still warm from the fires, sometimes burning my blistered soles. We ran into a thick, thorny bamboo brush, some of it still burning. Oh no, not again! We didn't know which way to go.

"We can't go any farther," said Sek.

"Let's go back," said Doeum.

I couldn't believe they were serious about returning down that cliff and back into the arms of the Khmer Rouge. An argument broke out among the men. I was sure they were going to kill one another. I had to step in. I didn't want to die. I also didn't want to see them fight to the death.

"Why don't we rest here for the night, Bawng? We're lost and tired anyway. We could wait until daylight and see where we are," I said. The men stopped for a moment and then lay down without saying a word.

"Who's taking the first watch?" I asked. The men already snored on the hard granite. Amazing, I thought: they took the word of this thin little boy. With that, I fell asleep in the cool, misty night on the majestic Dong Rek Range. I had not slept as well in four years.

The next morning, we pulled deer ticks off one another. A large tick, fat with my blood, was lodged on my right eyelid and caused me great pain. It took Moeun several pulls to dislodge it. I tossed the monster and eight others into the fire. There were eight small explosions and then a large one. I felt my pain avenged. Last night's row was forgotten, and no one brought it up again.

With the sun up, we could see which way to go toward Thailand. As an added bonus, we found five waterholes, pits on the granite mountaintop that were full of rainwater. Unknowingly, we had been sleeping no more than 20 feet away from refreshing water. We drank our fill. I loaded and plugged tight my two bamboo containers. Four days of thirst is one of the worst hardships one can imagine.

We even took a sort of bath, my first in weeks. It was a treasured moment for all four of us. We were at peace again and freedom didn't seem so far away anymore. Refreshed, we set off for the other side of the mountain range, for Thailand.

The early morning hike going down was effortless and almost enjoyable. We were still very hungry but the water helped very much. After about four hours, we saw signs of foreign civilization, the first of which was a new animal trap of nylon rope.

"Angkar has no new nylon rope," I said. "We must be in Thailand!"

My companions weren't sure. We were disappointed to find nothing in the trap. Then we came across a wide logging road with fresh tire tracks in the dust.

A truck or two had just passed by. We followed the road northward. A range of emotions began to surface despite my best efforts to suppress them. I had fantasized that we would reach Thailand today.

Doeum was seriously ill. We were all weak and tired. Our yellow fruit was completely gone. I couldn't remember the last time I had eaten real food. I felt I had been eating wild fruits and berries forever.

"Thailand! Thailand! We're in Thailand," Sek yelled, pointing to letters carved on a tree.

It was true. The sign read T-h-a-i-l-a-n-d. I thought I had forgotten how to read the Roman alphabet. My French reading skills had survived the years of fear and suppression, after all.[3] I couldn't stop rubbing the letters that were carved into the tree. "Thailand," it said.

My companions laid their hands on the letters, as though they were a magical gift from the heavens. We looked at one another. Then, like lunatics, we wept and danced with joy and excitement. I wept the loudest, not quite sure what it really meant to be free. The Khmer are generally uncomfortable with hugging, but the four of us did a huge group hug while jumping, crying, and laughing at the same time.

According to Doeum's Seiko watch, it was 10:22 in the morning of February 2, 1978. It was a moment I'd never forget.

The feeling of that moment can never be described by words. I, at sixteen years old, an orphan, had finally made it to freedom. At long last, we were free. Being in Thailand, even illegally, gave a sense of closure to my journey.

It was only much later, as an adult, that I realized I had been free since January 1, 1978—the day after my escape from the massacre—up to the moment I reached Thailand. I had decided which way to go. Now I was at another turning point. My life as a victim had ended; a new life had begun as a survivor.

After my little group had calmed down, we looked around. A sense of uncertainty shadowed us. The danger wasn't over, we knew this too well. The Khmer Rouge cadres, the so-called Angkar, wouldn't hesitate to kill us even if we had crossed the border.

Quickly, we moved on toward an unknown future.

14

Alien Worlds

Din Daeng, Sisaketh, Buriram, and Aranya Prathet

We woke up under a midday sun filtering through the forest canopy. A gentle wind shook the giant branches, scattered the light, and sent leaves and seeds spiraling to the earth. For ages, these ancient trees must have sheltered beasts and men like us, but perhaps few as exhausted or starving.

We returned to the road and continued our trek. Doeum decided to hide his rusty Colt-45 in a tree hollow by the road. His malarial affliction was getting worse. Although he was only thirty-four he moved like an arthritic seventy-year-old. I thought he would drop dead anytime but I sensed no quitting in the man.

At thirty, Sek was the youngest of my three companions. When he was focused, we were thankful for his military skills, but his concentration came and went. He became easily frustrated and angered. Several times, he had given up on our journey. It took all our efforts to bring him to his senses. Our minds can play terrible tricks on us during stressful times, and Sek was not immune. I had seen Sek dazed, counting leaves. Like me, he struggled to come to terms with the death of his relatives.

Moeun and I had become very close in the past few weeks—or had it been months? He was a barber, then a farmer-buffalo herder under Angkar, and finally a rebel senior leader. For a forty-five-year-old man who had just been through jungles for weeks with little food or water, he remained positive and never quit. He kept our group together. I felt safe and secure with him.

I was a mess of sagging skin and pointy bones. It was very easy to count my ribs. My shirt was abandoned somewhere in the northwest jungle, torn into many rotten pieces. My once-long cotton trousers were so tattered they barely covered anything. I still had my two almost-empty bamboo containers and a new Caveman Club, really just a stick to help me walk. Though not worth much, these wooden items were all I had in the world.

I lagged far behind my adult companions. My bruised legs were swollen, my blistered feet severely infected. Every step on the red clay dirt road was unbearable but I had no more tears. I could no longer cry.

Moeun often slowed down for me. "Don't give up now, Ah Khaoan," he said to me many times. "We're so very close to freedom."

"I'm so tired . . . my feet . . ."

Moeun was very persistent. "Keep going, Ah Khaoan," he said, often dragging me along. He was in no condition to carry me even if he had wanted to.

Two figures appeared ahead of us on the road, walking in our direction. I grew frantic. Should we run and hide? We had been intentionally avoiding people during our trek. Sek and Moeun ambled on, but I could tell that they were frightened, too. We all kept going, perhaps because of our physical weakness and our persistence in believing that we had come to a place of freedom. The figures came closer and I saw that they were a middle-aged couple. With their bright apparel, they did not look like anyone we'd seen in Cambodia. I tried not to stare. Even in my curiosity, I grew scared. I was very afraid of people and the harm they could do me.

I could clearly see the flowery pattern of the woman's blouse. I marveled at the clothes the couple wore. It was wonderful to see people in such brilliant colors again. Angkar had mandated black or dark gray clothing and they had strictly enforced this rule. I had witnessed cadres beating people for violating Angkar's dress code.

Sek and Moeun knelt and raised their palms in a *sampass* (traditional greeting). "*Sawady, Khun* [Greetings]," Moeun spoke softly in Thai, palms together. Doeum and I followed suit, kneeling and mimicking Moeun's unfamiliar words. They're Thai for sure, I thought, gazing again at the colorful clothes.

"There's no need for that." The couple spoke Khmer clearly, with a slight Surin accent. "Please, please get up," they said, bending down to help us straighten ourselves.

My feet hurt so much that my legs gave way. I lay on the red clay, my eyes blinking, hardly able to speak with my parched throat. I had been forcing myself to move during our mad dash to freedom, but now I refused to take another step. I just lay there, like a log.

The couple didn't seem surprised by what we did or how we looked. They unpacked their bag and laid out boiled rice, tiny grilled fish, and vegetables in hot chili sauce. Although I liked chili, the sauce was far too hot for me. I ate it anyway. The rice was moist, sweet, and flavorful. Jasmine rice, I was almost certain, and it was heavenly. It was the first time I had had solid rice in years. Again, it was every man for himself. We were all hands and tongues and tears coming out of our eyes.

"Slow down, please, Bawng," said the woman. "You might harm yourselves. Try and drink a little more water instead." The woman smiled at us. There was enough food for ten but the four of us ate it all. The man and woman seemed pleased.

We sat back, breathing heavily, enjoying our first full meal in years. Ten, fifteen minutes later, we vomited everything out. I felt drained. I had major regrets for vomiting all that delicious food because I hadn't had any solid food in sixteen, seventeen days. Water was all that I could keep in at the moment.

The couple took us to a clear pond just off the logging road, then left to give us privacy. We cleaned ourselves as much as possible. The couple returned in about twenty minutes. Doeum gave them his watch as a token of appreciation. The man and woman told us about the Thai Daeng (Red Thai), and the Thai communist guerrillas' growing power and influence around the area. They explained that the food we had just eaten had been intended to bribe the guerrillas, so that they and other villagers could farm in peace.

"You must go. If the Thai Daeng find you, they will force you to return to Cambodia, or they'll make you slaves."

We jumped up and turned back to the road as fast as we could. I was scared. I wanted to get away as far as possible from Cambodia and these communists who wanted to kill us. We walked so quickly that the couple asked us to slow down. They explained that we were in the village of Din Daeng (Red Clay) in Sisaketh Province.

Yes, we truly were in Thailand.

After about an hour's walk on the smooth clay road we came to a hamlet of about ten to fifteen houses. The midday sun was hot but a forest of big trees and open rice fields surrounded the homes. The smell of jackfruit was in the air.

A few hundred villagers came out, including old men, women, and the children. After the solitude of the forest and our habit of avoiding villagers, the presence of so many people shocked me.

My pants were torn, the cotton cloth rotted apart, only the elastic band and bits of cloth were left. I hadn't noticed my nakedness in the forest, but now I covered my private parts with both of my hands. We limped toward the town square while a crowd gathered around us. I was scared. I didn't know what to expect, how they would treat me.

People gave us clothes. I received an old pair of Thai kick-boxing shorts and an old T-shirt. The children laughed when I couldn't find a place to change. I hid behind my friends and changed quickly. These poor people were rich in heart. Some kids eating pickled mango gave me a piece of it. It was like gold to me. In a short while, I ran behind a tree and puked again. Water was all I could keep down.

The village had received refugees before, but we were the first to cross this particular stretch of the border for some years now. They organized a collection and brought more food. My stomach was still complaining so I ate little. However, I enjoyed sampling Coke, Pepsi, and other exotic food. It was like winning a lottery. Everything was absolutely wonderful—until the police and village officials came. They reminded me so much of Angkar Leu that feelings of fear and hate welled up inside me and killed the euphoria.

"*Khmen opah-youp* [Khmer refugee prisoner]!" said one of the policemen, pointing at us. Four men stood in front of us, two in uniform. They dragged us away from the crowd, asking us again and again if we were Vietnamese. The one who spoke Khmer kept asking me if Doeum was Vietnamese.

"He's a Vietnamese agent. What is he doing here?" he said repeatedly.

Over and over I said I was from Siem Reap, all the time eyeing their guns. The Khmer-speaking man kept edging me away from my companions even as I tried to get closer to them. I felt so threatened by these four big men. They frisked us, their hands touching us everywhere. I felt violated.

When they found Doeum's gold necklace with a Buddha pendant, they accused him of being a Khmer Rouge cadre, then of being a Vietnamese communist. I didn't know Doeum had such valuables on him. They escorted us to the bus station and handed us over to another man. They never returned the gold necklace or the pendant. Our first taste of freedom ended too quickly.

I felt much better when the policemen went away. Our new guide directed us to board the overcrowded commercial bus, but he did not tell us where to sit. We chose the roof. The wide blacktop road swiftly passed under us and the wind hit my face full blast. I was on top of the world and going at breakneck speed. I grabbed a steel bar. I was both terrified and excited at the same time. I had not been in a vehicle in almost four years, let alone on the roof top of a speedy bus.

All around us were men, women, and children, laughing, talking, and smiling. They wore nice shoes and clothes with vibrant colors. For years all I had seen was black and gray clothing, so different from those around me. Thailand cannot be a communist country, I thought. At stops people bought and shared food, but I couldn't take anymore.

Many times along the way, people and cargo went on and off the bus. The driver kindly stopped under a mango tree that overflowed with beautifully green fruit. Everyone on the roof picked mangoes off the heavily laden branches. As the bus rolled on, I grabbed a few. Soon I had stomach cramps again but at least I was not walking. My beaten legs at last got a good, long rest. My three friends appeared to be enjoying the ride, too. We didn't know where we were going. We didn't really care anymore.

Two hours later we were dropped off in the empty town of Sisaketh. It seemed that everyone was on a lunch break or taking an afternoon nap. We waited under a large tree. Classical Thai music played in the distance, reminding me of the good old days in my hometown. But the idyllic scene could not erase my worries. What's going to happen next?, I thought. Where will I get my next meal?

They left us completely alone for about half an hour, and we had time to think and talk about everything we'd seen. The policemen had reminded me of Angkar cadres. With no guard in sight, I found myself making escape plans again. I had become so used to hiding and escaping.

The towns' people finished their meals and awoke from their naps, then came by to stare at us. My lips tasted salty. We smelled pretty bad, full of grime and mosquito bites. I looked around at our bare feet, our long fingernails. My friends looked so thin. I saw the scars on my arms. I felt my head injuries, which were fortunately covered by long hair. Flies buzzed around the infected sores on my legs. I felt like a wild boy of the jungle.

An ice-cream vendor pushing his cart asked us, "*Kin mai?*" We understood enough to shake our heads. We had no money. The man rambled on in Thai. We could only stare as he scooped luscious ice cream on cones.

"*Khmen opah-youp! Khmen opah-youp!*" I parroted the words that the Thai police had said to us earlier. I also showed the man my empty pockets. The man smiled and handed the first cone to me. Tentatively, I reached out. Soon, we were all savoring the cool taste of ice cream. It was the most delicious ice cream I had had in four years.

Children came to buy ice cream from the man and I heard the phrase *Khmen opah-youp* again and again. More people came to look at the *Khmen opah-youp*. I felt like I was in a freak show.

Two stern-looking policemen in crisp khaki uniforms dispersed the crowd. Oh no, not them again. They had pistols. One carried a rifle, calling, "*Ma, ma* [come, come]!" We went to him. The other one, with an M-1 rifle, walked behind us. Escape would not be possible now, I thought.

We followed him past the town hall and to a light blue building a hundred yards away. The children followed chanting, "Khmen opah-youp! Khmen opah-youp!" I had thought it meant we were refugees. I was shocked to learn that it meant "Khmer prisoners."

I counted twenty steps up, limping painfully. Then I saw bars. Oh no, we were going to jail! The cop unlocked a big iron door. I wanted to run away, but, what the heck. I didn't care anymore. A guard stared at us, his rifle in his hand, not on his shoulder.

The door slammed shut behind us, and we found ourselves looking at Thai men behind bars, chattering like monkeys in cages. There were four cells. Two were crowded and two were empty. We were put in a cell that had an over-powering smell of urine. The toilet was clogged and filthy. Graffiti littered the wooden wall. The cell had no bed, but there was one barred window. We could see down into the street. Only bars separated us from the other men. Some spoke Khmer Surin.

"Where are you from?"

"Why are you here?"

We told them. "What about you, why are you here?"

They were murder suspects and criminals.

"I got drunk."

"I beat my wife."

"I was fighting in the bar."

"They think I killed somebody."

They asked for details about us. Some translated, others asked more questions. At some points in our telling, they were laughing, cheering.

About an hour later, a woman brought in food. There was a bony chicken, two *pla thu* fish, some vegetables with onions and coconut sauce, and a large amount of rice. The four of us fought over the food again. We didn't care about the smelly, overflowing toilet just a few feet away. The food wasn't enough. That was the first time I didn't vomit. Finally I was able to keep food down.

On the fifth day, we were moved to a 36 by 36 foot cell. Some of the prisoners shared the food their families had brought. Although a woman came to bring us food three times a day, there never seemed to be enough. We were soon gaining weight. I disliked being locked up and doing nothing but smelling the toilets and accumulating mosquito bites. However, we received clothes and a pair of plastic slippers in addition to food.

A week later, the district chief called on us to take care of the garden around his house, where he lived with his wife and a daughter, about two blocks from city hall. After a couple of hours, we were returned to jail. I was allowed to linger outside with the guards. They knew I wasn't going anywhere without my companions. They let me out after showing me an empty pack of cigarettes and giving me some money. They gave me the change, about two baht. Wow, I was earning money. I kept it all in my pocket.

We were called out whenever the district chief or his family needed a servant. We worked for the chief almost six days a week for about ten baht (less than fifty cents) a day. It was all right. At least we got out of the stifling cell. The chief's family treated us just fine.

The guards worked four-hour shifts and couldn't leave their posts. They would call me whenever they needed me to buy something. In about three weeks, I knew all of the jailers. They allowed me to roam around. I saved more than 150 baht in tips.

One day, when I was out of my cell, the jail commander arrived for a surprise inspection. My three companions were working at the house of the district chief. The commander shouted, kicked, and beat the guards, and sent the district chief to fight Thai communists near the place where we had emerged from Cambodia.

The four of us were never allowed out again. A week later, we were herded into a minivan with bars on the little window. "*Pai, pai, pai!*" said the guards. I wasn't sure what the words meant but it seemed they were telling us to quicken our pace. We hurried into the vehicle. It was very hot inside. We didn't know where we were going. I fell asleep along the way.

The door opened and we went through a tunnel, past two doors, and into a room where we were stripped naked against the wall. Always being a modest Khmer, I tried to cover my genitals and dared not look at others' naked bodies. Wherever we were, it was securely locked down. A man asked me for my name and birthday. I knew I was born in the Year of the Ox. Someone gave me a birth year of 1962, so I instantly became one year younger. I was completely naked inside this confinement center for hardcore Thai criminals.

The guards grimaced as they went through our dirty clothes. Coins and paper money fell out of my pockets. After the strip search, I didn't see my 150 baht again. They also took all of my companions' cash and valuables.

An orderly gave us dark blue cotton uniforms. The pants were too big for me. They were meant for adult convicts, criminals. The van took us deeper into Buri Ram Prison, past two sets of doors: one wooden, another of solid steel. I looked at the doors in dismay. Escape would be difficult, if not impossible.

On our thirty-second day in Thailand, we found ourselves in an open court-yard, amid more than seven hundred Thai criminals wearing the same blue uniforms and sleeping, working, or walking around with their hands in iron shackles. Around the courtyard were two-story buildings. The guards locked us in a cell big enough to hold a hundred people, and it was already packed like a sardine can.

I could hear traffic outside the jail. I heard people talking, horns honking, Buddhist monks chanting. Like the monks in my country, the Thai chanted in Pali (the liturgical language of Theravada Buddhism), so their words were a familiar, soothing sound from childhood.

We talked to some prisoners who spoke Khmer Surin. There were other Khmer refugees in the jail, also unshackled like us. The men around us were criminals, murderers, and rapists. I heard the sound of shackles everywhere. *Kling klong, kling klong.* I was glad the four of us were not shackled. After an hour, at about noon, an orderly opened the cell and showed us the bathing area at the back of the jail. It was screened off with a waist-high water reservoir. The water seemed to empty before our eyes as other prisoners bathed themselves. We stripped naked again under the watchful eyes of the guards. I did not feel comfortable unclothed in front of strangers. We scooped water from the reservoir with a small bowl and washed our bodies. A soap bar was passed around, but no towels.

Then we had lunch. We were very hungry by this time so we ate all the rice and soup they provided us. First we had to find a seat, and then we had to sing something before we could eat. I didn't understand the song, but someone told me we were giving thanks to the king and queen of Thailand for the food on our plate. We did this at every meal. I learned to sing the words of the song although I didn't understand them.

We were directed to make furniture. The first two days they taught us the basics, such as how to use a chisel. I quickly learned the routine. Before the sun is up, someone clangs on the bars. We clean up. A bell rings for breakfast and again for lunch. We line up for food, find seats, and chant thanks to their majesties before each meal, then put away the dishes. Food is always rice, vegetables, a few pieces of meat or *pla thu*. We make furniture morning and afternoon, and then it's bathing time. There's a dinner bell, then chanting prayers, and then off to bed by seven.

To avoid the rush at the bathing area, I went early. With the water still near the rim of the reservoir, I didn't have to bend down to fetch the water. On the sixth evening, as I entered the bathing area, about six men in shackles grabbed me. Four held me down on the rim of the water reservoir while two had their hands all over my body. I screamed all the while. They were laughing, chuckling, joking around. Nobody came to my rescue.

I found myself detached, watching a group of men molesting a teenager. He was yelling stop, stop, but the men didn't stop, they went on pulling and tugging at his penis, trying to get it erect. It went on for an eternity, and then they just let the boy go.

I grabbed my clothes and ran to my pallet. I skipped dinner. I couldn't sleep that night. I hated those men. I wanted to kill them. I would cut off their penises. I blamed myself for allowing the molestation to occur. From then on, I never went alone to the toilets and baths again. My companions suspected something happened when I began to stay near them all the time. I was too ashamed to say anything.

Lesbianism, homosexuality, and rape are taboo subjects in Khmer society. To be called a homosexual is a terrible insult. One who is sexually violated gets blame, not sympathy. The Khmer typically think that you must have done something wrong to invite such a fate upon yourself. You, the victim, are responsible, not the perpetrator. I didn't want to be blamed. I stayed quiet, suppressing my rage.

A few days after a group of Thai officials and International Red Cross workers visited the prison, about fifty of us Khmer refugees were herded into in an air-conditioned bus. I was happy to get out of prison. It was good to be outside and looking at Thai people on their bicycles. This is the way it should be. In Cambodia, I had not seen this anymore, this traffic and activity, people going about their business in a bustle of energy and splash of colors. Inside the prison, all I saw were criminals in shackles. That ten-minute ride into town was absolutely wonderful. I marveled at the scenery with pleasure and curiosity.

Still, my anger and shame wouldn't leave me. When I first stepped onto Thai soil, I had blocked anything Khmer from my mind. I felt deep shame for being Khmer. I had nobody, no home, no family, no relatives, and no country to call my own. I was a nobody. I had nothing to live for—not even the ability to avenge the death of my loved ones. Compared to that, the indignity at the water reservoir was so small I did not dwell on it. Still, I was angry with myself for being such an idiot, and I swore it would never happen again, that I would fight back and die trying.

We were brought to the Buri Ram Holding Center, an old, burned-out jail about ten minutes away from the prison. The roof leaked, but the original guard towers and barbed-wire fence were still intact. About three hundred Khmer refugees lived here, so the place felt like a refugee camp. The center was about 300 by 300 feet, roomy enough for us. (The size could be compared to three football fields.) I felt safer here because there were no Thai felons.

We had just a bit more freedom at the holding center than at the prison. Although we continued to be locked up at night, during the day we were allowed to play and exercise in the yard. Perhaps because I was the youngest in the camp, I managed to engage the guards and make money by running errands. Unlike Buri Ram Prison where we were isolated, we were allowed to plant and harvest crops in farms. I felt stronger and gained weight quickly, more than 40 pounds in six weeks. By June 1978 I weighed about 80 pounds at age sixteen.

Looking at the old barbed-wire fence one day, I saw a chance for more freedom. A gap near the ground gave me an idea. I envisioned crawling under the fence in the dark and then back inside later, before anyone figured out I was gone. Some of the men who had money did just that. One man paid off the guards, went out regularly and enjoyed the company of Thai prostitutes. He was friendly with the policemen. Every night he would go out and return late. Once I followed him under the fence.

The hole was big enough, no problem for me to get through. I was under that fence with my head out when a policeman saw me. He dragged me out from between the wall and the barbed-wire fence, yelling and pointing at my face, pushing me around a bit. I was embarrassed that I'd been caught and frightened that I would be tortured or killed if they returned me to the Khmer Rouge. The guards started counting people and then filled the hole with concrete. The guy I'd followed was really angry at me when he returned.

One day, I was playing with two Khmer kids in the yard after lunch. We looked up when the main gates began to open. This was a rare event. We ran to see who was coming. Some Caucasians and other people walked in with cameras and equipment. They looked around while a Khmer translator asked questions of the gathering crowd. I learned later that the group was creating the documentary *What Happened to Cambodia*, to be broadcast in America. Someone pointed me out. I ran away, but they caught me.

CBS News senior executive producer Brian T. Ellis came over with Peter Collins, the reporter, and the Khmer translator, Mr. Khem Savath (who was also from Siem Reap and had worked for VOA), as well as a cameraman and a sound crew. The camera light blinked to a glowing red color. I was made to show my injuries and scars to the camera. The translator asked me questions and more follow-up questions.

He caught me off-guard. I had left the horrors back in Cambodia, and I'd almost forgotten that my parents were dead. As I answered their questions I completely broke down. I couldn't help it. I bawled my heart out and they had to stop the camera. After a few minutes I calmed down. I didn't like crying in public. I was sixteen. I was tough.

I told them everything. Every question they asked me, I answered without hesitation. They asked me what I wanted to do next.

"Revenge," I said without the slightest hesitation. "That's all I want is revenge."

The translator stopped, pulled back a moment.

"What'd he say, what'd he say?" said the Caucasian.

"This boy wants to go kill somebody," said the translator. After that frozen moment, things returned to normal and the interview ended.

That afternoon the translator said, "Want to go out? We're taking you out for ice cream."

"I'm not sure," I said. "Are my friends coming along?"

"No, just you," he said.

Someone took a photo of me and my friends on my way out. Soon I was outside the prison wall, separated from my friends and walking with five strangers, including Brian Ellis. I felt both scared and excited at the same time. The vendor handed me some ice cream and I ate it.

After the ice cream, the friendly strangers brought me into a mall. I rode the escalator, my first ever. I went up and down, up and down that escalator while they watched me, bemused. I did it without asking anyone. Whee! It was fun. I felt like a little boy once more. I went up and down a couple of times more before they said, "Let's go. Enough cheap thrill."

Then we were inside the stores. "What do you want? What do you need?" they asked me.

I didn't want to impose. I looked around tentatively. "Is it all right if I get this?"

"Anything you want."

"Oh, I like that book, can I have that book? That ABC book with pictures?"

"Sure."

I got a Charlie Chaplin printed shirt and a pair of blue jeans that I associated with cowboys. I didn't dare get those wonderful rubber shoes, they looked too expensive. Instead, I got a pair of black Chinese kung fu shoes.

I put on my new clothes and shoes, thinking of the people inside the holding center. What would they need?

Then I saw the balls. The people back at the holding center wanted to play ball, life was so boring inside. Should I get a soccer ball? Maybe a basketball?

This dark one looked sturdier. I couldn't decide which one to take. I finally settled on three: a basketball, soccer ball, and volleyball. We headed back.

Before he left, Brian gave me a business card with a note on the back: "Any assistance to Mr. Yim Suthanakit is greatly appreciated," he wrote, doing his best to spell my name with the Roman alphabet. The card was signed "Brian T. Ellis, CBS News."[1]

After that two-hour shopping spree, I was back inside the holding center. "Let's play!" We went outside with the balls, and the cops chased us in. After two days of about three hundred people playing, the three balls were in tatters. I felt sad that the balls had been destroyed so soon. I should have asked for more. They might have lasted at least four days.

Some men talked to me about the interview. They praised me for speaking out, for showing my injuries and for crying on camera. "That's good, that's good," they said.

"What's so good about it?" I growled.

"Well, you told the world what happened to us. So you're like our speaker. You spoke for us, Poster Boy."

"I don't feel so good about crying in public, and I am no Poster Boy!" I said.

"That's all right, you did well for all of us."

The United Press International and *Bangkok Post* reporters came to the center a few days later to cover the Cambodian refugee crisis. When they interviewed me, I told my whole story without breaking down. I became that "Poster Boy." The reporters helped me fulfill a promise to tell the world about our terror, horror, and suffering. Now I had another promise to keep.

"What do you want to do with your life now?" Peter Collins, the CBS News reporter, asked. A 16-mm movie camera recorded my answer.

"Revenge!" I replied honestly. "Revenge for the death of my loved ones and friends!" I wanted vengeance even if it cost my life. I was consumed by rage. The reporter shook his head in disbelief.

In two weeks or so, my story came out in the *Bangkok Post* and in some international newspapers.

Seeing an opportunity to make some money, the prison guards allowed me out with an accompanying adult who could sing and speak a little Thai. I didn't want to be away from my three companions.

"Can they come with me?" I asked.

"No, they can't go. Just you, little man."

We spoke at the community hall, at the city hall, and at a temple a couple of times about our experiences and the reasons for our escape as refugees from Cambodia. I spoke through the interpreter. They would listen and afterward gave me money. Oh, this is good! I thought as my lips thanked them. I got used to speaking before an audience. People listened to me. My private pain wasn't private anymore. I found myself accepting more speaking engagements.

We went out to do this five times, and five times the Thai guards got their cut and I bought stuff for the people inside. I'd ask the others what they needed and they'd say cigarettes, or monosodium glutamate (MSG), which everyone in camp used to make their food taste better.

Those interviews and public appearances made me think. I had promised to tell the world about the abuses of the Khmer Rouge but I was shy about fulfilling that promise. You know the Asian philosophy about the "protruding nail getting the hammer." However, now I realized that people really did want to know. I did not understand why, but they wanted to know what had happened to Cambodia, what happened to me! But the opportunities to get out, taste a little freedom, and tell our stories didn't last long.

A few weeks later, when my Thai-speaking compatriot and I had been stuck inside the center for a while, a guard handed me a stamped envelope bordered with red and blue. I was surprised. Who would send me a letter? It had "Yim Suthanakit, Buri Ram Prison" on it, so I decided it was for me. This must be about those interviews, I thought. I opened the envelope and found ten dollars in it. "Oh! This is a lot of money! I can buy so much with ten dollars!" I was surprised that the Thai guard who handed me the envelope did not keep the cash for himself.

The letter was written in English so I searched the camp for someone who could read it. It was the first time anyone had ever written to me. People surrounded me and my friends. "What's going on?" They listened as the words were translated. The letter came from Bob Fonda of Los Altos in California. Bob had been on a plane to Paris when he happened to read the *Bangkok Post*. In the letter Bob offered to adopt me.

Everyone was impressed, envious, and a bit jealous.

"Someone cares about you."

"You're all set, you're ready to go."

"You'll get out of here soon."

"I don't want to go. My friends are here. Why would I go with a stranger?"

"Oh, I wish I had a pen pal like that. You're so lucky!"

My three companions were happy for me. "Luck is on your side now," they were all telling me. "If you can get out, go."

"I don't want to leave you guys," I said.

They nagged me.

"I'll go if you come with me." I meant it. We had a bond. We had gone through so much together. Leaving them would be like leaving my family all over again. I wrote back to Bob.

I received another letter, this time from Paris. I found someone in the camp who could read French. Like Bob, Philippe Poulin sent me money. I was very grateful that two strangers took the time to reach out to an orphan in a prison holding center far away. I felt that somebody out there cared. Philippe and I also exchanged letters.[2]

I kept those letters as mementos in my pocket, along with my marbles and pebbles, but people kept asking me for paper to roll their tobacco. I gave away Bob's and Phillipe's words in bits and pieces. But the monetary gifts were put to good use. Now that I was no longer getting out, I asked the guards to buy me MSG and marbles.

More Khmer refugees came. By July 1978 the new Khmer refugees crowded the holding center. Young and old, they were ill, thin, and traumatized. Many had been maimed by land mines; others had badly infected booby-trap injuries. And I thought I had problems.

Among the new arrivals were Khmer Rouge cadres and soldiers with their entire families. They had escaped either the fighting with the Vietnamese or the internal purges. They were instantly recognized by us. Here was a chance to get back at the destroyers of our loved ones.

Soon, the holding center was polarized into two groups of almost equal size and strength, attacking and counterattacking with anything they could find. Serious fights broke out often. Starting out small at first, the battles spread all over the tiny, crowded camp, terrifying many in the process. Some died; many were injured. Thai riot police came now and then, but the fighting and killing between the Khmer Rouge and Free Khmer factions went on day and night.

By the time the authorities finally decided to relocate the Khmer Rouge group, both sides had suffered greatly. I was not injured because I could run very fast when I was outnumbered. Though I did not kill any Khmer Rouge in that camp, I stoned many of them.

My adopted brothers Moeun, Doeum, and Sek and I were at the holding center for more than three months. In August 1978, five months after the four of us had arrived in Thailand, we became part of the group that was moved to the Aranya Prathet Refugee Camp on the Thai-Cambodian border.

This time it was a real refugee camp—a much larger area with hundreds of thousands of Khmer, Laotian, and Vietnamese refugees, all bounded by high-quality barbed wire. Thai officials ran the camp for the UNHCR (the United Nations High Commissioner for Refugees). Aranya Prathet was much better than Buri Ram. Here, I could see through the barbed wire fence. I could see forests and farmland and trees. Thai merchants came to sell stuff along the fence. We bought food and cigarettes for one another.

The camp looked well established and orderly. People had been there since 1975. By the time we got there late in 1978, housing was lined up and streets were laid out. They had wells, garden plots, subdivisions, and house numbers. I lived in a house with a Cambodian couple I called Aunt Chea and Uncle Mao. They wanted to adopt me. Aunt Chea took care of me as a mother would have. I also stayed close to my three adopted older brothers.

It was a pleasant little camp except that it was surrounded by barbed wire and guard posts with guns. Still, we held community dances, or musical events, or Khmer opera. We paid a baht or two to watch the plays or shows. There were markets and bustling shops where just about everything was available—except money, which was hard to come by. Except for the high fence and the gun-toting guards, life here was almost pleasant. It felt nearly normal again and I found it strangely difficult to adjust to this new feeling.

I still had the book Brian Ellis had bought me, even though I knew my ABCs well. I could speak some Thai and I tried out a couple of English phrases on the Caucasians working in the camp. But I began to feel tired more often. It was boring here. I didn't feel free. I was still under guard. I was depressed. I had long been depressed, but I did not know it. I did not know then about Post-Traumatic Stress Disorder (PTSD).

There is no pride or dignity in a refugee camp. We walked around the camp, talked, and hung out at the market. When we ran out of donated food and water, we went hungry. We didn't do anything but wait for handouts or the call to move elsewhere. A vehicle would arrive with the UNHCR's purchased food, water, and fuel. We would line up to get our share of the rations. A couple of days later, the vehicle would come again and we would line up again.

I was still on the alert for any chance to join the freedom fighter movement. Recruitment drives came and went but nobody would take me on; I was either too small or too skinny to be a guerrilla fighter. This feeling of rejection made me think of killing myself. But I knew that sooner or later someone would allow me to join and I would kill some more Khmer Rouge.

I had always seen both the Vietnamese and the Khmer Rouge as evil enemies. When I learned that the Cambodian Freedom Fighters had joined the Khmer Rouge to fight invading Vietnamese forces, I was very confused. My desire for blood lost some of its focus.

Some people in the camp had family members or relatives abroad and they submitted applications to go there. Because of the letters I had received, my friends urged me to submit an application, too. I went to the foreign workers and told them about my cousin Ang Khen, who lives in America.

"What's her complete name?" They asked me. "If she got married, she would have a different name."

"I don't know. Everyone knows Ang Khen. She's on the radio every day. She works for the Voice of America in Washington."

"Washington, D.C., or Washington State?"

"I don't know. I know Washington is where the radio broadcast is from."

"Oh, it must be D.C., then."

In September 1978, the International Rescue Committee received a cable and some photos from Cousin Ang Khen (Khen Chen was her married name) at the Voice of America Khmer Information Services in Washington, D.C. She had seen me in the CBS News documentary.

"Is this your cousin?" They showed me a black-and-white picture of a woman. She was a total stranger to me.

"I don't know; I haven't met her."

"Are you sure you don't know this person?"

"I know she's related to me but I haven't met her."

"Well, she put in an application to sponsor you to America."

"Oh. I don't want to go to America. But I'll go if my friends can go, too."

"Well, they can't come. But you, you can go. You can't stay here; this camp will be closed soon."

"But I don't want to go to America." I was being honest.

"You could go to the Surin camp; you have an aunt and uncle there. You want to go to your aunt in Surin?"

"Oh? I have an aunt there? Which one?" I was surprised to hear that I had an aunt in Surin.

"She's Yim Sayart, your father's younger sister, right?"

"I know her and Pou Ry."

"She's in the Surin Refugee Camp with her husband and children. You can write them and ask if they want to take you in."

"Okay."

I wrote Aunt Sayart and Uncle Ry. I wanted to stay with them in Surin so I could return to Cambodia as soon as possible and fight the Khmer Rouge. I never heard from them. Later I learned they were preparing to leave for America; Cousin Khen was sponsoring them, too.

After about a month of extensive paperwork, Cousin Khen was allowed to sponsor me, too. I wasn't too happy about it. I didn't want to leave my three companions behind in that awful camp.

The camp bored me, Aunt Sayart didn't respond to my letter, Aranyaprathet was closing, and my three friends couldn't come with me to America. What should I do?.

My companions nagged me. "Now you must go to America."

"I don't want to leave you," I said.

"You have to go."

"You're all I have."

"Your cousin's there, waiting for you," said Moeun. "You'll have a better future."

"Go, go, go, you must go," said Sek.

"There's nothing here for you here," said Doeum.

"You guys are here!" I insisted.

All of them offered dry smiles. "Just go on—without us."

I tired of their nagging. "All right, all right. What the heck, if I can't go back to Cambodia, I might as well go elsewhere." As if I had any choice: to return to Cambodia was sure death, but America meant opportunities and a new life.

The night before I left, we had a gathering. Aunt Chea and Uncle Mao were there, along with my three friends and many others. The whole camp must have known I was leaving. Whatever food we had, we shared: rice, *pla thu*, the hot sauce I now enjoyed, some cucumbers fresh from the garden plot, a little rice wine. We chatted, we got moody, we laughed. They all talked about what they knew of America, which was next to nothing. "A mere dishwasher job can earn you a car, or even two," said one fool. "You can go to school anywhere, have lots of money, and eat lots of food," another drunkard claimed.

"I don't care about having two cars in America." I was a bit depressed by then and reconsidering my decision.

"I want to go but I have no sponsor. You're so lucky."

"I just want to kill some Khmer Rouge." I was adamant.

"No, no, no. This is your best chance, your destiny. You're young; you have the chance to be great. You have to go," all of them nagged me.

So I relented. "Okay, okay, stop nagging." I left the party when they were still drinking. The bus would come at nine the next morning.

I didn't have much to pack. I cleaned my black kung fu shoes. In a bag, I stacked the clothes Brian had given me. When I lay down to sleep, all my friends were still out there, happy for me; I tossed and turned all night. I was scared about tomorrow, about leaving this familiar place.

The next morning, I waited for the bus with my three friends. I cried quietly when they put me on the bus. In other seats sat more Cambodian refugees going to the United States, to Australia, to Canada. My three companions were going nowhere. I left them at the refugee camp.

We arrived at the Dindaeng Holding Center in Bangkok. It was a wide open space with trees and grass. People were camping out, cooking. Mosquito nets were strung up. I had no pot, no food, nothing. I was confused about the name of the center because I knew the town of Dindaeng itself was far from Bangkok. The International Rescue Committee (IRC) representative told me where to stay, where to take a shower, where to eat. At a communal meal group I was introduced to another Khmer orphan. He was about fourteen, and he was also going to America.

Three days later, my IRC caseworker, Judy Kocher, arrived with her husband, Richard, to get me and the other orphan. We were invited to join them in the vehicle. I didn't know where we were going.

"We're going to their house," the boy said. He spoke Thai very well, much better than I. "I've stayed with them before."

"Oh, okay. How was it?"

"It's fine. They have a nice place, there's a hammock to sleep in, and food to eat."

"No gates, no locks, no guards?"

"Nope. You're pretty much on your own and they let you be. They take care of you."

"Oh, good, good. I like that."

We stayed at the Kochers for two days, played with toys and hung around. They had no rice and we ate sandwiches, which I really enjoyed.

The next day we rode in the Kochers' new, four-door car on an excursion. The boy and I sat in the back munching on chicken sandwiches. We were headed to a Khmer temple two hours away, near the border. However, after half an hour inside the "mother of all traffic jams" that Bangkok was, the stop-and-go movements made me vomit. I couldn't find the window control. "Eeew, what're you doing?!" said the boy.

We stopped the car. With the doors wide open, I retched again. I kept apologizing. "Don't worry, it's okay," the couple said. I spoiled the day. We returned home immediately, with me in the front seat this time, the window wide open just in case. I was embarrassed.

We enjoyed the comforts of the Kochers' home for a few more days before we were sent to the Din Daeng Quarantine Center. After almost two weeks there, we received our medical clearances. Despite all our time together, I can't remember the boy's name. By now the Kochers must be in their sixties. Judy had taken a lot of pictures of me and sent them to me.

I wish I could remember the place where I had crossed the border into Thailand. I can't recall the name of the district, the village, or the man and woman who had fed me and my three companions. I hope someone in that village will read the Khmer version of this book and contact me.

Our voyage to America began at the congested Bangkok International Airport. The other boy and I were placed on a plane to Tokyo Narita and then we were on a flight to Manila, where we spent the night in a Philippine hotel. The next morning we were on an early flight to Honolulu, where we spent the night in another hotel.

And then we were on yet another flight to San Francisco where we spent the night in someone's home near the Golden Gate Bridge. The next day, we were again on another airplane. After a short layover somewhere in the midwestern United States, the other orphan and I finally arrived at Washington National airport.

After all that flying and landing, I wasn't very sure where I was at any moment. All I knew was that it takes a long time to go to America.

My first jet plane experience wasn't very nice. I felt like a frightened bird on a journey across the Pacific. Airport after airport, the boy and I depended entirely on the kindness of the flight attendants—and they weren't always kind. The younger boy didn't seem very happy, either.

After an exhausting four days and three nights of travel, we were finally at Washington National Airport, wanting to use the bathroom very badly. However, the lady who brought us to the waiting area clearly said, in body language and hand gestures, "Stay here or else!" Neither of us wanted to go to the toilet alone or wait alone, so we twisted our legs for a long, long time.

A Khmer couple who smiled at us from afar turned out to be my young companion's long-lost uncle and aunt, who come to pick up their only surviving nephew.

The woman cried as they hugged. Like me, the orphan boy had been through much. Like me, all he knew about his sponsors was that they were relatives. He didn't cry. He was only relieved that the long journey was over.

"*Kmouy* [nephew]," said the woman to me, "your people will be here to pick you up soon. Don't worry, they'll be here." The boy waved good-bye. I did the same.

I felt frightened, lost, and alone in the mass confusion of Washington National. I was free but I felt terrified and excited at the same time. The feeling reminded me of the time I'd crossed into Thailand more than eight months ago. Free but terrified and excited. Then and now, I was unsure of my life, I was a scared refugee—now an immigrant—in an alien world called "America."

It was now the morning of October 29, 1978, the first day of my life in America, a brand-new step in my journey into light. I was almost seventeen years old.

15

Urban Jungle

Washington, D.C., Seattle, and Oregon State

Loudspeakers echoed through the cavernous airport. It was midnight. Last calls reverberated into a jumble of words and tones I couldn't understand. Masses of people went in all directions with the weary walk of zombies.

Exhausted after my first trip across the Pacific, I fell asleep in a plastic chair, holding a plastic tag printed with my native name Ranachith and my refugee case number in bold letters. Throughout my five-day transcontinental trip from Bangkok, this plastic tag took me from place to place, from airplane to airplane.

I woke up to incomprehensible paged announcements and hordes of humans. I wasn't sure where I was, but I knew my final destination was Washington, D.C.

My eyes scanned the crowds, fixed on anyone who might be looking for me. I raised my plastic tag high so many times that I slumped into my seat. Just then, I caught a movement.

Some 60 feet away, a short, rotund, middle-aged lady walked rapidly, followed by a tall man. She had Chinese features, shoulder length-black hair, and a light complexion.

She was smiling in my direction. I looked behind me but no one was reacting to her. I slowly stood up and raised my refugee case number with both hands. I hoped this was Cousin Ang Khen and her husband, Chun.

The couple came closer, almost running. I joined my hands in an uncertain *sampass* (greeting). "Welcome, welcome home, we're here, sorry we're a bit late," she said in Khmer, cheerfully giving me a big hug.

The tall, dark man smiled and spoke Khmer too: "How are you?"

"*Jumreap sour* [Greetings]," I said nervously, uncertain if my responses were proper.

"Come, come, let's go, you must be very tired." The woman cheerfully tugged at me.

"Yes," I said, thinking how talkative she was.

As we walked through the forest of people, I was reminded of my long trek through the jungles of Cambodia and how I walked just behind older strangers, afraid to be separated from them. I wondered what Moeun, Doeum, and Sek were doing in the refugee camp right now. I missed them already.

It was well past midnight when we got on the road in Cousin Khen's Chevy station wagon, and the car windows were slightly foggy.

The ride was very smooth, even at what felt like 60 miles per hour. There were no bumps or holes on the road at all.

Cousin Khen tried her best to cheer me up, explaining just about everything that passed by. I was silent in the back seat, answering direct questions only.

I had no clue where we were going, and I didn't pay much attention. I looked at the two strangers I'd be living with.

Cousin Khen talked on and on. I wasn't paying attention. She was so good at talking that she had talked for a living since the 1960s. I knew I'd get along with her.

Her husband Chun was quiet, only laughing sometimes when she delivered a good punchline. I called him *Nek*, for respected in-law. I didn't know if I'd get along with him.

Despite the car heater being on full blast, I was freezing cold. The up-down motions of the airplanes remained with me as the car sped onward. Engine noises still rang in my ears, which were hurting, perhaps from the air pressure changes of the various flights.

After a little more than seven months of living miserably in Thailand's finest refugee accommodations, I was at long last in the Land of the Free, the Home of the Brave. I was being taken to the home of two strangers, in a strange land.

The car went off the highway down the ramp to a place called Shirlington, Virginia. When we came to a complete stop, I saw a series of identical two-story brick duplexes.

I was still looking for the car door handle to let myself out when Cousin Khen opened the door for me.

"Welcome home, welcome home," she said, excitedly.

Was this, finally, home? I forced myself not to expect too much.

I grabbed my small bag, my plastic refugee tag, and stepped out, instantly chilled in my short-sleeved cotton shirt by the winter weather.

Cousin Chun was already unlocking the front door of their brick duplex. "Come on in," he said, holding the door open, "Please come in."

I walked into a very luxurious home, the walls full of oil paintings and framed photographs. Cousin Chun was a painter, Cousin Khen said. The couple hung their coats on a rack by the door.

It was cold even inside the house. I looked at their coats and fingered my pink Charlie Chaplin shirt. My eyes fixed on a tray of fresh fruit, the kinds of which I'd never seen—red apples and seedless grapes. It had to be about lunchtime in Asia. My stomach would not stop growling.

"The fruit tray is for you," Cousin Khen said happily. "Eat as much as you like. Do you like fresh fruit?"

"Yes, very much," I said shyly.

"Go on, have some."

"I thank you so very much," I said, grabbing the biggest apple and plucking some grapes, one at a time. "Thank you very much again," I said with my mouth full of sweet juices. Cousin Chun looked at me.

"Here we usually pick a small bundle of grapes to eat, not one or two pieces at a time like that," he said casually. "You can contaminate the whole thing if you do that."

"Oh, I'm so sorry." I said quickly. I couldn't decide if he was being critical or instructive.[1]

"Enjoy your fruit any way you like," Cousin Khen cut in cheerfully. I felt like the rope in a tug-of-war. I didn't want to be in such a position. A bad feeling washed over me.

I didn't dare touch the tasty grapes again. I sat quietly munching my apple, my pride hurt though I knew Cousin Chun meant well. He was only trying to teach the new kid the proper way of eating grapes.

Their many questions obliged me to elaborate as much as possible. I spent almost two hours telling them about my good and bad experiences in Cambodia and in Thailand. It was close to four in the morning when Cousin Khen showed me my room in the basement of their duplex.

My bedroom was amazing. It was a large, private room. Thinking of Cambodia's monsoon floodwaters, I found it incredible that I could have such a dry place so deep in the ground.

I crept into the extreme luxury of a sleeping bag on the linoleum floor. Just a few days ago, I had slept in a crowded, smelly, dirty room full of sickness and pain. Now I had an entire room to myself, complete with an indoor toilet, shower, and a nice washbasin. In an instant, I had shed my refugee skin. This was as close to heaven as I could get.

It seemed I had barely closed my eyes when two small girls shook me and pulled me out of my sleeping bag while screaming and yelling in English. I wasn't very sure where I was. The clock on the wall said 6:28. I had had a little more than two hours of sleep. My head was pounding.

The unruly girls, aged eight and ten, rudely dragged me up the stairs. They irritated me but I went along. They pulled me to a wide window in the living room.

"Snow, snow, look!" they screamed, pointing outside.

A white mass completely covered the ground. More cottony flakes floated down from the sky. After only hearing stories about snow, there it was, magical and white as can be. The first snowstorm of the year in Arlington, Virginia, had come to welcome me. I was mesmerized. I wanted to go out and swim in it. I was suddenly glad the girls had dragged me from my bed to see this wonderful sight.

"I see you've met Samini and Cynthia," Cousin Khen said, coming down the stairs in a blue-and-white checkered bathrobe. "These are my children. Sami is the eldest and Cynthia is the one who is missing her front teeth." She continued past us toward the kitchen. "How do you like your first snow?" Cousin Khen asked cheerfully from the kitchen, getting a cup of coffee.

We went outside. Soon I was freezing cold, but it was absolutely wonderful. We had a great snowball fight.

The girls couldn't speak Khmer and my English was limited to the alphabet and a few words, so we got by with sign language. Suddenly, I was the big brother.

They made me feel right at home in no time, but it was tough for me to adjust. After years without, I had to get used to family life again. "The Chens are my family now," I said to myself. It was slow and difficult at first, but I learned.

Cousin Khen and her husband had individually come to the United States as exchange students in the early 1960s. They met and married here. They returned to visit Cambodia a few times. Their last trip was in 1973 at the height of the conflict. When Cambodia fell in 1975, the Chens were already permanent residents in the United States.

Cousin Khen worked for the Voice of America's Khmer Language Services, which is under the U.S. Information Agency. Her husband, Chun, "a former starving professional artist," as Cousin Khen put it, was very proud of his coin-operated laundromats. "It pays the bills," he said, "and it's hard work."

Samini was their only child until they adopted a Khmer orphan girl, Cynthia, from a refugee camp in Thailand when she was three years old. And then, with my arrival on October 29, 1978, their cozy family of four had become five.

The snow came down for the next two days until it was knee deep. I had neither coat nor boots, but it was still fun playing with the girls in the deep, white powder.

After many hours in the local mall, Cousin Khen and I left with a new pair of boots, a pair of tennis shoes, several pairs of Fruit of the Loom underwear, a few shirts, and long pants. She was quite frugal and watched every dime carefully.

On the other hand, her husband bought me that very day a cherrywood bed-and-mattress set, a BMX bike, and many toys. I was very grateful for all these new and luxurious things. I didn't know how much it cost the Chens, but it must have been a lot.[2]

Soon I was immersed in getting the required immunizations, medical clearance, and riding the school bus to Wakefield High School in Arlington. I had my first brush with racism on that bus. The students from the neighborhood, mostly whites, didn't take kindly to the new kid on the bus who looked and acted different. They called me names, such as gook, Charlie, dirt bag, and shithead, names often derived from popular movies about the Vietnam War. Although I couldn't understand their words or their cruelty, I understood very well the intent to humiliate me, and the degrading laughter.

During my first few days in school, I saw students fighting in the yard. In the hallways, students intimidated other students. I didn't like that school. I bought a pocketknife for two dollars, needing it for self-defense. Many students from other countries were in this school, too, unlike the mostly white kids on my bus route. There were Iranians who spoke nothing but Farsi. There were some Mexicans and Guatemalans who spoke Spanish. There were Koreans, Arabs, and Africans. There were about four Cambodians. There was a tall Cambodian boy named Lim Peng Lee who knew karate. He liked practicing kicks on walls. I stuck with him.

I attended the class called "English as a Second Language." We had individual chairs with fold-out arms for writing. In Cambodian schools I had shared a long table and a bench with four people. Here we each had our own desk, and I had a writing tablet. The room had several pictures of presidents: Washington, Jefferson, and everyone else, all the way up to the current president, Jimmy Carter.

The teacher was a blue-eyed lady. I don't remember her name but she was very kind. On the first day, she asked us, "How many of you know the ABCs?" I raised my hand. I was sixteen, the same age as my classmates. "How many know some English words or phrases?" I knew how to say, "How are you" and "Fine, thank you," but that was all. So I again raised my hand. The teacher smiled broadly and I returned her greeting.

We all began with the basics. Soon I was bored; I wanted to hurry up the lessons. While we sat listening to the teacher day after day, a Korean boy would talk tough. I was completely and utterly annoyed with him. And I let him know it.

One day, while the teacher was temporarily out of the classroom, the same Korean insulted me and I replied in kind. He cocked a chair back, ready to bash my head with it. At that very moment, I had a flashback. Instead of the tough-talking Korean kid in front of me, I saw instead a young Khmer Rouge soldier who was ready to clobber me with a chair. I was back at Ta Source Hill, sweating profusely, and my pulse rate was off the chart. I pulled out my pocketknife, ready to draw blood.

Someone's loud scream brought me back to reality. The Korean kid backed off in shock. He could not believe that I had actually called his bluff and was prepared to slit his throat and spill blood.

The scream had come from our teacher. She sent me to the principal's office, where I stayed all day because of that knife. Cousin Khen was called in and I got an earful more, which I clearly and fully deserved.

Meanwhile, the name calling on the bus continued. I was even shoved and hit, often repeatedly. This went on for days, weeks, and months. The insults and physical attacks got so bad that I chose to walk the 8 miles to and from school, and later I rode my bicycle. Walking or riding alone, I talked to myself. I've done nothing wrong, why do they hate me? I asked myself many times. Is it because they think I'm Viet Cong? I am no "Gook"! I don't even like the Vietnamese!

The school cafeteria was the place I liked best at Wakefield High. There was always so much food. We could pick whatever we wanted to eat for lunch. I thought about my friends in Thailand. We used to fight over food. What were they doing now?

I'd bring food home. I couldn't help it—I was still in survival mode. Some fruit, a banana, or a piece of candy always went into my pocket. I hoarded the goods in my basement bedroom. Soon I was throwing away spoiled fruits and moldy candy. Again I thought of my friends in Thailand and how we quarreled over every little morsel or scrap we called "food."

The bright-blue-eyed teacher took us to Capitol Hill one day. She seemed to care about us, unlike the other teachers. She accepted us. I passed the ESL test with flying colors within a year, not the usual eighteen months. I advanced to regular high school classes. I took English literature, history, biology, math, and science. I did well. But even as I enjoyed my classes, I disliked the school.

What I hated most about this school was the bomb threats, the fighting, and the chaos in the hallways and the bathrooms. I had escaped the violence of Cambodia only to find it in an American high school. Guns were pointed at me a few times, but no shot was ever fired. I didn't dare go to the boys' room alone.

Fights broke out for the most trivial reasons. Girls fought girls; blacks battled whites, Asians clashed with Hispanics, and Arabs waged war against everyone. It was impossible for the teachers to stop them. The police would come in daily, but even the police couldn't stop them. What am I doing here? I thought. I shouldn't be here! I was wretched and confused. Instinct urged me to hit back, kill or be killed, but I wanted a better life. Why destroy all that I had struggled for?

Although the atmosphere wasn't conducive to learning, my grades were mostly A and B average. Once, when my grades dropped to C average, the Chens were so hard on me that I dared not let them slip again. I did my best to avoid trouble and mostly succeeded, but trouble often found me—like it or not.

I volunteered to tutor fourteen newly enrolled Khmer students not knowing that, in doing so, I became the de facto gang leader. Once I made the mistake of walking into the restroom alone. I ended up with a black eye and my head shoved into a urinal. Price paid; lesson learned.

The other Khmer students and I never talked about Cambodia or about life in the old country. I think we all wanted to forget that. There was too much shame, hatred, fear. We focused on what we could do this afternoon, where to go tomorrow. We concentrated on being as American as possible, as soon as possible. We wanted to complete the course and move on. I helped them with writing essays, some math, some English. I usually found myself leading.

I was taller than my Cambodian friends. I was skinny with facial acne. I wore my hair long, to my shoulder. I favored loose shirts and jeans. I preferred dark colors, nothing bright. I listened to rock music. However, I also knew well that my past was always just a step behind me.

I submitted some bland papers about Cambodia, Siem Reap, and the jungle, but they held no passion. I just turned them in to get my points. My teachers always said I could do better. I listened carefully when they talked, but at home I focused on TV. My priority was to learn the language, how to get along. I watched a lot of *Sesame Street*.

I didn't think of Cambodia. I didn't want a car. I didn't want to drive. I wanted to be just like that white kid over there. I wanted to speak English with no accent.[3] I just wanted to be accepted. I wanted a part-time job, but not at McDonald's. That was much too public. Cousin Chun kept pushing me. "I'm not ready for that," I said, "but I don't mind helping around at your laundry." I couldn't work at a hamburger place. I hated hamburgers. I couldn't face stranger after stranger, coming in to order burgers and fries. I was a loner. I could play basketball with my friends, but that was about it. I usually stayed in my room, reading books or watching my battered old TV—the Public Broadcasting Service (PBS) channel, mostly. That's usually how I spent my day after school, besides helping the Chens with routine chores.

Nothing in America was worth fighting for, I honestly thought. I felt trapped. My voice was changing; my body grew hair in places. I was growing taller, taller than an average Khmer. I had these agonies about growing up but could not talk to anyone about it. I did my best to put my terrible past behind me, but I still wanted to kill, to avenge the deaths of my loved ones. I was restless and all torn up deep inside.[4] Again, I contemplated suicide and came very close to doing it. What saved me was the thought that while I lived I had a chance to kill Khmer Rouge. I felt like a coward but knew I'd be a bigger coward if I killed myself.

It was an extremely difficult time for me. I had trouble focusing. At school I was harassed and chased. The Hispanics wanted to beat me up in the bathroom. The Korean guy wanted to beat me up in the hallway. At night, in my nightmares, Khmer Rouge death squads chased me. I would wake up sweating, shaking with fear. Many times, I couldn't tell whether I was dreaming. Thank goodness the Chens slept on the second floor. They couldn't hear my hellish screams down in the basement.

Some days, particularly in winter, I didn't want to get out of bed. I just wanted to hide. I wasn't a lazy person, I wanted to keep busy, but I didn't want to see anyone. I felt sorry for myself. I thought of suicide more seriously in the winter.

One night, my nightmare took a different turn. As usual, the Khmer Rouge soldiers were chasing me. As usual, I'd rest, they'd get closer, I'd run again. But then, suddenly, I could soar in the air. I could fly! From then on, every time I was chased in my nightmares, I flew and escaped the Khmer Rouge.

The role of being a dependent of the Chens was difficult to swallow. After years of surviving on my own wits, I felt suffocated by people caring for me, telling me what to do. I was a teenager with raging hormones. I wanted to be independent, to be free, but I felt hemmed in at home. If I didn't brush my teeth, someone would nag me. They weren't mean-spirited or anything, but I didn't like it when they told me to do things "now." I didn't like that "now" thing. For instance, the demands came when I was watching television.

"You need to take out the garbage."

"Wait, wait, I just want to finish this show."

"No, now!"

Resentment would flare up inside me. I became a rebel. I think they tried to guide me, but this living situation was such a big change from my independent spirit. I had been through things they couldn't imagine, but they treated me like a child. This made me frustrated and angry and confused, but I never lost my self-control. I did what they told me to do. I did my chores when I arrived home from school. I'd go to Cousin Chun's laundromat, wash the floor, and make things shine. I did this every time I could. I didn't mind doing it.

When I had free time I'd go to the nearby park, hang out at the benches, be by myself. Or else I'd call Lee, my friend the karate kid. He'd come to my house or I'd get on my bike and go visit him. Sometimes Cousin Khen would take me there or pick him up. My cousin was very accommodating. She gave me thirty dollars' allowance every month, which was a lot of money in 1979. We did family things together, such as playing games, having TV dinners, and even going on camping or fishing trips.

One day I went with Cousin Khen to the U.S. Department of Agriculture office. There I met with the USDA secretary and the chief of the USDA Forest Service. The secretary gave me some stickers while the chief gave me a Smokey Bear poster that said, "Only you can prevent forest fires" and another one with Woodsy Owl on it proclaiming "Give a hoot. Don't pollute." When we got home I took my prizes to the basement. I had lots of posters up in my room already. Colorful flowers mostly, a few airplanes, tanks, and guns, too. With Cousin Khen nearby, I stuck the stickers on my wall and tacked up Smokey Bear and Woodsy Owl in prominent places. I turned to Cousin Khen. "When I finish school, I'm going to join the forestry service," I said to her.[5]

Even with all the goodwill, even after a year had passed, the difficulties of adjustment continued. It was hard for me and hard for them. My growing pains and inner traumas got in the way. I couldn't always see eye-to-eye with Cousin Chun. He was strict, logical, and precise. I learned that from him, that logic and precision thing. Yet he treated me as a son. He took me fishing. Before we returned home, we'd always drop by a McDonald's.

I admired Cousin Chun for being a "self-made" man. Cousin Khen told me he had a hard young life, worked his way up, completed a master's degree, did this and that, then went into business. If he can do it, I said to myself, I can do better. He taught me many things. He was one of the few truly kind persons I knew. He was a father figure to me during the time I needed such a figure in my life—and he continues to be that father figure for me today. But I learned too much from him: the good, the bad, and the ugly as well. All of those things exist in each of us.

Cousin Chun was quick to change from nice to nasty. He had a split personality, and his transformation could be frightening. He wasn't violent toward people, only toward things. I prayed I'd never lose my self-control, my temper, and thus my cool. It was one of my greatest fears. I'd look at him and say to myself, "No way that's me." But in reality, Cousin Chun rubbed off on me. I, too, could easily and quickly become a madman. I hated and feared this tendency.

Cousin Chun's short fuse caused most of the trouble at home. On his rare bad days, I'd tiptoe around the house in my attempt not to get caught in the furies. Whenever he went into a rage, I felt that it was my fault, that I was in part to blame. What happened next was inevitable.

One August evening a few months after I turned seventeen, I was intently watching a PBS program in my room down in the basement. Samini, the Chens' daughter, came into the room and announced that it was time for her show.

I said, "No, I want to watch this show. You're are intruding on my turf!"

Again she insisted on watching her program.

"Let me finish mine, then you can have it," I suggested a compromise.

She would have none of it. She wanted to watch her show, and right now.

"Fine, go ahead," I said.

She couldn't change the channel because the channel selector knob was broken. She asked me to do it.

I refused, naturally.

This scene repeated itself the following night. This time, Samini went upstairs to her parents who were hosting a dinner party for their friends. Cousin Chun came down to my bedroom, his face red hot and steamed. He yelled and cursed, then smashed the old TV to bits in a fit of rage. I was in tears. It was more than just an ancient, almost broken TV that he had just smashed. He had also smashed my pride. Cousin Chun then went back upstairs and continued his dinner with friends, who were puzzled and dumbfounded by the whole scene.

I slammed the bedroom door shut and seriously contemplated my "counter move."

The TV had been very old, knobs broken, but still functioning. Now it wouldn't work anymore. I felt responsible for the whole thing, and I felt that it was probably my fault. I could have compromised, but he smashed the TV first. I felt humiliated. It felt like he had smashed *me.*

I had neither sleep nor dinner that night. I pondered the time I'd lived with the Chens, close to eighteen months. They had been good to me. However, I felt the need for independence. The TV incident was merely the last straw. I felt sadness, anger, pride, humiliation, and hurt. It was a little incident that had blown out of proportion, but it would be the last one for me, I decided then and there.[6]

I wrote out a note in Khmer thanking the Chens profusely, begging their pardon, but noting that I needed my space. It was time for me to move on. I was bawling while I wrote it, of course. Yes, I allowed self-pity to invade my space. The last time I'd bawled like that was at the camp during the *CBS News* interview in June 1978.

I put the note in an envelope with respect, laid it on the table so they could easily see it, and weighed it down with the house keys. Into my bag went my pictures from the camp, my old notebooks, and some clothes, two pairs of pants, and some knickknacks. I put into a tin can the pebbles and little toys on my window sill, my marbles, pens, and pencils.

At three o'clock that morning I left through the back door with my bag and $297, my school identification card, and my green card in my pocket. My worldly possessions. I locked the door behind me quietly, no key to get back inside. Now there was no turning back.

It was nice and quiet that August morning of 1980. I felt free. For what it's worth, I thought to myself, I'm out of that mess. They may not be too happy about it, but I'm done with them. Next stop: California. I walked till I got to the bus station and waited for the local Metro city bus. I was exhilarated but had a little tinge of sadness. I had turned seventeen only a few months ago. Now I was homeless and a runaway kid—like so many missing kids I had seen on posters on telephone poles. No one would look for me: I had decided to move out, I was not a missing kid.

I stayed on the bus for a couple of hours as it drove around the D.C. area. It was warm on the bus, and the ride was free. When it grew light out, I disembarked at Union Station. To my dismay, I found that I couldn't get a train to California, where Aunt Sayart was living with her family. I also knew a couple from the refugee camp who had settled in Seattle, Washington—some 3,000 miles away.

"How about a bus, can I get a bus to Seattle?"

"Yes, a Greyhound bus goes all the way there, but it will take a while."

"How long?"

"Five days."

"How much?"

"A hundred and fifty dollars one way." That's a lot, I thought; I won't have much money left. Think, think.

"Okay, I'll take it."

At the bus ticket counter I paid up and waited until the bus was ready to leave. "I'm heading out West!," I thought, imagining cowboys, California sunshine, and similar images I'd seen on TV. I was hoping I can stay with my friends in Seattle for a night or two so I won't have to sleep on a sidewalk.

"How long does it take to get to Seattle?" I asked the bus driver, to see if he might give me a different answer.

"Five days or so, depends on the traffic," he said. "You'll have to change buses five or six times."

It took me six days. I saw a lot of open country and fields after fields of sunflowers under the wide blue sky of Montana. At every bus change, I always sat right behind the driver. When other passengers asked about my broken English and strong accent, I was ashamed to be associated with the land of the Killing Fields, so I told them I came from Thailand. It wasn't entirely a lie; I had spent seven months there.

I slept a lot on the bus. I did a lot of thinking. My thoughts always stopped in Thailand, never going back to Cambodia. Sek was on his way to France. Moeun and Doeum were being sponsored by Cousin Ang Khen to come to America. It would take them about a year to get to the United States. If I were in camp with them right now, I thought, what would we be doing? Would I be happier? How much have I done since I arrived here in the United States? Am I doing the right thing? Still, I felt like I was my own man.

With teeth aching from grinding my teeth while sleeping on the long bus trip, I finally arrived in Seattle, a place I had only heard about through a letter from Uncle Mao, an acquaintance at the refugee camp. Now I was going to pay him and his wife, Aunt Chea, a surprise visit. The couple had wanted to adopt me when we were in the refugee camp. It wouldn't hurt to pay my respects. I didn't know anyone else in this rainy city.

Early that morning, as I stepped out of the taxi and stood in front of a small apartment, I recognized a middle-aged man who appeared to be on the way to work. He had put on some weight since I last saw him, but I knew who he was.

"Greetings, Pou Mao!"

He didn't recognize me. I had grown more than a foot since I last saw them in Thailand nearly two years ago.

"What do you want? Who are you?"

"Who do you think it is?" I said, smiling broadly. "It's Nachith."

"You . . . you?" Uncle Mao was stunned. His surprise turned to pure joy.

"Oh, my boy, so good to see you!" He gave me a big hug. "What are you doing here? How did you get here?"

I paid the taxi driver and Uncle Mao rushed me into his apartment.

"*Ming* [Aunt], look who's here," Uncle Mao said, his arm over my shoulder. Aunt Chea had a puzzled look on her face.

"*Jumreap sour, Ming,*" I joined my palms formally. "Hello, Aunt."

"*Cha, Leuk Dai Twaiy Preah, Khmouy,*" Aunt Chea said automatically. "Yes, Lord Buddha is praised." When she finally recognized me, I was choked in her bear hug. She had always been closer to me than Uncle Mao.

Uncle Mao was already late for work, so he called in sick. The childless couple looked me over, smiling broadly. "You have grown into a handsome young man, Nachith." Aunt Chea said.

"I have grown taller, thank you."

"So tell us, what has happened to you since we last saw each other in Thailand?"

I told them everything that happened to me in the new country up to and including becoming a homeless runaway. They were quiet, listening to me.

"May I stay and visit with you for a few days before I head down south to California? I have an aunt there. I haven't seen her since I was five or six years old."

"Stay with us as long as you like," they answered instantly.

"Thank you, but after a few days, I'll go south to California. I want to see that place," I said.

"Listen, Nachith. Come live with us. We insist," Uncle Mao said seriously.

"We don't have any children. We have plenty of room," added Aunt Chea.

"I'm not so sure," I said. "I want to see California."

"Well, stay here a while and go whenever you want," Uncle Mao said.

"That's quite fair," Aunt Chea said, handing me a cold soda.

That afternoon, two of their friends arrived and all urged me to stay in Seattle for good.

"All right, just for a while, then," I compromised. I didn't want to abuse their generosity. I wanted my independence, but I needed a starting point. The couple's small apartment seemed as good a place as any.

The couple then told me they were adopting three teens from a refugee camp on the Thai-Cambodian border. Chantha, an eighteen-year-old boy, and his younger sisters Savary and Savarin were family friends. With very limited English, Uncle Mao and Aunt Chea found it difficult to complete the paperwork required by the Immigration and Naturalization Service (INS). I translated and helped them fill out and file the sponsorship papers at the Seattle INS office the next morning. I also signed as a witness. I wanted to leave before the teens came, but the couple insisted that I stay and help.

I started attending West Seattle High School. After about two months, the three teenagers arrived. The couple's one-bedroom apartment became crowded. Despite the domestic problems beginning to surface, I stayed out of respect.

More paperwork followed. They sponsored three more: the teens' mother and two more of her daughters. I learned much about paperwork, and the unbelievable layers of bureaucracies at the INS, which would help me later.

Life in America had changed this Khmer couple very much, and in a bad way. Uncle Mao became an alcoholic and often beat his wife for no good reason. My intervention only led to more anger, although he didn't dare assault or hurt me.

After a particularly vicious episode, Aunt Chea prevailed on me to stay, hoping that my presence would deter his drunkenness, but he was back to his ugly self in a week. I left.

For several weeks, I lived mostly on the streets of Seattle until it became too cold outdoors. At high school I befriended Reth Chhlob, a Khmer refugee. (His name was pronounced "Chhlawb.") Chhlob's small, one-bedroom apartment became a safe haven for me.

Every day after school, I earned money picking cucumbers in the rain, on a farm just outside Seattle, and I did additional odd jobs in the afternoons and on the weekends. I helped the three teens living in Aunt Chea's apartment apply for welfare checks and food stamps. They enrolled in local schools. I took them on the city bus for vaccination shots and medical check-ups. In many ways, they also helped me cope with life in the new country.

One day in December, there was a knock on Chhlob's door. I opened it to find Aunt Chea, badly beaten and bruised. Her swollen face and lips gave away her embarrassment and pain. With the two teenage girls Savary and Savarin beside her, Aunt Chea begged for help. They feared for their lives. They needed a place to hide from Uncle Mao. Chhlob and I agreed to let them stay, and our tiny one-room apartment became their safe house. The teenage boy Chantha remained with Uncle Mao, who often drove around drunk, looking for his wife.

Seattle cops caught Uncle Mao driving drunk many times, but they usually let him go. The apartment manager condoned his behavior. I personally didn't care what happened to him.

Aunt Chea suggested we move to Beaverton, Oregon, where her Khmer sponsor lived. "Chith, I must get away from him," she said. "I must take these girls with me. You speak English. You know how to get around. You have traveled," she said. "Please help us!"

I agreed. I had wanted to head south all along. One morning, with nothing but the name, address, and telephone number of Aunt Chea's sponsor, we boarded a Greyhound bus bound for Portland. I bid my good friend Chhlob farewell and left town with three frightened people. Aunt Chea managed to cover the bus fares and lunch. We arrived in Portland late in the evening. Colorful Christmas lights were everywhere.

We found a phone and called Aunt Chea's sponsor, Mr. Sokhom Tauch, who picked us up in his tiny Chevy Chevette. We squeezed into the subcompact and headed for his house in Aloha, just outside Beaverton. Uncle Sokhom, as we all called him, told us that Uncle Mao had been calling repeatedly. At a stoplight Uncle Sokhom turned and looked at me. "So you're the tall, skinny guy who stole Pou Mao's wife and kids?" he joked.

"Uh . . . sorry, Pou, but what do you mean by that?"

"Mao said you stole these refugees from him," he laughed.

"It may look that way, but they made me bring them here. I didn't steal them, Pou," I said, and he laughed some more.

We didn't talk much in the cramped car. Aunt Chea wept whenever Uncle Mao's name was mentioned. I felt uncomfortable but my sense of responsibility to Aunt Chea and the two sisters was strong. I decided to see it through until I could make a clean break.

We remained with Uncle Sokhom and his family in Aloha for almost four weeks before we found an apartment. They helped us a lot. Uncle Sokhom, particularly, took it upon himself to set us up with just about everything we needed in our new three-bedroom apartment in Beaverton, where I transferred to Beaverton High School. Uncle Sokhom was the leader of a fledgling Khmer community in Oregon. We appreciated his kindness and personal efforts to get our lives going again. Then, in the middle of January 1981, our peaceful life at home was interrupted with a knock on the door.

When I opened the door I shouted out in surprise, "Pou Mao!"

He gave a dry smile and walked in. "Is Ming home?"

"No, but she should be back soon," I felt a bit awkward. I tried to be polite.

"How are you?" he asked, also uncomfortable.

"All right," I said. A long, awkward silence followed, interrupted by embarrassing attempts to start a conversation. We no longer had anything in common. I did my best to show him some respect, but it was difficult.

I was glad when the others showed up from one of their many shopping trips to the local Goodwill store. The shock showed on Savary's and Savarin's faces, but Aunt Chea appeared to have been expecting him. She had secretly been in touch with her estranged husband, like a good victim of domestic violence. I felt betrayed.

Two weeks later, Uncle Mao and Chantha (Savary and Savarin's brother) moved in with us. Days passed. Uncle Mao started drinking again. The household was in turmoil once more. The couple had a major argument one morning and somehow I got involved. Uncle Mao and I had a bout of pushing and shoving. He tried to punch me, but I ducked. I could not bring myself to strike an old drunkard. I worried that I might kill him. Aunt Chea intervened. With a large butcher knife, she sent Uncle Mao running out of the apartment. She cut his luggage to bits, tossed the pieces out, and chased him out of the house, locking the door behind her. I was pleasantly surprised. I never thought she had it in her. I gave her a broad smile as my congratulations for her newfound courage.

In June the teenagers' widowed mother, Mrs. Chak San, finally arrived from Thailand, with her two other daughters Thavy and Savara. Thavy was her eldest daughter and Savara was her youngest. The three-bedroom apartment in Beaverton became cramped with eight people, but we managed just fine. Within a few days of the new arrivals, Uncle Mao visited again. His wife, again, had been secretly calling him. She remained hopeful the man would change. I, however, had lost respect for Uncle Mao, and being in the same house with him day after day was awkward.

I decided to move out. The newly arrived immigrants and I found and rented an apartment about half a mile away. It was peaceful there with only Mrs. Chak San, her eldest daughter Thavy and her youngest Savara. Mrs. Chak San's three other children, Chantha, Savary, and Savarin, remained with their adoptive parents Uncle Mao and Aunt Chea, who received their welfare checks and food stamps.

Soon after, Uncle Mao and aunt Chea had problems with the three siblings and the newly arrived family. The couple left for Seattle without their three adopted children,[7] and the teens came to stay in our apartment.

Meanwhile, Thavy cleaned and cooked and washed dishes. She cared for her four siblings and her mom, and took care of herself. She was hard-working, responsible, and not shy about it. Nobody had to tell her what to do. She just did it, a real self-starter. We talked about school and lessons. I felt that I could teach her a lot, and she was a willing learner. I thought to myself, I can relate to this person and perhaps relate well.

While Thavy and I were dating, if you can call it that, we had a chaperone or two with us at all times. More often than not, we would have a car full of them. Sisters, brother, mother, aunts, cousins, even family friends—they all served as chaperones at one time or another. Our time together was not traditional "dating," as most Americans know it. But Thavy and I were infact pushing the cultural barriers as is.

I continued my studies at Beaverton High School, which Thavy also attended. I worked after school, on weekends, and on holidays. Life was improving for all of us.

I was good at yard work, painting, and doing odd jobs such as lifting or moving furniture. Soon, by word of mouth perhaps, I had way too much work to do on my own. I got Thavy and her brother Chantha, who had become my good friend, to help me out.

Two teachers at Beaverton High School gave me a lot of sound advice and support. Barbara Stevens, who taught physical education and ESL, asked me to assist other students, including Thavy and her siblings. My English literature teacher, Lindsay Peters, taught me literature, writing, and grammar. Both used their personal and professional time to help me with my studies. I did well in class. Ms. Peters, whom I called Lindsay, even taught me how to drive in her old stick-shift Volkswagon Bug. I often visited both of their homes and lent a hand with various chores and projects. No other students did these things. We became good friends.

In June 1982 I sat with several hundreds of other Beaverton High School seniors at the commencement ceremony. I was one of only thirteen Cambodian refugees to graduate that day.

Three people cheered when I received my diploma. I was happy to hear them calling my name. Thavy had a distinctive, high-pitched voice that carried over the crowd of over two thousand. I heard Lindsay's piercing cry as well. "Yay, Ronnie! Ronnie! Way to go!"

After the commencement ceremony, Lindsay and her husband Hugh invited Thavy and me to dinner. "Whatever you want to order, we'll pay for it. This is your day. Enjoy it, on us!"

Thavy came without a chaperone this time. Lindsay and her husband drove us to a nice restaurant, our very first fancy place to eat—ever. Thavy and I both ordered steak.

Lindsay and Hugh dropped us off at home, where an informal celebration awaited me. Thavy's mother and four younger siblings hadn't been able to come to the graduation ceremony because we didn't have enough tickets or available transportation. They had prepared a lot of Cambodian food at home, and Thavy and I had dinner again to participate in this Khmer party.

Meanwhile, I was thinking about college. I had applied to several of them, and all were far away. I'd be gone nine months a year for four years. I wasn't sure what was going to happen to thavy and me with all that separation. We had no formal plans, no serious commitments yet.

That summer Thavy's mother and her five teenaged children moved into a larger house much closer to the children's schools. When Thavy's brother, Chantha, moved out to his own apartment, the family had no car. We shopped around and Thavy and I split the cost of paying for a $2,000 Oldsmobile sedan.

After the joint purchase of the car, we bought a TV together. We sat in front of our "joint TV" often. We held hands in secret, which was a no-no in our culture. Khmers are not supposed to show affection in public. The family began asking questions, "What's going on between you two?" Of course when we went on a date, the entire family would come along—it was part of the culture.

That fall I received a full scholarship to attend Lindfield College, a private school in McMinville, Oregon, a small city about an hour's drive from Beaverton. I had been attracted by its academic program and champion football team. I enjoyed language classes and P.E., where I could blow off steam. I was now a college student.

I was very healthy, now weighing a comfortable 148 pounds compared to my former 123 pounds. In my now rare nightmares, I was able to fly to escape anyone chasing me—whereas before I could only run. I usually worked on weekends and was able to get all the work I wanted. I put money into my savings account, which peaked at a whopping $500, the most I had ever had at any given time. My biggest expenses at this time were food and rent. I cut my hair short to look dependable and more formal at work and school. I was more Americanized now, but not quite there yet as I still spoke with a strong Khmer accent. I still do. I always felt "less American" because of my foreign accent.

My weekday schedule was lengthy and complex. In the morning, I rode a bike to school. At three in the afternoon, I biked or bused to work, going to seven houses per week. I earned about $35 a day, working two to three hours a day. I did my English and math homework on the bus. It was eight o'clock by the time I got home. At seven the next morning, I'd get ready for school all over again.

I spent my holidays and breaks with Thavy's family, who treated me like one of their own. There was now more holding of hands between Thavy and me. It was just a silent agreement: "I'm here and I'm yours and you're mine," so to speak. Our "dates" still involved Thavy's entire family.

One day, I talked to Thavy. "Well, I'm in college now and it'll be a while till I finish. We have a joint car and a joint TV, might as well have a joint future. Will you be interested if I took you as my wife? Not now, I'm not ready, but later?"

"Oh, I have other options," she said. "I'll leave my options open."

"Okay, if you say so . . . me too, then," I bluffed.

I trusted the people I was involved with, and I trusted that my future would work out. I was beginning to appreciate Cambodian music. It took me back to my childhood. I felt I could do anything. Life was good—not great, but good enough. I had found love and it was comforting.

One day, I was alone with Thavy's mother in the kitchen. She was chopping up a chicken with her large butcher knife. "Now," she said, waving her big knife, "I know you like my daughter, but what are you going to do about it?"

The surprise pressure made me uneasy. I just wanted to relax with this girl and see how far it would go, and now her mother was hacking away at this chicken, asking about my plans. To be honest, I was a bit scared.[8]

"Well, I don't have a plan yet," I managed to say, looking at the messed-up chicken. "I like your daughter but I'm not ready yet. I have to finish college."

"How long?"

"Well, at least four years." I was logical and tactful. "Maybe when I graduate we'll get to something more serious."

"Okay," she said, finally putting down the knife. Whew, I thought, I'm off the hook!

My second year at Lindfield College was going to require additional shifts of work to pay tuition costs not covered by the scholarship, so I explored other colleges that cost less. Besides, I was eager to be part of more diverse student bodies than I'd seen in McMinnville, Oregon, even if they did have a really good football team. When I was accepted in 1983 to the University of Oregon, two hours away, I asked Thavy if she would like to live with me in Eugene and go to community college there. She was graduating from Beaverton High School that summer.

"I can't do that," she said. "Don't ask me that again."

"Just come and do the school thing, nothing more," I said.

"I want to be with my mother," she said. And that was that.

The end of Lindfield's school year was approaching and I made preparations to move to Eugene. Thavy's family said to her, often in my presence, "You better mark this guy before he's gone." Her mother, her sisters, other relatives, and the larger community wanted us to hold a formal engagement ceremony. I think they just wanted to party—at my expense. Someone decided that April, the Khmer New Year, was an auspicious occasion.

I didn't really want to do this costly and time-consuming ceremony, but I felt trapped. Reluctantly I went along, mainly to please Thavy and her family.

And so we became officially engaged in April 1983.

A Khmer engagement party is an expensive, elaborate affair and ours was no exception. It was like a wedding ceremony but on a smaller scale. It felt like I was getting married. It was our traditional way of announcing that we are spoken for, so everyone else can buzz off. We were not yet man and wife, "but please, nobody touch my fiancée. We have been spoken for."

There were a couple of Buddhist monks in orange robes, there was chanting and incense and flowers and blessings and all that. We tied ribbons and exchanged rings. Our Khmer and American guests got together and feasted on fine home-cooked dishes at the engagement party. Just about everyone in the Khmer community in Oregon knew about the event. We probably spent about a thousand dollars, in all. That was a lot of money for a college student to dish out in 1983.

We were now socially acceptable as a dating couple. Without an engagement ceremony, people would have talked, and that's not good at all in our culture. So I agreed to sacrifice my emotional well-being to make all these people happy when I wasn't all that certain myself. Perhaps I had "cold feet." In the end, it wasn't so bad. We had a good party. Thavy and I talked about general plans over the next four years: graduating, working, saving, starting a family. Thavy decided to attend community college in Portland to be near her family.

We visited the beach, went fishing and crabbing, and toured museums. The whole family still came with us practically everywhere. That's how we dated, as a pledged couple, for the three years following our official engagement.

The next year, in the midst of my sophomore studies and romance, a letter arrived with the most incredible news. My brother and sister were alive! I was shocked. I thought someone was playing a sick, practical joke on me.

Cousin Ang Khen, still a major radio celebrity in Cambodia, continued to receive letters from Khmer people seeking some kind of help. She had understood my decision to run away. I'm one of the reasons her own marriage was in serious decline. She hung on to her marriage to chun out of her loyalty to Khmer tradition. Larony had written her for news about relatives who might still be alive. He had heard rumors that I had survived and might be living in America. Cousin Khen got my address from a cousin and forwarded Larony's letter to me.

Reading his letter, my hands trembled and I wept. I was no longer alone. My brother and his wife and three children were alive. Also, my elder sister Mealanie had survived and had three children, all boys. She had reunited with her husband Voeun, whom I'd met in Keo Poeur in 1976. In an instant, I had ten close blood relatives. I was overjoyed.

Together with Larony's letter to Cousin Ang Khen, Cousin Chun had enclosed a personal check for $500 with a note: "Please, please accept this check and spend it as you see fit. I hope it helps." The note was signed "Cousin Chun."

Pride reared its head. My first reaction was to return the check with a thank you note. I did write the note, but cashed the check and sent it all to Larony. I could not forget that my cousins had rescued me from the refugee camp and helped me come to America, a debt of gratitude that could never be repaid.

Larony's letter began a five-year struggle and great personal sacrifice to bring my surviving family members to America. Thavy, who was good with paperwork, helped me with the numerous forms. We went to the INS nervously holding hands and grew even closer. We shared our frustrations, our family troubles, our finances.

Soon after the Vietnamese army invaded Cambodia in 1979, increasing numbers of refugees had fled, including my brother, my sister, and their families. Overwhelmed by hundreds of thousands of refugees, Thailand had closed its borders. New arrivals were forced to return and the Khmer Rouge butchered the returnees.

The two families had managed to stay in an unofficial border refugee camp loosely organized by Cambodian resistance fighters. However, the Vietnamese army shelled the camp daily; my family could be killed any moment. They would be safer in Thailand, even as illegal refugees. I had to send money so they could bribe their way into a U.N.-sponsored refugee camp in Thailand.

Six months after I'd received Larony's letter, my brother and sister found a guide to get them into the refugee camp and escape the shelling. The cost would be $1,200. They told me to send the money through a Jesuit priest in Bangkok, a Father John Bingham, who had converted them and many others to Christianity. The priest traveled to the border camp to give the money to Larony. But it took

$2,400, not $1,200, to get them into the Thai refugee camp. It might as well have been $2.4 million for poor students like us.

I began to skip lunch, walk, and skimp in many other ways. The financial cost was the least of it. I was also physically and emotionally exhausted now. It took our combined efforts to file papers, make phone calls, and pitch in money. We filed and refiled INS forms, had our fingerprints taken several times. It was a four-hour round trip each time we had to drive to the INS in Portland. We waited on the phone for twenty minutes at a time, produced and reproduced birth certificates and authentications, all on top of school and double jobs.

Thavy and I spent the summer and Christmas of 1984 working. I was on a work-study program at an architectural library, and I also worked as a part-time translator. I grabbed any work opportunity I could. The scholarship paid for my school and tuition, but Larony and Mealanie and their respective families required a lot of money to survive. Thavy cleaned houses. Twenty dollars here, another twenty there, put it in my pocket, and then send it to them in Thailand. Thavy and I skipped meals to save money, knowing full well that my siblings and their children had a more desperate need.

By 1986, our engagement was three years old, the longest ever, or so said those who I think only wanted to party. Once again, pressure from friends and the community pushed us, this time into the final stage of our commitment to each other.

And so on August 2, 1986, Thavy and I were married in an elaborate Khmer wedding ceremony in Oregon. Even Cousin Ang Khen and her sister came. Min Moeun, who had arrived in America, and his wife gave me away, while Thavy's mother gave her away. At long last, Thavy moved to Eugene to be with me as my wife and complete her college studies.

My brother and sister were not faring so well. Being illegal Thai residents meant that my siblings and their families had to hide in underground tunnels every time the Thai police searched the camp. Many illegal aliens were caught and forced to return to Cambodia. My family were safe in the camp, but only as long as they were not detected. They had to become legal refugees to qualify to stay in the refugee camp and to receive extra UNHCR food rations. More importantly, when they were legal refugees, I could sponsor them to come into the United States. And so Thavy and I had to send more money to Thailand every month so the two families could buy their legal refugee status in Thailand. This expenditure added severe financial strain.

For five years, we sent money in secret. Only two others knew about the transactions: the famed Jesuit priest, Father John Bingham; and Aunt Putsyar, my father's youngest sister. We sent money via these trusted confidants to safely get it to the two families. But one month our regular money order went missing and the two families went hungry and were in debt. The following month we were forced to borrow more money and send two months' worth. We endured the constant financial hardship on behalf of the two families.

Aunt Putsyar's husband, Uncle Sonn Nosay, was a high-ranking official in the border camps and had access to all the refugee camps along the Thai and Cambodian border. Thavy and I sent on average $200 every month, including bribe monies and extra fees, to help protect the families from abuse and deportation. It was a very large sum for us full-time college students.

A life of struggle was nothing new to me, but this process drained a great deal of my precious resources. In 1984 the poverty line in the United States was approximately $13,000. Thavy and I lived on or earned only $8,000 a year, and approximately $2,500 of that regularly went to the two families in the refugee camp. And so we were already living far below the established poverty line and were considered "dirt poor." We barely broke even after paying for rent, food, and gasoline. This fact escaped many people, including the two families that Thavy and I were supporting.

I thought about giving up school. But if I give up school now, I thought, I'll lose the credits I've already earned. I'll also lose time because the courses must be taken in a certain sequence in order for me to graduate. I decided I couldn't afford to quit school. Thavy understood. I took out as many student loans as I could qualify for to support the families of my two refugee siblings.

The office of the Honorable Senator Mark O. Hatfield of Oregon helped me with the paperwork to obtain legal status required for sponsorship. Thavy's family and countless friends pulled strings and pushed for support. Thousands of trips, phone calls, and letters later, my epic battle with the INS bureaucracy finally ended.

In 1988, after paying more than $18,000 in cash—an astounding amount for us—the two families were granted legal status in a refugee camp in Thailand. Thavy and I were worn out, emotionally exhausted, and nearly bankrupt with over $13,000 in debt, mostly in the form of student loans. It would take us over a decade to repay the lenders.

The two families were subsequently approved for resettlement in 1989 and relocated to a transit center in the Philippines for medical clearance and preparation for life in the United States. Thavy and I eagerly awaited their arrival, but at the same time we were also worried sick: we had no idea how to support them when they got here.

On June 12, 1988, a full year after the original date of my expected graduation, I finally received my landscape architecture degree from the University of Oregon. I was a special guest of Oregon's senator Mark O. Hatfield, the commencement speaker. The beaming senator greeted me under the glare of local and national television cameras. Over brunch, we chatted about the expected arrival of my siblings and their families in Oregon. "It's good to know influential people," I said. "Thank you for your assistance, sir." The scene was captured by a special *CBS News* camera crew.

Present was none other than Brian T. Ellis, the same senior *CBS News* Asia Bureau chief who, long ago, had bought me ice cream in Thailand. In fact, the ice cream event had occurred exactly ten years before. We had had no contact whatsoever over the past decade. A friend had called Brian Ellis to tell him of the commencement and Mr. Ellis had decided to surprise me. "I didn't think you'd survive the refugee camp," he said. "Now you're graduating from college. Ronnie, you're a reaffirmation of the human spirit."

Brian was by then a senior producer at CBS News. He decided on a follow-up story to the documentary *What Happened to Cambodia* that he had produced ten years earlier. Once again, I was prominently featured in his production. For three days, he and his news crew followed me around to record my activities, including the brunch with Senator Mark Hatfield, the graduation ceremonies, and the party that my wife Thavy and friends gave in my honor. It was aired later that month on CBS News's *Sunday Morning with Charles Kuralt*.

Concurrent with graduation, I completed my internship at the Willamette National Forest in Eugene, Oregon. This experience helped me find employment as a landscape architect and planner for the Deschutes National Forest in Bend, Oregon. This position was my first full-salary professional job. Thavy continued her studies at the community college in Bend.

On a freezing cold January morning in 1989, the two families—now including brand-new babies—arrived at the Portland International Airport (PDX). Once again, my family and friends were in the crowd. The *COIN 6 News* camera and crew had their bright lights on. *The Oregonian* sent a reporter and a photographer.

I had last seen Larony over fourteen years ago, and now he was making his way through the crowd, followed by his family and his new baby girl, named Amie Yimsut in my honor. We recognized each other immediately from the pictures we had mailed. The reunion included sobs all around and a quiet hug with Larony, then with my sister Mealanie holding her newborn son Lauro, barely a week old. We actually blocked traffic flow at PDX for a moment and some travelers stopped to watch and cheer. I continued to wipe my tears of joy.

America's newest immigrants were my family members. I held Lauro while Thavy carried Amie. My past, my present, and my future had come together in the choked traffic at the arrival gate.

The news reporters now rushed in to take pictures and ask questions. I obliged, pleased to share this happy moment of my life with the world. Although I was conscious of more challenges ahead to settle these pilgrims in their new home, I felt relief and a sense of closure. The twelve new arrivals shivered in their light summer clothing.

We lived four hours from PDX. Mealanie's brother-in-law Poeun lived only 10 miles away. My sister didn't feel comfortable staying at Poeun's house, so we chose to cram ourselves, eighteen in all, into my mother-in-law's two-bedroom apartment about 5 miles away. My poor mother-in-law, bless her big heart, was busy nearly twenty-four hours a day for two weeks, trying to keep everyone fed. She never once complained, not once, and she always had a big smile on her face. For this and for many other things, we all owed her a great deal. I will always be very grateful to this wonderful woman, the other mother in my life.

My longtime family friends the Mullers, the Stephens, and the Perkinses opened their hearts, providing cash and basic essentials. They were such angels, particularly Audrey Muller, who took it upon herself to help the two families settle down. Without their generous hearts, I would not have been able to cope.

After a slow adaptation to the cold, my siblings and their families settled down nicely and became economically self-sustaining, to my delight and relief. Most of the children did well in school and quickly took on American speech and behavior. However, their parents had well-entrenched Khmer cultural values, so life as new American immigrants was not a picnic. We encouraged them to learn and to rely on themselves, but we all pitched in to help when necessary.

I had now accomplished two of my major goals: completing a college education and bringing my siblings to America. I sat back and looked at my life. My times had been difficult, but I had done my best. I put myself through four years of high school and six years of college. It was a decade of hard work and sacrifice to support twelve people, not counting Thavy and myself. This made me feel good and increased my self-esteem.

After Thavy graduated in 1989 with associate degrees in accounting, computer science, and nursing, we decided to have a child. We wanted a girl, but either sex was fine. We decided to get a dog to practice our parenting skills, so we'd know how to take care of a living being.

Itchiewawa the puppy was all over us. He slept on our bed and became totally spoiled. We trained him until he knew where to go potty. He was our first baby.

By April 1990, the same month that we bought our first house, Thavy was expecting a baby girl. Perfect! She'd be able to help later with her younger siblings.

It was a pretty exciting time in our new home, with the baby kicking in Thavy's womb. Looking back, it was an easy pregnancy. However, late that July, I panicked—even with Lamaze birthing classes under my belt.

"I have a stomach ache, a stomach ache," Thavy groaned. We didn't know these were labor pains—after all, this was our first time.

When her water broke, I rushed her into our small car and headed for the hospital.

My first child, Samantha Rathanary, was born without complications.

Thavy's mother came. "Where's my granddaughter, where is she?" after seeing the baby, she went home.

"Oh," I said. "Is that it? Oh, okay." No grandpa or grandma to help us out as in the good old days.

By this time, I was enjoying the stability of a federal job for the Deschutes National Forest. I found my passion in social justice, civil rights, and environmental causes. Thavy found her niche, too. Life could not have been better for all of us. We had everything. Most importantly, we had each other.

Later, when our son Derrick Monorom came into our lives in December 1995, Thavy simply proclaimed, "No more kids! I have had enough!"

I had achieved the American dream. The orphan boy who ran for his life from Cambodia's Killing Fields now had a family of his own, a relatively stable professional career, and everything that he had ever needed or wanted. With much hard work of his own and some help from good people along the way, life couldn't be sweeter in the Land of the Free and the Home of the Brave. I should have been happy and content with my new life and role, as anyone else would.

I wasn't.

16

Back to the Past

Oregon State, Siem Reap, and Phnom Penh

The news sent arctic chills down my spine. A miraculous peace deal in Paris was to be followed by another miracle: Cambodia would have a democratic election that would install a parliament. If the news was true, then decades of warfare, genocide, and economic ruin were about to end for Cambodia and its traumatized people. This meant the end of Vietnamese invasions, liberations, and occupations; the end of freedom fighters, refugees, and infighting among the countless factions. After three decades, there would be peace by way of Paris.

In October 1991, Cambodia's warring factions, including the Khmer Rouge, signed the Paris Peace Accord. To help Cambodia get back on its feet, the United Nations was to spend $3 billion and send 25,000 peacekeepers, and about the same number of bureaucrats. The new foreign intervention in Cambodia was to begin in earnest.

How mind-boggling! I never thought I'd see this in my lifetime. Here I was living in Bend, Oregon, and my homeland was going through a huge change. At long last, the Vietnamese conflict in this troubled region ended with pen strokes by twenty-one nations, which, ironically, included most of the countries that began it all: the United States, China, the former USSR, Vietnam, and many others.

The news awakened the frightened boy in me. He'd been asleep, in a comatose state, really, for over a decade. No longer. Buried beneath the challenge of making it in America, years of suppressed memories broke out. For months I found myself crying often. Raw pain and anger assailed me with voices and screams. Thavy often woke me up because I was crying in my dreams and in my sleep.

Now I understood why I didn't feel comfortable with this easy life in good old Oregon, USA. I had been running away from my shadows. I wasn't at peace.

I had much anger and pain inside me. My past still haunted me, and now it had caught up with me.

I must heal something inside me, I thought. This is something I cannot do in America. I must return to where it all began, to Cambodia, whatever is left of it, I thought to myself. I realized that I couldn't deny my history any longer. It was time to reconcile with my past.

I accepted the fact that terrible things did happen to me. I used the voices and screams to fuel me when I ran low. I tried to figure out who I was and why I was still here. And I began to know that I'd been a victim, and now a survivor. I had been many things, but I hadn't been myself.

I began to speak out. I talked to strangers, to kids, to audiences at community forums near my home in Bend, Oregon. I cried openly, something I couldn't do before. People shared my grief. I communicated via newspapers and television about what had happened to my people, my family, and me. I wrote short essays of my bitter experiences. Later, after my first trip back to Cambodia in 1992, I wrote "The Tonle Sap Lake Massacre." This story was published by Yale University Press in Dith Pran's 1997 anthology *Children of Cambodia's Killing Fields*.

I began to feel worthy of being alive again. I began to return to my past. I started with the Chens because I felt that I still owed them. Since 1984, Thavy and I had visited once a year at the Chens' house on the East Coast, some 3,000 miles away. Later, the kids went with us. The Chens still love and care for me, and I feel the same about them. They love my children very much. I'm a bit jealous that Thavy gets along with them so well.

Cousin Chun and I became close again. The couple was proud of my accomplishments. When I told them I wanted to see the old country, they questioned my sanity and feared for my safety. Since the big migration of 1975, the Khmer have just not returned to Cambodia.

"We escaped with our lives," said Cousin Khen. "No matter how much we miss Cambodia, we do not go back. We just don't."

My siblings objected, too. "We can't understand why you'd risk everything for a trip to that dreadful place, no matter how brief," said my elder sister Mealanie.

"There's nothing there for you," my elder brother Larony said. He described Cambodia as hopeless and evil, a chasm void of light, a place to stay as far away from as possible. "Why do you want to return to that black hole?"

I had no good answer. News from Cambodia is rarely good. It is no wonder that very few Khmer Americans like to talk about the old country. Many friends and family have refused to return; there is nothing to gain by looking back to the old country, they say. Who can blame them?

"Your life is here now," said my American friends. How could I share what I felt with my fellow Americans? Before they met me, few knew where Cambodia was, let alone its bitter history.

"I have to," was all I could say. The urge was so primal I had to go. But whatever I found there would not matter to me one way or another.

I boarded a jumbo jet during a cold morning of February 1992, terrified but resolute. Cambodia was still the source of my darkest fears. It was the place of my darkest nightmares.

After many restless hours of plastic-tasting food, transit stops, and connecting flights, Thai Airways flight 875 from Bangkok approached Phnom Penh Pochentong International. Fourteen years ago, it had taken me two weeks of dangerous treks through jungles, seven months in prisons and refugee camps, and five days of flying and landing at international airports to reach America. To return took only nineteen hours.

In February 1978 I had left, a frightened boy. In February 1992 I returned, a scared man. Ready or not, I was now here, a tourist on a four-week search through rubble. My years of waiting and longing would end here in the old country that I had left years ago.

The jet plane began its descent. I found it impossible to steady my emotions. Will I be accepted in my native country? What will I find here? How do I behave? How do I handle these feelings that threaten to burst?

I still had no answers by the time we were on our final approach to Pochentong International Airport. I looked through the small window and saw open rice fields and slender palm trees. I felt tears on my cheeks.

"First time back, huh?" a voice next to me boomed in Khmer. I was surprised that the words had come from a smiling, middle-aged white man beside me.

I nodded and turned to the window, savoring my reunion with my Cambodia.

The wheels of the Boeing 737–400 slammed on the tarmac, rolled for a few moments, and came to a full stop. While in Bangkok, I had set my watch to Cambodia time. It was two o'clock in the afternoon.

The passengers began to stir. I took a deep breath to compose myself. For the many overseas Khmer on the plane, it must have been their first trip home, too. Excitement was clear in their eyes and voices. I also sensed their apprehension. Like lost children, we were afraid yet happy to return home.

I was the last to disembark. A blast of hot, humid air and the smell of jet fuel hit my face. I descended into the heat with trepidation, thoughts rampant, heart quickening.

I hadn't really planned to do it. A spur-of-the-moment impulse drove me to kneel and kiss the black tarmac. I rose to see people smiling at my act of self-indulgence. One even applauded. I nodded politely and tried to smile in return.

A gentle breeze blew. The scents of Cambodia cut right through the airport smells. I filled my lungs with the aroma of just-harvested rice from the open paddies and the sweet smell of the tall sugar-palm tree flowers that marked the harvest season.

I'm back, I thought to myself. After fourteen years, I'm back.

I took off my jacket and walked to the tiny terminal's customs sign, which had both Khmer and English words. For a moment I felt as though I were in a foreign country.

I was last in line, sweating, searching for a familiar face in the crowd. Cousin Thie had not come to pick me up. Of course, I was only three days late.

When I sent my itinerary to Cousin Thie earlier, it had taken a month for his reply to reach me: If we missed each other at the airport we'd meet at Hotel Sukhalay in Phnom Penh where another cousin worked. Perhaps my response about schedule changes didn't get to Cousin Thie in time.

"Passport! Visa form!" said a chubby customs officer in a light-green Vietnamese uniform. I handed him my papers.

"What country you come from?" he said in English, flipping through my U.S. passport.

"Bangkok," I said. "It's on the visa form, sir."

"Where do you live?" he asked in Khmer. "Cambodia or United States?"

"I'm a U.S. citizen living in the USA," I replied in English and then quickly switched to Khmer realizing that he had spoken to me in Khmer.

He glanced at me, looked at my passport photograph and handed my passport to another uniformed man. The man took a quick look and passed my passport on to another agent. There were ten of them in a row.

This could take some time, I thought. I walked along the line until I got to the last two green uniforms. One stamped my passport and the other collected the $20 tourist visa fee. My ears rang at the inefficiency. Ten people and twenty-five minutes for something that could be done in less than two minutes by one person!

This is Cambodia, I told myself. Shut up.

At a counter toward the exit, two dark-green Vietnamese-looking uniforms sat waiting. One took my passport; the other took my entry visa form. I thought that after ten years of occupation and tens of thousands of deaths, the Vietnamese "liberators" had left Cambodia. But they were still here.

"Twenty dollars," one uniformed thief said in Khmer, looking away from me.

I was puzzled. "I paid the visa fee over there," I pointed to the ten officers sitting behind the long counter.

"Twenty-five dollars," the man said, a bit louder. The other began to flip the pages of my passport violently. "Twenty-five or thirty?"

I was dumbfounded. They were demanding ransom for my passport! Then I remembered . . . that's how it works here: the more I resist, the more I pay.

"Well?" he said arrogantly.

Anger welled up inside me. I pulled out two fives and a bunch of one-dollar bills and tossed them on the counter. They went after the flying notes. I grabbed my passport and bags and walked to a door jammed with people.

Another uniform stopped me. "Come this way, please," he yelled over the noise. He asked me to open my two suitcases. Four uniforms rummaged through my neatly packed items, mostly gifts for relatives. They had questions for just about everything they pulled out of my bags.

I controlled my temper pretty well. I was getting tired of the charade but I followed him to see how far this would go. When one asked for money "to stop the search," I finally lost it.

"Please! Lauk [Sir], please do your job, this is your duty!! I have nothing to hide, just do your job, Lauk!" I fired out in Khmer.

The inspectors looked at each other. They didn't want to draw attention to themselves. I raised my voice even more. "Are you through, Lauk? May I go now . . . ? Lauk?" I emphasized the Khmer term for "Sir" to show my disgust and frustration.

"You may go now," one said, pointing his open palm to the exit. They looked so stunned I almost forgot my anger. It took me a while to repack my suitcases. I cursed in English and Khmer, loud enough for all to hear.

"Passport, please," a police officer by the doorway stopped me. I gave him a sharp look. He waved me out the door, into the crowd.[1]

"Taxi, sir!"

"Taxi, taxi!"

The mob of drivers yelled, rushing at me. Two of them pulled at my suitcases. I yelled and quickly, pointed to a scrawny man, choosing him as my driver. I can beat him if I have to, I thought to myself.

The little man grabbed my luggage. For his size, he had amazing strength. I quickly got into the taxicab.

"Sir, one hundred riel, one hundred riel, sir," the two who had pulled at my suitcases ran alongside the cab. I laughed, shaking my head. Welcome, indeed, to Cambodia.

Strangely, the driver didn't ask where I was going. I had been to Phnom Penh a couple times when I was a boy, but I had no idea where in the city I was now.

"Bawng, Hotel Sukhalay, please," I said in Khmer.

"*Baht tean* [Yes, sir]," he replied respectfully.

Cars, trucks, motorcycles, and bicycles were all over the road every which way, blowing their horns as loudly as my driver did. I decided I would never drive here. But Phnom Penh is not Cambodia, I told myself.

The taxicab stopped abruptly in front of the hotel. Thump! A bicycle crashed into the taxi's rear end. A young woman was flat on her back and very upset. She didn't have a helmet on. In fact, none of the bicyclists here wore helmets.

The cab driver disembarked casually, wiped the dent on his bumper, and opened the trunk to get my luggage. The woman got up, furiously straightened her old bicycle and left. I was dumbfounded.[2]

The driver followed me into the Sukhalay, an old, run-down hotel, and set my large suitcases on the floor next to the counter. A woman smiled from behind the counter.

"How much?" I asked, remembering that I should have negotiated the fare before I got in the taxi.

"Five dollars, *tean*," he said quietly.

I turned to address the hotel clerk. "What's the going rate from Pochentong to here?"

"Oh . . . between four and seven dollars," she said cheerfully.

I gave the cab driver seven dollars. We had traversed about 4 miles of a very congested road. He counted the money twice.

"You pay too much," he said, returning two dollars.

What an honest man, I thought. Then I remembered that tipping was never part of Khmer culture.

"No, Bawng, that's for your extra effort," I gave him back the money. "Please keep it."

The big smile on his face made my day. I forgot Pochentong's customs officer altogether.

I asked for Sinoun, the cousin I had not yet met. She was a maid at the hotel, which her brother-in-law owned. The clerk went to find her. A middle-aged woman appeared and greeted me in the traditional Khmer way, with her palms folded together and her head bowed.

"*Soursdey*, Bawng Srei." I returned her sampass. "Have you seen Thie recently?"

"They've been waiting for you the past few days," my stranger cousin said excitedly. "They didn't think you'd come."

"They? Who are they?"

"Ming Sross and Nek Gnoy were here with Thie, waiting for you. Thie left by boat for Siem Reap early this morning. The others left to buy a boat ticket to Siem Reap, too. So sorry, you just missed them. Oh, there they are!" she pointed across the busy street.

We went to the sidewalk and I waved at the two vaguely familiar faces. It was indeed Aunt Sross, the wife of my late Uncle Thongdy, with her son, Cousin Gnoy, the elder brother of Cousin Thie. Quickly, they dodged bikes and motorcycles to get to my side of the street. They hugged me unabashedly. I hadn't seen them in nearly seventeen years. They looked so much older. Life is tough in Cambodia.

"You're here, finally! I can't believe it!" Aunt Sross cried. By a crowded street choked with people and traffic, my past finally caught up with me. I was now with my relatives in my old country.

Aunt Sross and Gnoy decided to delay their departure a day or two. We spent a few nights in my hotel room, which had two double beds for $25 per night. They couldn't believe I was paying $25 a night for a room. As a civil servant, Cousin Gnoy earned that much in a month.

"You must be doing well, Nak," Aunt Sross said, addressing me by my nickname. "You live in heaven and now you've come back." She always carried herself like a princess, perhaps recalling her youth as the only child of wealthy Sino Khmer parents.

To Aunt Sross and everyone else here, America is heaven, Cambodia is hell, and, of course, anyone from America is wealthy. I felt duty-bound to open their eyes.

For three days and two nights, I told them of the America I knew as a boy, orphan, and immigrant: a great place, but nowhere near heaven. I told them of the more than two million Americans and some Khmer in prisons, with more than two million on probation due to the lack of space. I told them about the more than four million homeless Americans, begging or living on charity, and of the millions more in debt. I had to give them the good, the bad, and particularly the ugly about life in America. I described the racism, the rat race, the materialism, and selfishness. I tried to show them the big picture.

I failed. They didn't believe me.

Before Aunt Sross and Gnoy left for Siem Reap, I gave $250 to my aunt for her family. It was, perhaps, the biggest sum of money Aunt Sross had ever held. It only proved that dollars grew on trees in America. I didn't tell them how long it took me to save that amount. I did not want to rain on her parade about the growth of dollar trees.

There were three choices for my trip to Siem Reap: an ancient Russian airplane, an old bus on a long, bumpy road infested with Khmer Rouge guerrillas, or a long and dangerous ride on an old, leaky boat. I chose the thirty-minute flight. I prayed the whole time I was airborne.

I had expected either Aunt Sross or Cousin Gnoy to ask Cousin Thie to pick me up at the tiny Siem Reap municipal airport, but he wasn't there. I took the hotel bus to town.

Siem Reap looked just the way it had when I was a little boy. Children still herded oxen and water buffalo in the rice fields. The ride to town was short and pleasant, much shorter than I recalled. Along the sides of the road, vendors sold sugar palm and other treats. Memories brought on tears. The sights, sounds, and smells were just as I remembered. I was truly back in time.

It had taken me more than fourteen years to return to my old village, but here I was. My spirit had never soared so high, my mental anguish was never stronger with the great fear of the boy still inside me.

I checked into a hotel, took a quick shower, changed into fresh clothes, and walked out with my backpack. I could have walked the two miles to the old market where my home had been, but, for sentimental reasons, I chose to ride a *romork*, the local version of a rickshaw. Hard to believe that romorks were still hauling people and goods around my hometown.

About a half mile down the road, an old Honda motorcycle caught up with us and drove alongside the romork, its driver flashing me a bright smile. I thought we were about to be robbed.

"Is that you, Nak?" the smiling man asked, waving the driver to a stop. Only family called me "Nak."

"Yes, it's me," I said, getting out of the romork for a closer look.

"Nak," he said, standing up with a wide grin, "I'm Thie, your cousin." He was a bit taller than me.

"Cousin Thie? I didn't recognize you at all." I hugged him awkwardly. "Where have you been? I was looking for you in Phnom Penh and in Siem Reap."

"I waited for you in Phnom Penh," he said, "and I waited for you at the Siem Reap airport. I saw you, but I wasn't sure if it was you, so I followed you to the hotel."

I was so happy on the bus that I hadn't noticed the motorbike close behind. Thie was expecting a "tall guy with shoulder-length black hair," as Aunt Sross and his brother Gnoy described me. But the heat had driven me to a barbershop the day I got on the plane to Siem Reap. I had my hair cut very short, almost shaved.

After paying the romork driver, I hopped on Cousin Thie's Honda motorbike and off we went. At his house a good crowd of people had already gathered from near and far to greet the Khmer from America. All claimed to be related to me in some way or another, but I couldn't figure out who was who.

I planned to spend the next three weeks with Aunt Sross, whose family had built a home right where my old house had once stood. I was born right here, on this very spot.

I had a strange experience on my first night on my old turf.

At about two o'clock in the morning, I was still wide awake. It would already be daylight back in Oregon. A dog howled. Soon another dog and then another, and another, until the entire neighborhood was completely filled with howling. I became even more fearful when Aunt Sross began to curse. Her foul language used against the annoying dogs unnerved me. Almost an hour went by before quiet returned. I felt like a scared child again. A lost little boy who had run for his life not so long ago.

I must have dozed off momentarily in the chilled morning Siem Reap air. Suddenly I woke up, hearing a commotion on the dirt road in front of the house. The repeated thumps scared me. I felt like I was back at Ta Source Hill, hearing the beating and clubbing all over again. I felt like that little boy again, and I wanted to run for my life. I struggled out of the mosquito net, trying to figure out what timeframe period I was in. My mind was playing tricks on me. I was back in time and running for my life—scared shitless.

"Where are you going, Nak?" Aunt Sross whispered.

"Something's happening down the road, Ming," I whispered back, prepared to get out of there.

"Stay where you are," she said. I ducked back inside the mosquito net. The beating sounds went on. It sounded like a baseball bat hitting flesh. The massacre scene at Ta Source Hill some fourteen years earlier returned to me. I was sweating, panting. I began to shake uncontrollably—just as I had as a boy.

I stayed awake long after everything was quiet again, but finally fell asleep. When I opened my eyes, it was late in the afternoon. No one had dared to rouse me. They had politely allowed me to sleep peacefully.

I took a cold shower sourced from my old well, remembering how I had hauled water for the plants around the house so many years ago, in peacetime. I had a late lunch alone. My relatives sat around, watching me eat my lunch.

When I described my worries from the previous night, they laughed their heads off. It seemed that a couple of drunkards were killing a dog for meat.[3] These bastards couldn't have picked a worse moment to bludgeon the poor dog to death. In the daylight, surrounded by my family's laughter, I felt foolish.

After the tasty lunch of rice, pan-fried lake fish, and sour fish soup, Cousin Thie took me around the old hometown on his aging Honda. We visited relatives I knew well, far and near.

Honorable Brother Som in Krobey Riel and the family friends in Dorn Swar couldn't believe their eyes. I enjoyed their astonished faces, as they at long last recognized me, a ghost that had come back to life. I was no longer the skinny boy they remembered. They never thought I was alive, let alone back in town in the flesh.

I could only thank them again and again for helping me after I escaped the massacre. "When you took me into your home that day fourteen years ago, you became my family," I said. We shed tears together.

We spent a good part of the day reliving old times and mourning the deceased. Every one of them was surprised that I'm still a living ghost to them, as they continue to be even to this day.

I thought I had plenty of spending money but I was forced to sell my $600 Olympus camera and accessories for only $250. I was seeing too many poor relatives, including people I wasn't even sure were related to me.

Before I left Cambodia, I wanted to visit Tapang, where I had suffered the most physical and mental anguish during my childhood. I told Aunt Sross and her family about my plan. "I want to let the Mith Chass know that there's one witness to their atrocities who's still alive," I said.

Cousin Thie brought me there on his trusty motorbike. What years ago had taken me three days of walking now took a mere two hours.

In Tapang I spent half the day with Phan, the former Mith Chass who had helped me survive those dark two years in that town long ago. Phan was a small, skinny guy. We were about the same age. Although he was a Mith Chass, he had taught me how to take care of a palm tree, how to make sugar palm, and how to catch frogs and crabs; in short, how to survive in Tapang where very few Mith Thmey had managed to survive.

Phan was still skinny and an even smaller man now. He had a wife and four kids. He was shocked to see me alive. I told him my story. He couldn't believe it. Then and now, whenever we meet, he hugs me repeatedly to make sure I'm real.

Almost the entire town came to see me. Many of the older people recognized me. They found it amazing that, of the hundreds of Mith Thmey forced to go to Tapang, I alone survived and actually returned to the miserable town.

"Don't you remember me?" a man called out from the crowd.

"No, I'm sorry I don't," I said. His face was only vaguely familiar.

They had no school, no clean water, nothing but the little rice they grew in this poor region. Their Angkar's Great Leap Forward had reduced them to a pathetic rubble. They could no longer torture Mith Thmey like me. They no longer had the power of choosing life or death for others.

"You must remember me, we used to do things together," another called out.

"Sorry, I don't remember. I came to see my old friend here," I said politely. I felt sorry for them. I wanted to help them improve their lives, these people who had hurt me and my family.[4]

When Phan took me to the site of my old hut, I cried. This was where I had lived in absolute misery.

I secretly gave Phan some gifts and 35,000 riel—about $50. The money would save his family from starvation when a devastating flood came the following year.[5]

Thie said we had to leave. Tapang was in a remote part of the countryside, and he didn't want to be here after dark. His usual grin was gone.

"It's only two o'clock, Thie."

"Yes, that's right. Still, it's time to get out of here."

On the way back, I asked Thie to take me south to the edge of Tonle Sap Lake where my family and neighbors were killed. We passed Kok Poh and I recognized Aunt Samon's home. This village was where I'd befriended that little dog years ago.

"About fourteen years ago, this family gave me a tiny meal. I must thank them," I told Thie. He was anxious to return to safety, but he pulled over.

Aunt Samon was flabbergasted. She introduced me to her youngest daughter, who had been only two years old when I came to her home early in 1978. Angkar had killed her husband and sons soon after I left. I hugged her, feeling her pain and loss.

"It wasn't because of you, Nak," she assured me. Angkar killed indiscriminately before the invading Vietnamese Armed Forces kicked them out.

I gave her my last $20 and prepared to go to the killing site. "Oh, no, no, you mustn't go there," Aunt Samon was horrified. "There are bandits in that area; they'll take your liver and eat it raw."

"They eat human liver? Raw?" Then, I reminded myself, anything is possible in Cambodia.

"Please, don't," Aunt Samon pleaded. "You mustn't go there."

"Are you coming, Nak?" Cousin Thie was on his bike. "Hurry up!" he yelled, nervously puffing on a cigarette.

Perhaps it was because it was getting late and we were very tired that we headed for Siem Reap and I didn't get to see the place where I had almost died so long ago.

As I prepared to leave Siem Reap, I realized that I still owed my affluent cousin Yim Sary $300 that I had borrowed during my stay, but I was still joyful. I had come home. I got to see most, if not all, of the relatives and friends who had survived the Khmer Rouge, and I quickly repaid my debt.

I looked nostalgically at my old town. The Spean Thmor (Concrete Bridge) was still a big landmark in Siem Reap, but it looked smaller, shorter, only a third of what I remembered it to be. A hundred yards away, sugar palm was still being sold and people bought and drank it there. Chinese merchants were still rich and becoming more powerful. People still resented them. I walked on that bridge and looked down.

The river had taken on a character I don't like. Because of a dam downstream, it was more stagnant than before. There was more trash, including plastics and bags. Mosquitoes bred there. Water was sparse, even in the rainy season. If I were mayor of Siem Reap I'd have had that river cleaned up in a minute, the dam opened, and to hell with the dry season or the Khmer Rouge.

I'd kept my promises. I had expressed my gratitude to those who took me in when I escaped the massacre. The site of the Tonle Sap Lake Massacre still haunted me. When the time is right, I thought, I will return and come full circle. Silently, I promised my deceased family and friends that I would return to the massacre site one day. I'm not very religious but I do know I've been given another chance at life.

A second life is like being reborn, but with renewed wisdom. Life can be so brief. Each breath is borrowed time. I know the difference between living and existing. I learned not to take life too seriously, not to focus too much on the little things. I learned to prioritize.

And yet, many times, I find myself complacent and taking things for granted again and again. When I see myself slip, I kick myself. And, when anyone asks, I share what I have learned. This sharing is, I believe, most significant of all.

17

Back in Time

Oregon State and Phnom Penh

I was driving home to Bend, Oregon. Thavy and I were talking about the great Thanksgiving weekend we had just had with family and friends in Portland.

The snowfall continued but we were nice and warm inside our 4 × 4 Nissan Pathfinder. Samantha, now two years old, dozed in her car seat in the back, next to the terrier Itchiewawa, who was a year older than she was. I glanced at the dark sky. Snowflakes continued to blanket the Oregon Cascades. The Cascades Pass, which goes by Mount Hood, was familiar to us in all kinds of weather. Heck, we had driven over 50,000 miles on this very same road. In fact, I knew just about every curve and turn of this particular stretch of Oregon's Highway 26.

Going downhill, I was irritated. The car in front of us had no tire chains and it was slipping and sliding in the slushy snow. I decided to pass him.

I slowed down, gently tapping my brakes. Since I had obtained my license in 1981, I had always been a careful, defensive driver. I had my foot on the brake, so the Pathfinder was running at about 30 miles per hour, not very fast.

I was negotiating a slight curve when I saw oncoming headlights and automatically hit the brakes. I couldn't stop the car. It continued to slide in the slush; I had no traction. To avoid a head-on collision, I spun the steering wheel to the right.

Like a movie stunt car, my trusty 4 × 4 turned 180 degrees in the opposite direction and came to a complete stop on the shoulder of the highway. After about two seconds, the soft shoulder gave way.

"Hang on!" I yelled to Thavy. The car sank to one side, and the driver-side door hit the earth. Thavy screamed.

The vehicle rolled over the steep embankment, picking up speed. We bounced, held tight by our seatbelts. It felt like a roller coaster.

God bless whoever designed seat belts, I said to myself. My mind remained clear as the vehicle rolled over and over down the embankment. Thavy continued to scream.

"Hang on!" I yelled again as the windshield began to crack before my eyes. The roof started to buckle and collapse. Then a small tree stopped the vehicle. We hung upside-down.

Fearing a fire, I quickly shut off the engine. I put the transmission into "park," unbuckled my seatbelt, and kicked the door open.

"Are you okay, Thavy?" I said, reaching into the back. Thavy was still screaming, so I knew she was fine.

Samantha was swaying upside-down quietly, her black eyes round and reflecting light. I unbuckled her as quickly and as gently as I could. Itchiewawa jumped up and down, excited as usual.

"Everyone all right?" a man asked.

"I think so. Could you hold my daughter, please?" I grabbed the dog while Thavy got out on her own and took Samantha from the stranger, hugging her tightly. Our baby girl yawned, her nap interrupted.

Except for a few bruises, we were all right. It was a miracle. The vehicle, on the other hand, was a total wreck. It took two tow trucks four hours to haul the Pathfinder out of the embankment.

It was the closest I had come to death since the 1978 lakeside massacre nearly fourteen years ago. Really, it wasn't even close, but it was close enough to jolt me. I had been taking my life for granted. We got a ride home, and on the way I reflected how unpredictable life is. A split second could change it forever. The jolt got me thinking: Why am I still alive?

Again, Cambodia was on my mind. I had given time to my loved ones, now I had to give time to myself. But I could heal myself only in Cambodia. I was certain of these thoughts that night after the accident, even before we got home.

The tree that stopped our vehicle had lost almost 50 degrees from its straight-up position. For years I checked out the tree when I drove Highway 26. It long outlived the Pathfinder.

I became restless. I wanted to go back to Cambodia, but I felt guilty. This need to resolve my "issues" was completely for my benefit. But what would I do about my family, my friends, and my job? On the other hand, if I didn't attend to my inner traumas, I might never heal.

The accident pushed me into making a decision. I decided to put our lives on hold and applied for a year of sabbatical leave.

Thavy said, "I don't like it, but I understand. You do what you have to do." She had been married to me long enough. She understood, and that was enough for me.

Thavy and Samantha moved closer to my in-laws in Portland, Oregon. Thavy continued her career with the Forest Service in Portland for the time being, until it was safe for them to join me in Cambodia.

On March 18, 1993, four months after the accident, I was on my way back to Cambodia. For this second trip, however, I was not a tourist.

I applied and was accepted as a volunteer of CANDO, the Cambodian-American National Development Organization, which was generously funded by USAID. U.N.-sponsored Cambodian elections were scheduled for May 23, 1993. Along with 25,000 U.N. peacekeepers and bureaucrats, I faced a daunting task in helping with the elections, in human resource development, technology transfer, democracy, and with human rights. Cambodia was awash with problems, but I was more than ready.

In fact, I was eager, willing, and—whatever it would take—I was determined to do my best to help Cambodia. Along the way, I hoped to come to terms with my private pain.

Departure day was a rush. At the tiny municipal airport in Redmond, Oregon, I had less than five minutes to bid Thavy and Sam good-bye. My little girl had not yet turned three. Thavy was either sad or boiling mad, I couldn't quite tell.

I hated farewells so I quickly went aboard, all torn up inside, keenly conscious of my separation from Thavy and Samantha.

In San Francisco, I had exactly thirty minutes to run and catch a United Airlines flight that would take me some 9,000 miles from San Francisco to Pochentong, with a stopover in Bangkok.

Rushing madly through the cavernous airport, I felt a sort of déjà vu. I was here some fifteen years ago, a young refugee. Then, I was also lost and rushing. I found my departure gate barely in time.

My seat was in the midsection of the jumbo jet. It was only after I had tossed my duffel bag in the overhead compartment that I was finally able to relax and read the CANDO directives and list of volunteers.

Seven other volunteers were supposed to be on this flight. I read the names to myself. Tony DeRapp, Steven Hollister . . . wait a minute, these are American names! Oh, here are Khmer Americans: Peter Chea, Fahrid Sou, Suling Khou, and Sophia Lor.

I was pleasantly surprised that we had two Khmer American women volunteers. I admired their guts. I knew it took much just to get this far.

When we landed in Thailand, the resourceful Suling left to spend the night with her Thai friends somewhere in Bangkok while the rest of us got ready to check into those six-hour rental rooms near the airport. However, a woman at the counter said our room reservations were no good.

"No good? What do you mean, 'no good'?!" Fahrid yelled at the woman, demanding a room. She was almost in tears when I stepped in and all of us dragged him away. The group was embarrassed.

We finally managed to get a few small twin bedrooms.

At Pochentong Airport in Phnom Penh, a Khmer-Chinese-American woman in her late forties stood at the doorway, smiling broadly at me. "Ronnie?"

I had a feeling she was the director of CANDO, Thida Khus. I had never met Thida before, but we had corresponded a few times. I smiled back.

"Yes, I'm Ronnie. *Jumreap soeur.*"

She introduced Potong Chhun, Sophia's fiancé, and Wayne Wright, the first Caucasian CANDO volunteer, who was from Long Beach, California. We shook hands.

We packed the minivan and sedan with our baggage. Soon we pulled into the driveway of a huge, fenced villa. Orchids bloomed in the elegant, petite garden. I thought that we must be at the wrong house. At best, I had expected to stay in a wooden house, a thatched hut at worst. Here we were about to enter a massive mansion.

"Welcome to your new home," Thida said loudly and with pride.

"This is it? We're going to live here?" Fahrid was attempting sarcasm. We looked at him. No one laughed.

"Let's go inside. Everyone please grab a room," Thida said.

The villa had six sizable bedrooms, each with a private Western-style toilet and bath. On the first floor was a kitchen, a large dining room, and a living room area with a portable fan, color TV, and a VCR. The second floor had another living room with all the same furnishings. In the back, a utility shed housed a diesel generator, among other things.

I found out that CANDO rented the place for $2,500 a month, a huge amount of money in Cambodia and far too expensive by Cambodia's standards.

The group that had arrived two weeks earlier was now called CANDO I, and we became known as CANDO II. Each volunteer got $725 a month as a spending stipend and complimentary health insurance, which included a medical emergency airlift. We also had sick and annual leaves. It was not employment, but it was close enough to a full-time job, with quite decent compensation. Our "volunteer stipend" was twenty times the earnings of an average local Khmer.

Each volunteer put in $80 a month for communal meals and about $20 to cover salaries for the head cook and the night guard, who were paid very well by Cambodia's standards. These positions would get a starting salary of $40 a month, a sizable sum for locals. There were no other out-of-pocket expenses for us volunteers except personal expenses. CANDO paid for the rent, a daytime guard, and a live-in housekeeper who also doubled as cook's assistant.

Director Khus suggested that CANDO II elect a resident adviser (RA). Being a strong advocate of woman's rights, I nominated Suling, the sole female volunteer in the house. She wouldn't even consider it. Again and again, she adamantly refused to be nominated.

Then I was nominated, but I declined. I had chosen to work in the Forest Service to get away from politics, definitely away from having to deal with people. This aversion to politics was also why I volunteered for CANDO, a nongovernmental organization (NGO), instead of getting a well-compensated but more serious job with UNTAC. I also knew that the RA position would bring me nothing but headaches, for no extra pay or credit. Unfortunately, I won by a landslide—like it or not. Except for two votes, all were in my favor. One was my ballot for Suling with "NO RONNIE!" written on the other side. I think the other vote was Fahrid's.

I accepted the challenge, reluctantly, since no one else was willing to do this dirty job. I made sure everyone in CANDO II had a voice and a vote. The first order was ground rules for the communal life, hiring a cook and a night guard. Since we were new to Cambodia, finding a head cook and night guard wasn't easy. I asked all members of the household to nominate or suggest someone they knew and trusted. No one did anything about it except for Suling and me.

Suling nominated two relatives for head cook. I nominated one of my wife's distant relatives who had some guard experience. I didn't know anybody else even remotely qualified for the position. Except for Fahrid who chose not to vote, we agreed to hire one of Suling's relatives as cook and my nominee as night guard. Democracy worked its magic, or so we thought.

A couple of days later, Fahrid decided that we had practiced what he called "nepotism." (Before that day, I had not heard the word. I had to look it up.) "We shouldn't hire people we know or who are related to us," said Fahrid. A serious debate ensued and then a major argument broke out, with tons of yelling and shouting. Ultimately, it was six votes to one to retain the original vote. Fahrid became angrier and miserably bitter. His frustration boiled over and drove CANDO II practically to insanity. He blamed Suling and me for the turmoil when he himself was his own one-man band.

Being a Muslim, Fahrid did not eat pork so we made sure the cook prepared special food for him. It was a chore to accommodate a single man, but we did our best to show respect. He resented our eating pork in his presence. He spent much of his spare time arguing with others at CANDO II. I was his prime target and sort of a punching bag—either because he simply hated my guts or because of my RA title. I thought he would resort to violence at any moment. He had been a football player in high school, and he had a stocky, powerful body. Also, one could easily hire a hit man for less than $100 in Cambodia; I was warned by Fahrid himself. I worried about attempted murder and expected at the very least an assassination of my character. I did not know how to handle Fahrid's repeated outbursts of anger.

I couldn't help but see myself in Fahrid, the boy I was when I'd first arrived in America. Then, I was also very angry at the world for my dead family, my pain, and my loneliness. I got over much of that, but Fahrid was still under pressure. I could clearly see his struggle to deal with his previously suppressed emotions, which were no doubt amplified by being in Cambodia.

I discovered that, of the seventy-eight CANDO volunteers, Fahrid was the only ethnic Cham-Khmer-American. Now I began to understand his rage even more.

The ethnic Cham, a mostly Muslim group, see themselves as a badly mistreated minority in Cambodia. Like so many of us, Fahrid had been through hell and back during the terrifying Khmer Rouge years. The Cham were specifically targeted by the Khmer Rouge and were nearly wiped out. Even though Fahrid never shared his story, I sensed that he was struggling with long-term effects of many traumatic experiences. I understood him because I had my own demons to deal with.

Our return to Cambodia brought out raw emotions in all of us survivors of the Khmer Rouge's genocide. Some directed the pain and anger to do good. Sadly, Fahrid directed his anger at people around him.

With the consensus of the rest of CANDO II, I wrote a formal complaint letter to Director Khus detailing our concerns about Fahrid. This last resort to resolve the conflict didn't make any difference in his behavior.

Time passed. All of CANDO II shunned Fahrid. He decided to move out. For some reason, he couldn't get into CANDO I and moved in with CANDO III. Within a week, the new group of volunteers wanted to return Fahrid back to us. We politely refused, of course.

After a year in Cambodia, Fahrid's anger eased somewhat. He wasn't a changed person by any means, but his attitude improved. We all changed somehow through this volunteer work in Cambodia. Fahrid and I were only two of so many survivors who had to heal old wounds, face deep angers once and for all, and then get on with our lives. We did our best.

18

Turning Point

Elections in Phnom Penh

My mornings started with a light breakfast, usually a bowl of steamy hot Phnom Penh noodle soup and fresh fruit. A slice of tree-ripened papaya, a banana, a steamed sweet rice cake, or a roasted banana cake with a glass of cold water held me together until lunchtime.

I thoroughly enjoyed my early morning walk through the bustling Bung Kang Kong market, the constant frenzy of people and fresh produce coming and going. It was my favorite time of day and the best time to take photos, a hobby of mine.

The market people were watching me, too. First, they tried their sparse English on me, then their broken Thai and even Russian. When I replied in Khmer, explaining that I was born in Siem Reap, the looks on their faces were precious. Most of them adamantly believed that I was a foreigner who learned to speak Khmer. Hearing that I was actually from Siem Reap was a bit of a stretch—in their minds. No one really believed me because of the way I looked and how I carried myself as an overseas Khmer, or what the locals termed a "Khmer Anickachun."

It took a few months to convince a few fruit merchants, those I got to know well, that I really was from Siem Reap.

"You don't have the Siem Reap accent," one challenged me. I did my best imitation of the famous Siem Reap accent followed by the Phnom Penh one. Everyone cackled. A crowd formed.

It was the same everywhere I went. At first I felt insulted, particularly when they said not very nice things behind my back, thinking I didn't understand them. Later, I enjoyed surprising them with a punchline in Khmer, which usually drew a blast of good laughter from all.

By midmorning, I was longing for the cold freshness of an Oregon winter. I had forgotten how the April heat bakes Phnom Penh so much that, in our first few weeks, we worried about dehydration and heat stroke. I showered at least twice a day, drank buckets of water, and sweated as much. The nights were agonizing.

In the evenings, the heat that was trapped in the concrete buildings by day escaped to warm up the air. We slept well when electricity was sufficient to drive the Chinese-made air conditioners. More often, we had hardly enough power to turn the blades of the electric fans. Rolling blackouts were very common throughout Phnom Penh at all times of day and night, which made city life even more miserable. We learned to endure, as always.

During the hot nights, I lay awake thinking of my wife, Thavy, and little Samantha. One night I thought to myself, I miss them so much and I have 330 days to go. This separation was more difficult than I thought it would be.

A phone call home cost $6 a minute. A ten-minute call of $60 was impossible on my $725 stipend, half of which went to Thavy and Samantha. At $6 to $12 a letter, faxing was also pricey. The last resort was handwritten letters via diplomatic or organizational pouch for 32 cents. Although this option was the cheapest way, regular mail could take weeks or even months to get to America, much longer coming back to Cambodia. The e-mail revolution was still in its infancy and very few had access in Cambodia.

I wrote once a week, religiously, in the first three months, twice a month in the next three months, and finally once a month until Thavy and Samantha could arrive in Cambodia for their first visit. For six months, I kept busy so I wouldn't miss them too much. It worked for a while, but lonely nights persisted.

I spent my first two weeks as a CANDO volunteer at meetings and orientations. We toured schools, clinics, and the orphanage. We met students, teachers, directors, staff, and orphans. We also met many of the hundreds of local and international NGOs that worked with UNTAC, the United Nations Transitional Authority of Cambodia, which was sponsoring the general elections to be held on May 23, 1993.

Cambodia's first election in three decades had everyone jittery, and it got to us, too. When a group of mostly Caucasian UNTAC well-wishers came to visit, they seemed to talk more with the white volunteers Tony, Steven, Wayne, and Paul, than with other Khmer American volunteers. All the naturalized citizens in the three CANDO groups openly discussed their fears that, if the elections ignited a civil war as it had in 1975, we would be treated as second-class citizens and would be the last allowed to board the evacuating planes, if at all. I hoped the moment that tested this theory would never come. Meanwhile, the debate raged.

A proposal to Director Khus went around for our signatures. It looked like a petition. It said that we, the CANDO volunteers, wanted to be sent to Bangkok a week before the election and return the week after. The security concerns were valid. The situation was volatile, and it could explode at any moment.

Many of us remembered the chaos of 1975. However, I felt that it was all a scam, with the security issue exaggerated to get the volunteers a free, two-week vacation in Bangkok. CANDO was a volunteer organization with a limited budget. I spoke out openly against the petition. I could not, in good conscience, remain neutral or silent.

"I will not stop you from leaving, but I will not be with you. I support your concerns with reservation. We must remember that, in the first place, we volunteered to come. In the second place, we came because we wanted to help Cambodia. Third, we knew that we faced some risk." I made it clear that I didn't plan to leave. "If we take off for Bangkok, what will our local staff think? It will not instill confidence in the people we are helping. In fact, we could trigger a panic."

Fahrid considered my speech an insult. During the earlier debate about hiring the cook and house guard, he had called us paranoid about safety and security. Now he insisted that we all hide in Bangkok, together. I wondered: who is running scared now?

Director Khus politely rejected the petition. I could not have been more pleased. Some volunteers shunned me for a while.[1]

Weeks before the elections, we volunteers were invited to a pleasant barbeque dinner at the headquarters of PACT (Private Agencies Collaborating Together), which directed the CANDO program. The guest speaker, U.S. Ambassador to Cambodia Charles Twinning, assured us Khmer Americans that we have and would get equal treatment as U.S. citizens. Although I had my doubts, his pledge did make me feel better.

I could not vote during the election because I was no longer a Khmer citizen, but I joined the campaigns and the rallies. I was everywhere. On May 21, 1993, two days before the election, I joined the Peace Walk led by Samdech Moha Ghosananda, the Supreme Patriarch Buddhist monk and three-time Nobel Peace Prize nominee. It was an exhausting and yet exciting day. I joined this first-ever organized Cambodian Peace Walk in front of the Royal Palace as the participants formed a prayer circle on the most holy grounds of Wat Phnom, the historic center of the capital.

The newly recrowned King Norodom Sihanouk, Queen Monineath, and their son Prince Norodom Ranariddh, as well as Prime Minister Hun Sen and other dignitaries, were there to greet the marchers. I was right in the front row when their majesties walked by with arms outstretched to touch everyone. I grabbed King Sihanouk's arm with both hands and held him for the second time in my life. The first time had been in 1968, when then-Prince Sihanouk had received French president Charles de Gaulle in Siem Reap. Sihanouk had been reaching out to his subjects, so I reached back to him. This time, however, I felt the ravages of old age. The king's sagging skin and flesh marked his sunset after years of roller-coaster politics. I bid farewell to the man who, as king and as politician, had brought Cambodia to the brink of both good and bad times.

On another sunny day shortly before the election, I shared a taxi with Steven Hollister, Wayne Wright, Peter Chea, and Dec Ly—my fellow CANDO volunteers. We were going to Battambang in northwest Cambodia. There were five of us with the driver in his tiny white Toyota sedan. It was cramped at best.

The four-hour trip was bone jarring on the pothole-ridden National Highway 4. I counted twenty-three army checkpoints (legal and illegal) on the 95-mile stretch. Most of the men who manned the checkpoints wore the new Royal Cambodian Government Armed Forces uniforms and carried AK-47s and B-40 grenade launchers. The soldiers were often drunk, with bloodshot eyes, most likely from the potent local rice wine. Our driver said soldiers were known to shoot out the tires of local taxis when the drivers didn't pay the "toll fee."

Dec Ly, a scrawny man in his early twenties, and I sat in the one-person front bucket seat. Wayne Wright, Steven Hollister, and Peter Chea shared a more comfortable back seat. The first few legal checkpoints just outside Phnom Penh were not so bad; the soldiers waved us off after seeing the two white men in the back seat.

"Let the UNTAC people pass," a soldier yelled to his colleagues ahead. The soldiers called all white visitors "UNTAC people," assuming that all whites were employed by the U.N.-deployed governing body.

I became tired of AK-47s in my face and the cramped front seat with skinny Dec virtually on my lap, so I asked the white men to take a turn. Having Wayne or Steven in the front bucket seat produced instant results. The taxi didn't have to stop at checkpoints now; the soldiers simply waved us right through. After we passed one of these soldiers, I leaned forward. "The power of the white man's magic is strong!" I said, to a loud outburst of laughter.

After the first few moments of tension, Steven and Wayne enjoyed their newfound power. Our first trip across the countryside, to and from Battambang, was very pleasant. All we needed was a couple of "UNTAC faces" (fake ones though they were) in the front seat, and that did the trick. Simply magical!

One rainy day shortly before the election, I saw people playing games outside. A ball floated in the floodwater. I thought to myself, we don't do that in America. I saw people dancing in the warm rain. I did the same. I played with children in the downpour, something I hadn't done in almost thirty years. It was fun with those kids in the rain, with the lightning and thunder all around. The rain was nice and cool here, not freezing cold like it was in Oregon. I had forgotten how much fun it was in the monsoon season, watching the boys running around in the water and falling. I was a little kid in Cambodia again—if only for a brief moment. I remembered with fondness how often I had played in the rain, once upon a time in Cambodia—some three decades ago.

After a year of constant intimidation by the Khmer Rouge, May 23 arrived. It was a cool day with a light drizzle. At the last minute, the Khmer Rouge decided to boycott the elections, hoping to sway the rest of the population to do the same.

Despite the threat of heavy monsoon rain and the promised violence by the Khmer Rouge, the lines at the polling station were long. Men and women arrived early in their brightest and best outfits, carrying colorful umbrellas. Hundreds and thousands went to the polling stations manned by U.N. volunteers and peacekeepers with guns and metal detectors. My people were showing up to determine their future. After thirty years of bitter conflict, more than 94 percent of the registered voters cast their votes, an amazing turnout, if not a world record. The falling rain hid my solemn tears of hope in my new moment of pride. I was here in my homeland to take in this historic election, to savor this special moment in time.

A few days after the election, the United Nations pronounced the FUNCINPEC Royalist Party of Prince Norodom Ranariddh as winner.

The Cambodian People's Party (CPP) lost after eighteen years of rule despite its predictions of a landslide victory. The CPP and its party leader, Prime Minister Hun Sen, immediately cried foul. When the CPP made it clear that it still had full control of the armed forces and all the security apparatus, everyone once again braced for another bout of violence, if not a full-scale war. To avert a major bloodbath, King Sihanouk—with a blessing from UNTAC—pressured his son, Prince Ranariddh, and his party to share power with the CPP equally. The prince's choice was either to share power or to be expelled or die. The prince gave in, wisely if not enthusiastically.

Cambodia created history. Now we had two premiers: First Prime Minister Prince Ranariddh and Second Prime Minister Hun Sen. This uneasy marriage of convenience wasted the year-long U.N. effort, $3 billion spent, and the efforts of 25,000 peacekeepers and volunteers. Cambodia stayed on the same old road, practicing its own brand of democracy. Rather than lose face, the United Natons proclaimed the election a success. The world body did not have too many options.

Under the bright lights of local and international media, the new parliament convened for the first time. Security was tight. The diplomatic corps were present for the opening of Cambodia's first assembly in many decades. Thousands marched to stage a cheerful demonstration in front of the parliament building with banners and placards asking only for a peaceful Cambodia.

As fate would have it, I managed to get myself pushed into the rear entry of the parliamentary building, amid a group of Japanese newsmen. The parliament building was the kingdom's tightest and most secured bit of real estate, but I passed through security with my backpack and camera. We were not inspected.

I ended up in the front row, a mere 10 feet away from King Sihanouk in front of us and the newly elected 126 parliamentarians in the rows behind. I decided to make the most of this opportunity of a lifetime and exposed all of my precious two rolls of Kodak Ektachrome slide film.

King Sihanouk preached about peace and development for Cambodia. In his thirty-minute speech, he mentioned justice for the Khmer survivors only once, and I'm not even certain if he meant it.

Except for the Khmer Rouge leadership, it was a reunion of everyone directly or indirectly responsible for the suffering of the Cambodian people these past thirty years. Co-Premiers Prince Ranariddh and Hun Sen sat in the front row with top political leaders, former rivals, and bitter enemies.

They were all in one big building now, right in front of me. If the Khmer Rouge leadership had joined them, and if a high-explosive device were hidden in my backpack, I might have decided to exact revenge for my murdered family with my own hands.

However, I wanted justice, not revenge. I didn't have explosives, but who can predict the whims of fate? If I had been a terrorist, I could easily have taken out the entire Cambodian political leadership, including the king and queen. A dozen hand grenades could have been hidden among my photographic equipment in my backpack.

But I was just a nervous, lucky intruder who happened to be in the right place to witness Cambodia's history unfolding before his eyes.

I came out of the parliament building into the crowd of wild cheers and waving placards and banners. CANDO director Thida Khus, fellow CANDO volunteer Steven Hollister, and the noted activist Madam Mu Sohua were surprised to see me walking out of the building with the politicians and reporters.

"How did you get in there?" Thida Khus asked me, her round eyes wide with wonderment and amazement.

"Fate, perhaps?" I said with a wide grin.

Fahrid and some other CANDO volunteers had left for Bangkok on their own dime. They missed a chapter of Cambodian history that they had signed on to witness. They probably had to settle for reading about it in the *Bangkok Post* instead.

Of those who remained to witness history unfolding, I must have been one of the happiest and most proud.

The next day, while waiting for dinner at home, I decided to sweep the street clean and get rid of a huge pile of garbage just outside the fence. If I wanted to start cleaning Cambodia up, there was no better place to start than here, where I would be living for the rest of the year.

The domino effect could be very powerful. If I started with my front yard, my sidewalk, my street, who knows? The city and the entire country could be next. My fellow volunteers and my neighbors simply laughed.

"Pay someone to do it for you," one called out.

"You can afford it," another said with a grin.

"I can use the exercise, won't you join me?" I engaged the neighbors politely, but only a few children came out to help in the fun. Most came to watch the spectacle. "Look at that idiot," I imagined them thinking.

At least I got my neighbors' attention. Perhaps they even felt a little guilty watching me work so hard on the large rubbish pile. I hoped they would also clean up and get rid of growing piles of rotting garbage in and around their neighborhood. After all, they lived here. I was only a visitor. Who should have more ownership? I felt good when the city dump truck removed the big pile of rubbish that blocked the dirt road. The dump site at Stung Meanchey was another place that badly needed social engineering.

I quickly grew attached to my neighbors across the street. Their eight kids were all scrawny boys, ranging from two days to fifteen years old. The younger ones often went without clothing and the elder ones wore rags. Their meals were very basic. Their home, which took up a portion of the street, was a wooden shack covered with plastic tarp and sheets of flattened cardboard boxes.

The father, Prum Samnang, pedaled a cyclo for a living, while the mother stayed home caring for the eight children. In her spare time, she sold bottles of purified water and pieces of candy from a display right beside her shack. They were just one of the urban poor natives in the expatriate community. They soon became my adopted family.

I have an assortment of vitamins and minerals for my personal use, but the mother needed them more than I did, so I gave them all to her. Each morning after a brisk walk in the small Bung Kang Kong market nearby, I would return with an assortment of snacks for the children. It soon became a daily routine, which felt good and awkward at the same time. I didn't want this family to be dependent on me, and so I began to investigate ways in which I could help this family and others like them to be self-sustaining.

I went to the other side of the river for a better view of the Royal Palace and saw a woman sweating in the sun, growing vegetables in a plot of land near the river, just across from the palace. Her name was Khy Som-Oeun. All of her four small children had a high fever and red eyes. They were hungry. Som-Oeun's husband had abandoned her and the children for another woman. The neighbors said he had burned down the family home and possessions because they refused to move out. The family had nothing but some handouts from the neighbors who were dirt-poor themselves. Som-Oeun gave half of her crops to the landowner and sold her share at the local market. Her home was truly a cardboard shack, to put it mildly. I saw how hard Som-Oeun worked in the open field. I gave her some medicine and some cash, $50 it was, which was a lot of money in Cambodia—even for me at the time.

During my bike trips around the city shantytown, I met more families with similar stories. They struggled for survival in the crowded city, living from day to day without knowing where the next meal would come from. I felt compelled to help. I couldn't possibly help them all, but for sure I could try.

I obtained a small grant from the Trickle Up Program in New York for an experiment in urban, micro-economic development. Along with my own $500,

I had a $1,000 operating budget, a good chunk of money in Cambodia. Each of my five sponsored families received a one-year $200 no-interest loan. They all came up with plans of action to start businesses. I advised them on the basics and provided a lot of encouragement.

For another four families who were interested in pig raising, I provided pairs of piglets that cost $20 each plus some money for pig food. I told them that I expected to get a fully-grown pig in return. Imagine me going after the tiny piglets in the middle of the street in Phnom Penh. That's exactly what I had to do to get the project going.

Prum Samnang, the cyclo pusher with eight kids, decided to take four piglets for himself. I thought it would not be easy to raise them, but he claimed to have some experience in pig rearing and felt he could do it again. He also decided to return to his traditional drawing and producing fine Khmer religious sculpture, in which he was very talented.

With a $100 loan from CANDO director Thida Khus, Mr. Prum began his own pig and art business. In less than a year, he repaid Thida Khus and was running a thriving business with the help of his older children. His wife became a retailer in a nearby market. All the older kids attended school, and their diet improved a great deal.

The following year when I visited, Prum Samnang's home was almost completely remodeled with a tin roof and hardwood planks for the walls and floor. He had upgraded from the old cyclo to a used motorbike. The family was still poor, but they were becoming self-sustaining, even thriving.

Som-Oeun turned out to be a better seamstress than farmer. The loan fueled both endeavors. She rebuilt her home with real wood and all four kids attended the local school.

The other three families were not as successful, but they held their severe poverty in check. Of course, I didn't take the grown pigs—what would I do with five squealing, 200-pound pigs. Also, I didn't take back the $200 no-interest loan from the five families, which they had expected to repay. Instead, I asked that they use the money to help the less fortunate achieve some economic freedom once they were better off themselves economically.

After a while, I began to adjust to a lot of things. Despite the temperamental diesel generator's noise, I was able to sleep again. My constant sweating had eased somehow. I began to acclimate to Cambodia's weather conditions.

I knew just about every neighbor on the block—except for the Russian pilots who were either away or occupied with their Khmer and Vietnamese girlfriends who clung to them. I also got used to the Phnom Penh traffic and its "controlled chaos" flow pattern, as Steven Hollister called it. I was now able to go faster on my bike, particularly without Suling nagging me from behind.

Time was always at a premium. I was always short of time and money. My monthly budget was only $350. I spent most of my money on what I felt were worthy causes. It was extremely difficult at first for me. I was used to living on more, but if the local Khmer could live off $30 a month, I surely was going to try to survive on $350.

Despite their $720 monthly stipend, my fellow volunteers didn't fare as well, so I didn't feel too bad. Compared to them, my spending was very disciplined. In six months, I was busy with work and little social projects.

After my morning class at the Ministry of Planning, I taught basic planning, design theory, and drafting until late into the evening at the once-proud Royal University of Fine Arts. When I saw the lack of instructors at its Faculty of Architecture and Urban Planning, I volunteered to teach there. One hundred nine second-year architectural students—more than 100 percent overflow—signed up for my class. My students addressed me as "Lauk Sastrajah Ronnie" (Sir Professor Ronnie).

The class began at precisely 1:00 P.M. with an hour of theory instruction. Two hours of studio time followed, after which came the critique session in class, and finally the question-and-answer sessions, which usually ran overtime. I often arrived early to class and returned home late, but I enjoyed teaching. Being a respected teacher and bureaucrat is in my bloodline, I suppose.

I gave the class the very first project I had learned at school. After an hour of specific instruction, I had the students team up in twos to plan, design, and construct a contraption out of a box of toothpicks, a sheet of paper, and a bottle of glue. The objective was to protect an egg from being crushed when dropped from thirty feet. I gave them forty-eight hours to do the project: drawings, text, construction, and all.

I would never forget the blank looks on their faces. The class was absolutely quiet. What have I done? I thought.

"Is this a joke, Lauk Sastrajah?" one asked politely.

"Nope, it's for real and it should be fun," I said. "Get to it!"

The blank looks turned to polite smiles, and then an outburst of laughter. Two days later, more than fifty designs were all over the large studio for final review and critique, from the most popular parachute design to the Houdini death box. Bets were made for who would get the highest grade.

The late afternoon show was as loud and noisy as can be. One at a time, the projects were dropped from the second-floor window; each release was accompanied by loud cheers as egg after egg flew off and splattered on the ground below. The noise was so loud that it disrupted other classes.

Annoyed at first, students and teachers came out in groups to witness a most peculiar spectacle. Nervously, I looked for ways to end the proceedings. Unfortunately, the occasion had a life of its own. The other classes began to cheer even louder. Fortunately, the dean was on an official visit in Italy.

Can they actually fire a volunteer? I asked myself.

I don't know how his Royal Highness Prince Norodom Ranariddh heard of the egg-tossing incident. The prince, now the co-prime minister of Cambodia, wanted to visit the school and "meet the instructor personally."

I heard about it when I came to class one afternoon. His Highness had showed up without warning earlier that morning. To the deep embarrassment of the school staff, they could not find the key to the room, or the teacher.

"Samdech Neyuk Rothmentrey Tie Muy was here to see your class this morning," the deputy dean said.

"Huh? Who?"

"Prince Ranariddh was here."

"Oh. . . . Why?"

"His Highness wanted to see you and your class."

"Well, he should have made an appointment or something."

"Where were you?"

"I have other morning classes elsewhere. You know that."

"Oh," he said. "His Highness will be back tomorrow. Be here. And get all your students and class in order."

The prince, who is the son of the reigning King Norodom Sihanouk, was a no-show the next morning. An apologetic aide said he had a "last-minute, urgent affair of the state." Everyone was disappointed, but it suited me just fine. I didn't care much about royalty.

About four weeks later, the aide made an appropriate appointment, and the entire Royal School of Fine Arts turned out to welcome the prince and the princess. It was almost like a Sunday parade. The students lined up along the official route, the males in white shirts, khaki slacks, and ties, and the females in their best traditional Khmer silk dresses.

Two hours went by before lights and sirens blared to signal the arrival of the prince/prime minister and his cabinet ministers. He was late, as usual. A student smoothed his trousers. I looked down at my jeans. I was the only one wearing jeans and a T-shirt, the CANDO logo emblazoned in front. Perfect, I thought to myself, just perfect!

Perhaps my choice of apparel was a subconscious form of protest. Royalty may have been a good thing in the Angkor period, but it became too expensive to maintain. Still, royalty has always been a part of Cambodia.

Four motorcycles carrying policemen wearing white uniforms pulled into the schoolyard accompanying a light-blue Mercedes Benz, followed closely by a herd of fancy sedans. The chauffeurs parked their vehicles and then stood by. The prince's door was opened first, followed by all the rest. The prince stepped out into the sunlight and wiped his forehead with a white handkerchief. Princess Mary stepped out of the limo, smiling broadly, just behind her husband.

The prince began to touch the crowd, grinning widely—his papa, King Sihanouk's trademark. The long entourage moved sedately behind the royal couple, until they reached the platform and special chairs. No one dared to sit until the prince had sat under the clicking shutters of the press corps cameras. The prince gave a long speech about the importance of education and the development of Cambodia.

I smiled to myself. The royal government had allocated less than 11 percent of its national budget to education. The armed forces and other security forces received more than 54 percent in the 1993–94 fiscal year. It was the rhetoric of a politician, which I did not really care to hear.

I led the parade to my classroom on the second floor. The prince's aide told me quickly what the prince wanted to see my classroom, including the students' work. I opened the double doors and the crowd poured in.

"Who's the instructor?" the prince asked casually without looking at me.

"This is our instructor, Mr. Ronnie Yimsut, Your Highness," the class president, Mean Ravuth, said in a matter-of-fact tone, motioning toward me.

All eyes were on me. The room was quiet. I was a bit unsettled. I had no formal instruction about proper behavior or the Khmer terms of royal address. Cousin Ang Khen had met the prince several times in the course of her reporting for the Voice of America. She told me that the prince expected everyone to address him using the proper Khmer royal terms of address, but I had not asked for details. However, I had spent hours watching Chinese classical movies with Khmer voice-overs, and I now recalled the royal terms they used.

"Your Highness," I placed my palms together in a Khmer sampass and bowed my head a little lower than the prince, who was a foot shorter than I. The prince glanced at me and nodded.

He moved on, looking at my students' best drawings on the wall and the scale models on the table. Princess Mary smiled at me, nodding her approval. I bowed slightly to acknowledge my appreciation. I followed the prince and princess as they toured the students' work.

The prince stopped at a model for a bridge and gazed at its detailed construction drawings. "This is marvelous, absolutely wonderful," he studied it closely and then glanced at me, smiling broadly.

"Don't you all agree?" he turned to his cabinet ministers. Heads nodded.

"Good work, good work!" said His Excellency Van Molyvann, the undersecretary of state, as he tapped me on the shoulder, smiling.

"These are all my students' hard work," I said, smiling back. "I just guide them."

"Where are you from? Who do you work for?" the prince said, looking at the projects.

"I'm from Oregon, USA. I'm a CANDO volunteer," I pointed to the logo on my T-shirt. The prince glanced at the CANDO logo and then continued his tour of the scale models.

"And how long will you be teaching here?"

"After about six more months, I'm returning home, Your Highness."

"Your home is in Oregon, right?

"Yes, in Oregon."

"What will it take for you to stay and teach longer? How much do they pay you?" he rubbed his fingers in the "money" gesture, which drew another outburst of laughter from his entourage.

"My contract ends early next year, and then I have to return to my family."

"You're married? Oh, that will make the negotiations difficult," he said. More laughs and cheers. The cabinet also doubled as cheerleaders. They hooted and applauded just about every time the prince opened his mouth, which only encouraged him to continue his clowning.

I was embarrassed but I held my ground with a broad smile. The prince and I continued the tour side-by-side. He came to a complete stop in front of a scale model of a wooden bridge. He studied the model and the drawing for a long time.

"This is wonderful," the prince said. Studying the listed name, he asked, "Who is Mean Ravuth?" The prince looked around.

"I am Mean Ravuth, Your Highness," said the student body president, bowing very low, with palms together in a sampass.

"Did you do all of these?" he gestured across the drawings and the model, not looking at Ravuth.

"Yes, Your Highness."

"May I buy these drawings and the scale model from you? I like this simple design. Cambodia needs this kind of bridge!"

"Your Highness has to speak with my professor about that," Ravuth said, to my surprise. All eyes were again on me, the room quiet for my answer.

"How much are you willing to pay, Your Highness?" I replied jokingly, to a burst of laughter from around, the prince laughing the hardest of all.

"Seriously, I want these drawings and the model," he said.

"Seriously, Your Highness, you cannot have them before I give Ravuth a review and a grade first. Then we'll make a deal," I said. More laughter ensued.

"Okay, okay. What do you need around here?" he said.

This was my best opportunity to help the school. "Your Highness, this place is known as the Royal University of Fine Arts. However, the condition of the school does not fit its royal designation.

"I have 109 students in a classroom designed for 50 at most. The roof is leaking. There are not enough drafting tables or chairs to go around. Lighting is very poor because there is no electricity. Need I go on, Your Highness?" I asked poetically.

The prince nodded, smiling. "Three days ago I went to this village outside Phnom Penh," he said. "They told me that the road to this village was terrible but they fixed it when they heard I was coming.

"If I provide this school with a generator and fix the roof, others will demand things from me too. When I visit them, the roads might be terrible simply because no one will fix it!" The entire room cracked up.

"At least, please help us get the roof fixed and give us a decent generator so we can work better," I said. "We can probably manage the rest."

"Let's make a deal," he said. "I get the drawings and the model. Your class will also help me design the Royal Riverfront Park in four weeks."

I stood silently.

"And I'll fix the leaky roof and give you a generator. Deal?"

"Deal," I said, smiling politely. Everyone laughed.

I formed the class into ten teams. For four weeks, they worked on the plans, the designs, and the model construction of the Royal Riverfront Park. They spent a lot of time and money—something they didn't have much to begin with—on the scale models.

I had never seen a more dedicated group of students. Some even slept at the studio and went out only to grab a bite or take a bath. I found myself hanging out late with them into the evening. Time was too short. I had to practically force them to stop working and prepare the displays, but we made the deadline. After four weeks, on the morning the prince was due to arrive, we were ready.

First came a large generator with all the trimmings. Then we heard the noisy convoy of European sedans. The prince and his entourage reviewed the ten designs and scale models one at a time. He selected and took away the three best designs.

The leaky roof was never fixed but the generator worked fine. We got a good deal.

It took the local contractor only two months to construct the Royal Riverfront Park at a bargain price of $45,000. Before the actual construction, the "clearing and scrubbing stage," tearing down existing structures and hauling them to the dump, had cost a lot more.

The resulting 3-mile open, green space along the waterfront has became a joy to all visitors. I am proud to have played a small role in establishing it. How wonderful!

This architecture class was working on the very concepts I had studied for six years—the same concepts I had also been examining daily in my professional employment these past four years. I didn't want to return to the English classes and mediocre assignments at the Ministry of Planning anymore, but they were part of my CANDO assignment. The architectural students were so hungry for knowledge that they kept me on my toes.

One day, during a class at my design studio, John Sanday paid me a visit. Before I came to Cambodia we had been in touch by mail and by phone. The Briton was project director for the New York–based World Monuments Fund (WMF). Mr. Sanday asked me to help with the conservation and preservation work at the Angkor Wat, now a U.N. World Heritage Site.

This was my chance to give something back to my birthplace.

I became an environmental consultant for the WMF. My responsibility was to write a management plan for the conservation of the Preah Khan temple, one of Cambodia's most important monuments. To fulfill this responsibility before my return trip to the United States, I found a way to complete a management plan before my term with CANDO ended.

By the time I started working with the WMF, hundreds of locally hired laborers had already begun clearing the forest around the project site. The ten-year WMF conservation and preservation program focused on the Preah Khan temple, built by King Jayavarman VII in 1227 to honor his father.

Fellow expatriate consultants received good consultation fees. I was happy enough with the free meals, lodging, and travel allowance. I was the only Khmer among the eight consultants. Using my management plan as the blueprint, we designed, built, and managed a visitor center, trails, put up interpretive signs in various languages, and planned travel and access corridors throughout the temple grounds.

We helped train Phnom Penh university students and local laborers, hoping that they would inherit the project when the WMF pulled out. The hard-working laborers and student interns were crucial to bringing heritage conservation to Cambodia.

The American project became a showcase of heritage conservation. Soon, the Indonesian, Japanese, German, Hungarian, and French governments followed suit and began conservation work under the watchful eyes of UNESCO's and Royal Government of Cambodia's APSARA representatives. Although competition among the international conservators was strong, professional cooperation continued. I worked with the best of them.

During a trip to visit the Kien Khleang Orphanage across the Tonle Sap River, we passed the distroyed Chroy Chongvar Bridge, which brought back a flood of bitter memories from my trips to Phnom Penh before the war.

The hopelessness in the eyes of the 138 orphans made my eyes water. I saw myself in each and every one of those faces. It was me, my own face, just fifteen years earlier. When I returned home that evening, I had a good cry alone. It was time for me to do something.

With Suling's assistance, I founded the first Big Brother and Big Sister Program in the kingdom. Just about every weekend, with the help of Suling and my students from the Ministry of Planning, the CANDO II villa became a fun haven for the orphans of Kien Khleang.

In groups of twenty to thirty at a time, we bused them to tourist attractions in Phnom Penh, took them on boat rides, or hiked with them along the edge of the river. We took pictures, played games, served hot meals, and had them bathe before returning to the orphanage at the end of the day.

One weekend at a time, each group of orphans became kids again, away from the high walls of the orphanage. With our limited resources, Suling and I did what we could. However, funding and resources were scarce, so the group rotation was too slow for me.

My CANDO term was finishing up. I had been in Cambodia for a year now, spending part of that time with Thavy and Samantha. I had enjoyed going through an entire cycle of planting rice seedlings, tending the growing rice, harvesting, and cooking rice for the New Year celebration. I must have directly touched the lives of more than five hundred people during my stint as a CANDO volunteer from 1993 to 1994. And they, in turn, enriched my life beyond measure. I gained much more than I expected.

I went to Cambodia for my sanity, for healing, and to reconcile with my past. I found peace in helping those less fortunate and regained my identity as a Khmer. Cambodia will always be a part of me. I will always be a part of Cambodia.

We returned to Oregon and continued our lives. Soon we tried to have another child.

In December 1995, our son Derrick Monorom Yimsut was born. Grandma San came with Thavy's sister, Savarin.

"Where's my grandson, where's my grandson?" said Grandma San. Then they left.

We were on our own again.

The children are older now. We don't do much hugging and kissing anymore. My dad didn't demonstrate affection, either. I didn't like the lack of fatherly warmth when I was a kid, but I see that today I'm the same as my father. Amazing, I'm actually a chip off the old block. I continually struggle to find a balance between being a Khmer and an American father to these American-born children.

Besides this emotional distancing from my kids, I'm also like my father in other ways. We both like nature. He hunted, I fish. I don't talk much but when I speak, I mean it and can't shut up, especially when I know what I am talking about. He let my mother make household decisions. Thavy does that in our household, too, most of the time.

As the years passed, I kept in contact with a few of my fellow CANDO volunteers. Sadly, no one has heard anything from Fahrid Sou, my fellow volunteer, housemate, and nemesis. I still wish him all the best as he moved from being a sorrowful victim of the Khmer Rouge, to being a survivor of the Killing Fields, to living his life to the fullest as a Cambodian American.

When I visit Cambodia, as I try to do yearly, I still run into a few of my former students. My greetings and thoughts are with them all, as I know for a fact that these young Khmers have to carry the weight of Cambodia's future on their individual and collective shoulders. They represent a more hopeful and better Cambodia.

The roof of the Royal Phnom Penh University still leaks. The park by the river front near the Royal Palace is now a fine tourist attraction, an open space, a wide promenade for all to enjoy. I'm proud to have been a part of that. Thavy and I started the Cambodian Orphanage Fund, which is still running and raising funds.

Our house in America is made of wood. Like my childhood home, it has a wooden polished floor that I can slide on. We clean and wax our floor every week, just like I did in Cambodia when I was a boy. Derrick and I created a garden in the back. We grow many good edible plants, while Thavy grows beautiful flowers. The difference is that Derrick doesn't have to lug water. A knob, a switch, and the plants are watered automatically.

Samantha's doing well in school and will break many more boys' hearts before her time as a college student is over. She wants to be a teacher and is very good with kids, just as her grandfather had always been—even if she never knew him. Teaching is in our blood.

When I pause and look at my family and my own life in general, I seem to be doing exceptionally well—considering what I went through at a very young age. Where I am now is nothing short of a miracle. Deep inside, however, I still wonder: How am I really doing? Will things turn out all right? Deep inside me is still that scared little refugee and orphan boy from Siem Reap.

19

Facing the Khmer Rouge

Siem Reap, Ta Source Hill, the Massacre Site, and Pailin

There's nothing like a morning in Siem Reap. It's the most peaceful time of the day. Tree leaves drip dew and the moist soil releases a delicate fragrance I find hard to describe. The taste of mornings in my old hometown is a magical mix of smells, of sounds and sights. I feel a sense of belonging here, but my memories of this place can drive me away at the same time.

The Tonle Sap Lake is peaceful now, but the screams, faces, and terror are still incredibly raw in my mind. The remains of my family, my friends, and hundreds of neighbors are still in mass graves around the lake. I am the only known survivor of the "Tonle Sap Lake Massacre."

A few months before this day in Siem Reap, when I was still in Oregon, a phone call from someone in California's Central Valley surprised me. Mr. Greg Douglas called to say that he was leaving for Cambodia for the third time that year and wanted to know more about my story of the massacre, which he had read on the Internet.

I drew the stranger a crude map of the area with as much detail as I could remember and sent it to him. About three weeks later, Greg called from Cambodia. He was very excited. He had just found the killing site.

"Your map was most helpful, Ronnie. I'll send you the photographs as soon as they're developed." We were on the phone a long time. "There's no physical danger," said Greg. "It's easy to get there by motorbike."

I was impressed by his determination and by the fact that he actually found the site. Just talking about it excited Greg.

"I got there at dusk," he said, "about the same time the massacre happened. I was reading your description of that terrifying December night and it gave me the creeps. My hair just stood on end, man!"

A few days later, I received Greg's photos, and we had a much longer phone conversation. One of the large trees in Greg's snapshots, which I marked as a landmark on my map, stood out hauntingly against the lush rice fields.

Greg encouraged me to visit the site and he sent me $1,000 to help finance my trip. The place still terrified me, but Greg's sincerity and generosity touched me in a big way.

Thus it happened that, one morning in January 1999, I was at my cousin Sal's home in Pouk, about 10 miles west of Siem Reap. With me were a reporter from the *Phnom Penh Post*, two Western journalists, and a documentary filmmaker.

The previous day we'd been at Dorn Swar on the outskirts of Siem Reap. The group had filmed an interview with my old friend Brother Som and the group of women who had helped me to escape death from the Khmer Rouge twenty-one years ago.

I remembered discussions with my brother Larony, a true Republican who wants Cambodia to be a republic again. I'd argue with him, we'd raise our voices, we'd get to the point of killing each other, but in the end we're still brothers. I want the former Khmer Rouge to be that way, too.

I visited my old friend Gnoy Phan in remote Tapang, my second trip in seven years. Again, almost the entire town showed up to see me, the sole survivor among the hundreds of "New People," the "Mith Thmey" who were forced to become slave laborers here.

"Oh, my friend, I missed you so much," Phan hugged me again and again. He had not changed much. Cambodia was more peaceful now and had a market-oriented economy, but his family still struggled to survive. It was a truly miserable place in summer when wells and ponds dried up and clean drinking water was hard to come by.

"Always nice to see you too, Phan. How's your family?"

"Fine, fine," he was excited to see us. "Have you all had anything to eat yet?"

"Don't worry about us. We came prepared," I said. He and his family would go hungry just to feed us one meal. "We had our meal prepared down the road."

"I can cook some rice for you and your friends," he offered.

"No, no. My escort has a friend near Wat Yieng. They are preparing a meal for us. It will be ready by the time we return," I said.

When Phan saw that we didn't have enough drinking water, he climbed up his coconut tree. I remember him offering me a drink from the same coconut tree seven years ago. We had better luck then; the green coconut had had a little liquid. But the current hot season was too much. No liquid came from the coconuts. Phan tapped the few sugar palm trees nearby until he had an almost-full bamboo container of sweet juice.

"So sorry. It would have been more honorable if, instead of sugar palm juice, coconut juice was served to my honored guests," Phan said.

"I personally prefer palm juice," I said, "but I appreciate your effort very much."

Two flat tires on one of our rented motorbikes gave me more time with my old friend. He still eked out a living in this poor region by rice farming. For extra income he worked the sugar palm trees for juice. Phan and his family barely survived, but he was willing to share what little he had. He is the kind of man one may count on, whatever the circumstance. His honesty, kindness, and unselfish acts kept me returning to this desolation.

I had only two friends in those two long years I'd spent in Tapang: Laive, who was killed by Angkar, and Gnoy Phan. Despite his poverty, Phan never once asked me for money or assistance. This is why my heart stays open to him.

The flat tires also gave the reporters time to film an interview with the townspeople about the impending international tribunal to judge the Khmer Rouge leaders they had once supported. Surprisingly, the answer was a mix of positive and negative. "Peace and reconciliation" appeared to be the motto of the year for all Khmer Rouge, former or otherwise.

I also had time to conduct a straw poll for fun and found that I could easily be elected the town's commune chief on a simple platform of economic development and self-help.

We had lunch at Wat Yieng, the same temple where I'd found my family twenty-one years ago, even as we all marched toward death. It's a peaceful temple again, with Buddhist monks and incense and flowers. A community thrives around it. People worship there now. Its days as a torture place or an execution center are a fading memory.

That night, I dreamed of my beloved family. My father, mother, and brothers lined up on a pathway in their best clothes, smiling and waving at me. In the dream, I floated on the path toward them. The next day I woke up wondering what it meant.

Over lunch at my cousin Sal's home in Pouk, the journalists talked about filming an interview with Ieng Sary, Noun Chea, and Khieu Samphan, the last living leaders of the Khmer Rouge. They urged me to go with them as translator. The filmmaker wanted a few shots here and there in Pouk before sunset. On the table was the pile of photos that Greg had sent me.

"I'm going to go to the killing site this afternoon," I said.

After a moment of astonishment, the Western journalists scrambled for the bikes. Two left for Siem Reap to buy fresh batteries and film.

"I'll get my equipment ready," the filmmaker said. "Give me two hours." They had been waiting for this moment, but they were surprised just the same.

I had never been so relaxed. After a cooling shower, I took a nap in the hammock strung up between two coconut trees. My decision to rest was very unusual. I do not take daytime naps.

At about five in the afternoon, we went south on our rented motorbikes toward the lake. I instantly recognized the low anthill mound of Ta Source Hill. Here I had killed two Khmer Rouge soldiers. For a moment, I was back in time, to that day when my rebel group attacked this hill. The raucous sound of gambling and drinking soldiers at the new guard post on the hill jolted me into the present.

At an easily identifiable turn-off, I got off the motorbike and came to the familiar low dike, now called Thnoal Beng by locals. My eyes misted as I recalled how, just days before our march to death, my hungry family and thousands of others had labored here.

I felt the helplessness once more. The screams and groans returned, but I knew only I could hear them. I had to summon all my strength and courage to go down the narrow path. Some twenty-one years earlier, at just about this time of day, I had walked this very same path.

My cousin Thie and his wife followed; they wanted to see where our relatives had died.

And then I saw the tree. It is the large tree that stood, and still stands, as a silent witness to the senseless slaughter of my kin. It was a haunting landmark.

My consciousness slipped in and out, between past and present. I clamped down on my terror and walked ahead of the group toward the spot where I was left to die. I felt fear, bitter pain, and sharp anger. The grief brought me to my knees. I wept.

A feeling of relief came over me. I had returned at long last.

"Nak, we must leave soon," Thie said gently. I looked around. My cousin's eyes were wet. His wife wept quietly behind him. The three Westerners were quietly filming. The *Phnom Penh Post* reporter Christine Chameau was under a tree, wiping her eyes.

It was getting dark. I had lost track of time. I remembered that it was dangerous to be here after dusk. I walked over to the tree and lighted three incense sticks.

"Ieng Sary, Noun Chea, and Khieu Samphan tell us to forget the past, to let bygones be bygones," I said to the lady reporter. "Their families are alive and well. They enjoy their lives inside Khmer society as though nothing happened. The cowards. Let them all come here and tell me to forget," I said, weeping uncontrollably.

"How can I forget January 1978, twenty-one years ago," I said, laying a lock of my son Derrick's hair beside the tree. I burned a page from a calendar for all those who died here. "I have not forgotten!" From the small fire, smoke rose to the sky. "I'll never forget."

A phantom government run by shadowy figures destroyed my village, abolished property, freedom, money, homes, schools, temples, and families. Children became slave laborers toiling till they died. Laughter and family meals were gone. Boy soldiers gave us torture, starvation, illness, disease, and death. In less than three years, I became an orphan, sick, emaciated, with only my memories and my promises. How can I forget? I thought to myself. I'm back as I had promised, I said to the dead, and these people are my witnesses.

I looked at the five people around me.

"Let's go," I said. "If I remember right, the mosquitoes here are terrible." We left quietly, in respect for those who lay there.

I turned for a last look. The place was in complete darkness, just as it was when I last walked here twenty-one years ago. I bid the place farewell. We got on the motorbikes and raced back to Siem Reap.

In the city, we dined at an old family favorite, the Banteay Srei Restaurant. Everyone around the table felt my lightness of being. And then I told them that, although I was still a little apprehensive, I was ready for Pailin.

Pailin is a remote town rich in gems and timber. It is also the heart of the autonomous Khmer Rouge government, run by local war lords. I thought back to my forced labor days in the Mobile Brigade. In less than four years, the mad dash toward agrarian utopia had killed nearly two million through starvation, disease, and summary executions.

I reminded myself that I was not here as a massacre survivor but as a member of the press. The Frenchwoman, Christine Chameau of the *Phnom Penh Post*, had been to Pailin three times before. She suggested that we keep our cameras and video equipment hidden. She didn't want to give the Khmer Rouge any excuse to kick us out before we met with the last surviving senior Khmer Rouge leaders, Ieng Sary, Khieu Samphan, and Noun Chea, who had recently defected to the government side.

After changing into fresh clothes at the hotel, I decided to tour Pailin and get my bearings, just in case. I offered a driver 5,000 riel to cruise through town for an hour.

After about twenty minutes, he said I had seen it all. I was a bit disappointed. I asked the driver to do another round or so. It was approaching 10 P.M. when he dropped me off near my hotel, but there were still people on the street.

I walked across the street to a shop where people sang karaoke in Khmer and Thai. I sat down and asked for the wonderful fruit shake called *teuk kroluk*.

I spoke with the middle-aged shopkeeper and was surprised to learn the town stayed open twenty-four hours a day, seven days a week. However, City Hall recently ordered a 2 A.M. curfew when some people were killed in a nightclub gunfight. The authorities clamped down hard, mostly on newcomers. She said petty crimes were few. Criminals were shot, no questions asked. Khmer Rouge soldiers have been known to empty a 30-round magazine in less than three seconds.

I found her stories hard to believe, but I felt safe enough from crooks and petty criminals.

Those who had killed for their communist ideology for over thirty years had now switched to extreme capitalism. Just across the street was a casino, an attached dancing bar, and shops with blinking neon lights that offered all sorts of massages. Khmer, Thai, and Vietnamese women were available for a small fee, Thai baht or U.S. dollars accepted.

Money was now king in Pailin. The provincial governor, Commander Eeh Chien, a hypocritical defender of the communist ideology, had seven mansions and villas. His private stash of gems and timber was reportedly worth millions of U.S. dollars. He was said to have fat bank accounts in foreign countries. Even the armed forces of the Royal Government of Cambodia feared him.

Had the Khmer Rouge changed? I doubted it. Their image was friendlier, yes, but changes in their ideology? Impossible!

I had a restless night. Neither the hard bed nor the jumbo mosquitoes bothered me. It was in a place and with a people who could become violent in a split second. I know what they are capable of, and they had guns.

A racket started outside. The morning was still dark but I had to see what made all that noise. I concealed my 8-mm video and 35-mm Pentax camera in my cotton *kroma* (scarf) and went outside.

Not too far away was a gigantic gem-mining operation. I had read in the papers that the Khmer Rouge had signed a concession for a few dozen Thai nationals to run a twenty-four-hour mining operation. Giant milling machines and hydro cannons blasted the earth and muddied the rivers.

A Thai worker told me the mine had stopped in the night, but the mechanical failure had been fixed early that morning. Three hundred and sixty-five days a year of this? I was appalled to see the remains of a hill that had mostly melted into the Sangke River, which ends in the Tonle Sap. I quickly shot some video footage and slides.

Cambodians live each day with little regard for the future, plundering natural and cultural resources, killing off forests, fish, and gathering gems for individual gain. Severe drought, floods, and failed crops are common. People go hungry again and again. Once self-sustaining and proud, Cambodia is now a "beggar state," as King Sihanouk often said, waiting for handouts from the international community.

On the way back to my room, I met a group of people of all ages walking with their gem-mining implements. I quietly took a picture and a short video clip of the group. Just in case they saw my camera, I pretended to be Thai.

"*Pai nai, khrap?*" I said in Thai, asking "where they were going." They smiled but kept on walking. A little boy replied in perfect Thai that he was "going to dig for gems." The woman with him, his mother perhaps, knocked him hard on the head.

I followed them just a little way to the mining site, next to the main boulevard of downtown Pailin, not very far from city hall. The little boy was rubbing his head. About a hundred people worked the small-scale mine.

Back at the hotel, I met my group, talking about what to do next. We ended up spending a good part of the morning openly filming the crowds digging for Pailin's famous rubies.

We split up after about 10 A.M. The three journalists decided to attempt a meeting with the Khmer Rouge leaders. That night the journalists told us they had arranged a meeting with Ieng Vuth, deputy governor of Pailin and son of former Khmer Rouge leader Ieng Sary. It was better than nothing.

The next morning, the desperate group urged me to serve as press corps translator-interpreter. I reluctantly agreed.

Sary's son was very upset when the press kept referring to him and his colleagues as Khmer Rouge. I was certain that he was going to shoot me, the translator.

"We are no longer Khmer Rouge. We are just ordinary Cambodians now," Ieng Vuth said several times during the interview. His glaring eyes showed his anger. I only saw evil and insincerity.

At the end of the interview, the deputy governor asked me: "Where did you study your English, brother?"

"Uh . . . in a foreign country, Your Excellency," I gave him a smile. According to his aide, Ieng Vuth wanted us to call him "His Excellency."

"You speak English very well, brother. Do you live in Phnom Penh?"

"Yes, in Phnom Penh, Your Excellency," I responded with a polite smile. I didn't trust him or any Khmer Rouge, former or present.

"We need people like you to help us improve our image a little, people who know the Western language well. We are Cambodians now and not Khmer Rouge anymore," he said yet again.

Not for a million bucks, killer, I thought. It was difficult to keep my anger hidden behind my smile. I couldn't wait to get out. Those twenty minutes were agony. The Khmer Rouge had killed my loved ones twenty-one years ago but it was only yesterday to me.

In an interview just before he died in April 1998, Khmer Rouge leader Saloth Sar, better known as Pol Pot, said: "My conscience is clear." Like his top lieutenants, he acquired the "Selective Amnesia Syndrome" and simply blamed the "Vietnamese, KGB, and CIA agents" for his atrocities against his own countrymen. Sadly, he and other Khmer Rouge are not alone. Many other Cambodians have the same syndrome and simply refuse to accept the fact that Khmer killed fellow Khmer—for whatever insane reasoning.

The United Nations continues to gather evidence after signing an agreement with the Royal Government of Cambodia to create a tribunal to try the Khmer Rouge leaders. Again, Chinese, former Soviet, and Khmer leaders protest this tribunal. It is good that the United States, Vietnam, and Thailand are seeking. These countries helped create the Khmer Rouge, after all.

China invokes national sovereignty to oppose the tribunal: "The Khmer Rouge issue is Cambodia's internal concern." China's military advisers, hardware, and funds helped the Khmer Rouge. Each minefield, each rotting mass grave, each maimed, limping Khmer is a curse on China. Cambodia's narcotics, human trafficking, child prostitution, AIDS, homeless and landless people were caused by direct and indirect Chinese intervention.

During the half-hour drive through a dusty but pothole-free road between Pailin and the Thai-Cambodian border, we heard a loud boom every now and then.

"Land mine," the driver said, bored.

The land in and around Pailin had to be the most mine-infested area in the world. From early 1979 to the end of 1996, this stretch to the border saw several battles between the Vietnamese invading army and the resistance, which included the Khmer Rouge and two other factions. The road itself became mine-free only in early 1997, after Ieng Sary supposedly defected to join the government.

By the roadside, damaged tanks and armored personnel carriers lay scattered along with chunks of metal wreckage. What was once majestic rain forest along the road was almost barren as far as the eye could see. The source was not war damage—it was progress in the name of capitalism.

At the border, we saw two live land mines on the roadside, a mere 5 feet from a drink shop. I was told not to go off the road; more land mines were around.

We went into a Khmer Rouge–owned casino just 300 feet from the border. For a remote jungle casino, security was very tight. No cameras of any kind were allowed. Hundreds of Thais and some Khmer gamblers were bused in. The betting currency was Thai baht, each wager worth between one and two thousand U.S. dollars, considerably more than I had seen in Las Vegas casinos.

Fancier casinos were being built, financed by a son of Theng Bun Ma, Cambodia's richest and most notorious businessman who was well connected to the ruling party. When a communist turns into a capitalist, he goes all the way to the moon.

I felt dirtied by my visit. I will not return to Pailin, not as long as the authors of death roam free.

I returned home to Oregon deeply and utterly disgusted by the fact that these criminals, the murderers of millions, including my own family, are still wandering throughout the country with full impunity. They have gotten away with murder.

No matter. Karma shall undo what has been done.

One cold morning in January 2001, back in the United States, Thavy woke up completely blind. "I can't see! I can't see anything!" she said. The diagnosis: multiple sclerosis. MS is a terrible autoimmune disease whereby your own immune system feeds on and attacks your body. The disease mechanism mirrored what the Khmer Rouge did to their own kind. MS represented an "auto genocide" feeding on itself. We were as shattered by this diagnosis as the Khmer Rouge had shattered our lives.

The slow return of Thavy's eyesight was another miracle for which we were immensely grateful. Her illness had changed our family's life. It affected not only her vision but also her mobility, and those around her. A lesser person would have given up, but my wife fiercely and bravely fought on.

So goes life's journey with its ups and downs, challenges really, that we all must overcome. It is not about how hard we fall or have fallen, but rather it's about how well we get up from such a fall that counts the most. We survived the Khmer Rouge and so we can very well survive any other curve ball thrown at us.

20

Lights

Siem Reap and Phnom Penh

One breezy morning late in 1994, Cousin Thie introduced me to the owner of a 2.4-acre plot of land near National Highway 6 and the Siem Reap international airport. The lot was about fifteen minutes away by slow motorcycle from my old home in Siem Reap.

It was a flooded area filled with wild grass and rice stock. In the center was a large hole 6 feet deep, where people had carted away soil to raise their houses from the flood.

"You can have it for two *chi* of gold," the farmer said.

"How much is that worth, Thie?" I asked my most trusted cousin.

"Oh, about 90 U.S. dollars."

"Sold. Here's $100," I said. Thus I became a landowner. The law says I can't be one. According to the new Cambodian Constitution, only a Khmer citizen with proper papers may own real estate. I didn't have such papers so Cousin Thie owned it for me.

In giving the farmer my hundred-dollar bill, I made real my trust in a stable and peaceful future for Cambodia.

Cousin Thie built a hut on my maturing property and lived there. He married a polite girl who lived just two doors down from my piece of land. "Nak Farm," as it is now known to the locals, has seen serious improvement over the years, transforming a once flooded rice paddy to a fully mature orchard.

Over these past years, I have spent time and money, pouring sweat into the land. It's filled up now, no longer flooded. The temporary fence cost me $300, three times the cost of the land. The deep hole is now a fishpond with waterlilies. Five years later, a more permanent fence and a fancy gate cost me $1,200.

Following a family tradition, I plant trees for my wife and children whenever I visit Cambodia, which I try to do at least yearly. The coconut, jackfruit, mango, and banana trees now grow all over the little farm.

Aside from trees, the little farm now has vegetables and chickens. Besides the $23,000 I have thus far invested to develop it, I also developed emotional ties. The property is now the envy of the neighborhood, and it is priceless as far as I am concerned. I don't intend to sell anytime soon. The farm is my personal pride and joy, a symbol of my return to Cambodia—even if it is only for brief visits now and then.

The Khmer belong to the land. By taking the land away, the Khmer Rouge and the next regimes had crushed us. But now, I have a piece of land that I call my own. I proudly and joyfully show and share this land with others.

There's more work to be done before it will become a bed-and-breakfast for tourists. I'll be spending my time on that land when it's cold in Oregon, six months a year.

In November 2001, Thavy and I and the kids entered Cambodia all together for the first time. The kids were now old enough to get in touch with their roots. When Thavy and Samantha were in Cambodia for those three months in 1993, my daughter was only aged three and remembered little as she grew, while Thavy was fearful and jumpy, so they didn't enjoy their visit very much. This twenty-one-day vacation promised to be a better trip.

On the day we arrived in Siem Reap, Derrick wanted to climb one of my favorite fruit trees.

"Can I climb the tree with Bawng? Please?" Derrick was referring to my little second cousin.

"I don't know," Thavy said. I, too, wasn't sure. We were a long way from hospitals or medical supplies.

"Let the boys climb the tree in peace. They'll be just fine. Don't worry," Cousin Thie said.

Like me, Samantha Rathanary and Derrick Monorom turned out to be natural tree-climbers. It's not easy to find a good tree to climb in America. If there is one, Thavy and I worry about falling, about broken limbs and medical expenses.

We watched our youngest kid climb the *ko kup* tree cautiously. His little cousin was way up, munching. Derrick soon joined him, enjoying the sweet fruits. I was reminded of myself when I was six. Then Samantha, eleven at that time, also went up the tree, and our nervousness doubled. She spoke better Khmer now, but Derrick only spoke English. However, my little cousin understood their hand signals well. Seeing that kids will be kids everywhere, Thavy and I began to relax.

Derrick said the tree-climbing episode was the highlight of the trip. He frequently complained about the heat—and this was midwinter in Cambodia— while the locals wore up to three layers of clothing. Yet, later he wanted to return to Cambodia again and "climb the many fruit trees."

Samantha's report on Cambodia, prepared to make up for the classes she missed, earned her an A. Besides learning to speak Khmer, she also enjoyed authentic Khmer dishes. She got to know more about the country, its beauty, its grinding poverty, its age-old culture, society, and her hundreds of new relatives.

"I never thought we'd have so many relatives!" she said many times. She wants to return, and that's a good sign.

In 2003, Thavy and I took a trip to Cambodia on our own. We plan to retire there one day when the kids are grown. We already built a large-two room suite right next door to my old Angkor High School, in my native Siem Reap, for that purpose. Thavy seems to feel better when we are back in the old country. I always feel whole and meaningful again when I am back in the old place. In the meantime, we will visit Cambodia as often as we can and help rebuild that country in any way we can.

In the 1998 U.N. development index, Cambodia ranked 140 out of 174 nations. One hundred ten infants died out of every 1,000 live births, and only a third of the nation had access to clean and safe drinking water. Most children were malnourished. A study by the UN-FAO says Cambodians get the lowest average calorie intake in Asia, 35 percent of the population is illiterate, and one in 240 is a land-mine victim. Cambodia has the highest HIV/AIDS infection rates in Southeast Asia due to a sex industry involving men, women, boys, and girls. Sex tourism is illegal, but unscrupulous officials have deep pockets to fill.

However, there are changes. The communist ideology took to capitalism and market economy like fish to water. Leaders found wealth more enjoyable than ideology, and there is a slow shift from dictatorship to plural democracy. Over three hundred local and international NGOs are in the kingdom, which is now a member of the U.N. and the ASEAN and wants to join the World Trade Organization to improve trade. The economy grows between 4 and 6 percent each year with aid, foreign investments, and tourism. Inflation remains low, in line with the gross national product.

The future looks a whole lot brighter. There's more political stability than before, and faction infighting is almost gone. They're busy making money instead of waging war. Peace has prevailed, for the most part. The former top Khmer Rouge leaders who are still alive are looking for ways to avoid prosecution, and the rest are in jail awaiting trial.

To build a solid, civil society will take much time, perseverance, hard work, and luck, but Cambodia will get there. The Khmer are a resilient people with a culture thousands of years old.

Prince Sihanouk became a king again. He later retired to focus on his poor health before giving the throne to his youngest son, Sihamoni. He made some seriously big mistakes in life, learned to live with them, and dealt with them all. I only hope he will admit his errors and do something about them soon before he moves on to another plane. History shall judge him accordingly, regardless.

The old Sangkum Reastr Niyum flag is back. The white Angkor Wat is in the center once again, just as I remember it, and we have come full circle now, after the new flags lasted only three regimes. I hope this is a sign of the regeneration of Cambodia's spirit and pride, unity and peace. Things always come full circle. It is the law of nature.

I hope to return to Resin Mountain someday. I imagine the mountain as still there, with people still tapping resin—if there are any trees left. I'm sure the son of that old man is still there, maybe in his sixties now. I hope he will read the Khmer version of this book and contact me. We were the four strangers crossing his path during that dark time in Cambodia's history. I'm sure he will remember his father giving the four of us that lighter, essential for keeping us warm at night, if not saving our lives. He'll remember his father teaching us the chanting verses, the verses designed to protect us as we traveled through the valley of the dead and the deep jungle of northern Cambodia.

Kok Poh is still a small hamlet in the countryside. Aunt Thet is in her late seventies now, still looking tough, always looking for ways to make money. She has not found success, but she never quits, either. Something I learned from her.

National Highway 6 has lost its blacktop, in many parts, and is being rebuilt into a superhighway to link Southeast Asia with China to the north. The road still disappears when it rains. It used to be that after the rains, people dumped soil to cover the huge potholes. And yet the road is still there and still being used as of April 2009, the last time I traveled to drop off this book, in the Khmer language, to many of those described in this book—including Aunt Samon of Kok Poh.

My old school, Sala Komrou, is gone. The land is now someone's private property. Bicycles are still a major mode of transport, particularly in the countryside. The site of the refugee camp in Aranyaprathet is now a huge market for imported goods to and from Thailand.

I returned to Krobey Riel under Brother Som's guidance. Brother Som is now living in Siem Reap with his wife and three grown kids. I asked him to be my guide. He was the only one who was familiar with the places I walked through as a boy from the place of my near death to his home in Krobey Riel.

On separate motorbikes, we backtracked, retracing my route that night but in reverse, all the way to the killing spot. The haystack hideout still stood in Dorn Swar. The big canal in Keo Poeur was smaller than I remember, about 60 feet wide, maybe 15 to 30 feet deep, sloping inward to the bottom.

It was an easy journey, physically. The distance that I walked all day and all night as a little boy back then was now completed in an hour. Emotionally, it was something else. I only realized Brother Som was just as tense as I was when we separated where the track diverged. He was panicking when we met again. He felt that he was my protector, and he did not want to lose me again.

Tonle Sap is now a UNESCO-designated biosphere reserve, a wildlife sanctuary booming with ecotourism. Silting is still a concern. The government is doing something to stop people from cutting down too much firewood too fast in Prey Roniem, the unique flooded forest. Its ecosystem includes fish and wildlife, still one of the richest in the region. But this grand lake is dying a slow death as I write this chapter.

I still watch tapes of those old UPI interviews of me, and find things I didn't notice before. Sometimes I watch them with Derrick and Samantha.

Meanwhile, in the comfortable routine of life in America, the screams and terror dim and slowly fade away. I've become more complacent, but little things annoy me. Like most Americans, I complain, expect what is due me and want more. And then some. There's never enough. Every now and then, when I least expect it, the terror returns. I use it to give myself a kick in the butt, back to awareness of my purpose in life.

For every bad Cambodian, there are tens of thousands of decent people working to improve their homes and communities. Decency and kindness live on. This is one light I found in my journey.

My journey has been long and difficult. I too needed much time, perseverance, and luck. When I escaped the death squad, a strong desire for killing and revenge kept me going, but I was a puppet driven by a past. I had made no decisions about my life.

Today I see things in a clearer light. The dead don't call for more blood. The bloodshed should end, they would tell me, and I should end it. I'm still angry. I still hurt, but I accept that a very terrible, awful thing happened to me. I have tried to move on beyond revenge. This is another light I found.

I can't forget, but I've learned to forgive. First I forgave myself. For what I have done, for the terrible things I was forced to do, I forgave myself.

Second, I forgave the Khmer Rouge, its rank and file, those who hurt me most. I can't kill them all, but I can forgive them all. They are my own people. In killing them, I kill myself.

Third, I have learned to use my anger and hatred to rebuild, to regenerate, and to share my light with people I meet in America and in Cambodia. I try to help end violence, hatred, and grudges. This is also a light I found in my journey.

Today, I see the variety of choices I have and I try to make wiser decisions. It is my family and not revenge that keeps me going now. The warm light of knowing keeps me alive and well.

These are some of the lights in my very dark journey. Someone once said: "Life is a journey, not a destination." I expect more ups and downs, challenges and rewards. I have seen the worst, so the journey must be downhill now. I will enjoy this ride with my lights guiding the way.

My past fuels my journey, which will only end with my last breath. My present is a continuing struggle to maintain humility and focus on my lights. My future is unclear so I live in each moment. My past, present, and future intertwine in everything I do. My motto is: Consider the past, present, and future, always!

Those who hear my story usually find it difficult to accept.

"How could this be possible?" says one.

"I had no idea what you and your people went through in Cambodia," says another.

"Now you know," I say.

Hope is my guiding light. It has shown me the way, even during my darkest hour. It guided me through turbulence, ups and downs. Without hope there is no journey. Without a journey there is no life.

Hope will always be within me. I am certain there is a light within you as well. To see your light in your own journey, you only have to reach deep within.

And the journey shall continue. . . .

Epilogue

Our life's journey never ends. It is like a rushing stream fed by the annual monsoon water or the melting water from the great glaciers. Even during the driest of seasons, the stream continues to run. Only when we die does our life's journey come to an end.

We can choose to enjoy the journey by overcoming all obstacles, adversities, challenges, and tragedies in our own way, or we can fall flat on our faces. For it is not how hard we fell but rather how well we got up that counts the most. If you are still breathing, then it is crystal clear that you have a choice. Hopefully, you'll make the right one and move on with your life, regardless of life's circumstances.

My own guiding light took me back to Cambodia, home to memories I had actively and foolishly evaded for years. It was 1992. A U.N.-sponsored democratic election was scheduled for the following year, and I signed up with a USAID-funded nongovernmental organization (NGO), which was working to ensure a free and fair election process. The trip would be the first of many regular voyages to do volunteer work, to heal, and also to reconcile with my past. During my year-long stay in 1993–94, while I did my part to help rebuild Cambodia to its best potential, I witnessed history unfold before my eyes. I once again became a part of Cambodia, just as Cambodia has always been a part of me.

But Cambodia today is not the place I knew as a child, no matter how hard I look. As I said when I first stepped out of Pochentong International Airport in 1992, "It is a very sad world out here!" Even National Highway 6, the familiar road by my hometown, reflected the country's instability through its new ruts, and depressions, and monstrous potholes. My old Cambodia, like my family, has long been dead. Gone! A new one has risen in its place, this much I realize.

I can no longer afford to live in the past, but I can well dream about it, gain strength by it, and look to build a better future. I can make a difference in

Cambodia, and in this world, no matter how tiny. For a "good person" always looks to draw a "small circle" around him and his family. A "better person" always looks to draw a "larger circle" around him that includes his family, his friends, and his community. A "great person," however, always looks to draw a "great big circle" around him that includes his family, his friends, his community, his nation, and his world. I intend to do my very best and I have made an honest effort. I will always consider the past, the present, and the future in everything I do.

Pol Pot, the head of Angkar (the organization also known as the Khmer Rouge), died in April 1998. "My conscience is clear," Pol Pot said in an interview before his death. Like many other senior Khmer Rouge leaders, Pol Pot, also known as Saloth Sar, refused to take blame for his evil work. He and many other Khmer Rouge leaders like him blamed the death of millions, including this survivor's family, on others—namely "Vietnamese, KGB, and CIA agents." He honestly believed what he did was for the good of Cambodia!

Sadly, they are not alone in this "blaming game." Many others refuse to take responsibility for what happened in Cambodia. Worse yet, some do not believe that this genocide, one of the worst in modern time, ever happened in the first place. "It's propaganda," these individuals say. People are easily blinded by ignorance. More reason for mass education by those who managed to survive genocide.

There was not a scintilla of remorse by the mass murderers of millions. Many of Pol Pot's top henchmen and women, his top lieutenants, are now dead. The few who are still alive are sick, aging, or infirm. Yet they are still very much defiant. They still blame others for the blood, including the blood of my loved ones that stained their evil hands. They take no responsibility for their atrocities and crimes against the Khmer people (their own people) and against humanity. These people have no morality or conscience, absolutely nothing. They feel no remorse and feel no shame for what they have done, individually or collectively. They have no right to exist among humankind. They should not be allowed to share our civil society, ever again! These devils don't deserve to live and walk among us. And yet, most of them still walk freely, still taunt and torment those of us who managed to survive.

The Khmer Rouge as a revolutionary organization and a fighting force ceased to exist after the death of their arch leader, Pol Pot. Their rank-and-file has defected to the Royal Government of Cambodia by the thousands. Their top leaders, those who are still alive, if not well, are looking for ways to save their skins. They are attempting to get away with genocide. Ironically, some of the former leaders are now back in power with the Royal Government of Cambodia, headed by former Khmer Rouge cadre and longtime prime minister Mr. Hun Sen. Will the Khmer people find justice for their dead? I have my doubts, but I am also hopeful at the same time. For hope is all that I have got.

The world community must not be silent about crimes against humanity any longer. How can we live with ourselves if we do? We can no longer afford to be the so-called indifferent bystanders. We can no longer afford to look away and pretend not to see or care. We must not allow history to repeat itself. Never again! Cambodia and her people have suffered enough from our individual and collective silence. Let's not allow this to continue on or allow it to happen to other people and in other places.

The wheel of justice for the Khmer people moves slowly, very slowly, simply because of ongoing geopolitical drama and involvement by foreign powers. The United States, China, the former Soviet Union, Thailand, Vietnam, and others must bear some responsibility for the brutalities and atrocities committed in Cambodia. These foreign powers played a key role in creating and keeping alive the monster that we now call the Khmer Rouge, among the most notorious regimes known in modern times.

The day of reckoning is finally here.

As of this writing, March 2010, the Royal Government of Cambodia (RGC) and the United Nations (U.N.) have signed an agreement and secured most of the funding needed for a tribunal of the surviving top Khmer Rouge leadership. With the full support of the United States and many other nations—with the exception of communist China—the United Nations and the RGC have begun to gather evidence for prosecution of those senior leaders within the Khmer Rouge regime deemed "most responsible."

With the help of the dedicated Documentation Center of Cambodia (DC CAM) staff and investigators, including Youk Chhange, DC CAM director and a personal hero of mine, who provided much of the evidence against the Khmer Rouge regime, the United Nations and the RGC have set up the Extraordinary Chambers in the Courts of Cambodia (ECCC), a unique hybrid court in Phnom Penh for a tribunal against those who led the Khmer Rouge during the period of 1975–79.

The ECCC has at long last arrested, detained, and put on trial five of the top Khmer Rouge leaders. These key planners and policymakers, the architects of the Khmer Rouge genocidal regime, are being charged with war crimes and crimes against humanity. And they are all being treated very well under ECCC's watch. Indeed, even a slimeball criminal deserves his or her day in a civilized court of law with their basic human rights respected—contrary to the Khmer Rouge belief and attitude.

And I am happy to report this fact directly from my private and guided tours of the ECCC courtroom chambers, prison cells, defense and prosecutor offices, medical facilities, and even the kitchen facilities where daily feasts are meticulously prepared for these high-value prisoners and former high-ranking Khmer Rouge cadres. I was allowed nearly unimpeded access into ECCC premises in April 2007 and practically handed the prisoners a Khmer version of this very same book. I had heard that they were "bored almost to death" in their respective prison cells and I thought that a good read would surely help reduce the boredom and possibly a premature death. No one wants the former KR cadres to drop dead before their time is up—certainly not before the tribunal conclusion.

As of March 16, 2010, the five top Khmer Rouge leaders being held by ECCC for the tribunal include the following:

1. Khieu Samphan, former Khmer Rouge head of state and the public face of the Khmer Rouge regime. He has a doctorate of economics from Paris, France, and he acted as the architect of a failed economic policy under the Khmer Rouge regime, which led to severe starvation.
2. Noun Chea, former Khmer Rouge chief political ideologue known as "Brother Number Two"—the man next to Pol Pot and the person most responsible for the Khmer Rouge regime's political and policy development. A former Buddhist monk, his policy initiated the destruction of most temples, eliminated all religious activities, and oversaw the murder of many Buddhist monks and laymen.
3. Ieng Sary, the former Khmer Rouge foreign minister responsible for many deaths at Bung Trobek concentration camp, where thousands of intellectuals and diplomats were lured back to Phnom Penh under false pretenses.
4. Ieng Thirith, former Khmer Rouge social affairs minister, whose policies directly and negatively affected millions of lives on a daily basis; she is the wife of Ieng Sary and the sister-in-law of Pol Pot. Some even referred to her as the "Queen of Terrors."
5. Khaing Khek Ieu, also known as Duch, former Khmer Rouge security chief of the Tuol Sleng prison (also known as S-21), where an estimated 16,000 lives, both young and old, were snuffed out under his direction. Duch is the most infamous Khmer Rouge executioner, a very proficient professional.

The ECCC, after many moons of court proceedings and controversies, has at long last put Duch on trial. He is the first ever senior Khmer Rouge official to sit in the docket and answer for crimes committed on behalf of the Khmer Rouge regime. To date, Duch has confessed to many of the charges for crimes committed as director of the Khmer Rouge's most notorious prison, S-21.

Comrade Duch was found guilty by the ECCC court and sentenced to a very lenient forty-year prison term since Cambodia does not have the death penalty. This sentence is not justice for humanity, but a bargain for a serial killer, no, a mass murderer. The fact that Duch practically got off with such a light sentence points directly toward his willingness to accept his role and responsibility under the Democratic Kampuchea regime. Hey, he is a "converted Christian," after all, and his preacher told him that Jesus Christ had already forgiven him for all his earthly sins, including crimes against humanity (and at least eight known foreign/white Christians he ordered killed). His testimony against his former bosses will no doubt be part of the deal.

Sadly, there are still hundreds more professional executioners like Duch out there, still walking free and with impunity. Ironically, these executioners live among many of their former victims throughout Cambodia, those who survived the Khmer Rouge's madness.

The trial comes some thirty years late, but for the sake of justice, it is better late than never. As a victim and a survivor of this terrible regime and its evil leadership, I strongly believe that this process will be expensive, slow, long, difficult, emotional, and painful. And yet, I also believe that the ECCC exercise will be worth every dollar, every minute of the years-long process, for ECCC is the last, best hope for many Khmer, both dead and alive. If we refuse to look into our past and learn from it, we are already doomed, for we "human animals" are very capable of self-destruction and repeating the same mistake.

Whether the verdict at the ECCC is guilty or not guilty is irrelevant. I have already moved beyond the killing fields and the Khmer Rouge regime. Regardless, I have already forgiven these bastards, simply a bunch of sick and pathetic old men and women, really. ECCC is simply a symbol of justice, an exercise. For justice delayed is justice denied, and symbolism is better than nothing at all.

My life, my survival, and my being on this earth are not without purpose. I survived to tell the world what happened to my beloved family, my people, my country, and me. I have done that in the past, present, and shall continue to do so in the future. I cannot rest until all those responsible answer for their crimes against humanity. The architects of this genocide must be held accountable, with absolutely no exception. My life is for such a purpose. Justice must be served. Until then, the Khmer people, both dead and alive, can never rest in peace.

I escaped from Cambodia, my own beloved country, to preserve my life so that I could seek revenge against the Khmer Rouge. I left it far, far behind—not by choice, but by necessity. As Dorothy said in *The Wizard of Oz*, "There's no place like home, there's no place like home." My home was in Cambodia and so I also say, "There's no place like Cambodia, there's no place like Cambodia." Cambodia is my home. My physical body may be far away from my beloved Cambodia, but my soul and spirit have always been with my Cambodia.

Much like Dorothy in the Land of Oz, I went through life's wonderful and often frightful journey. I made the most out of my life in my own Land of Oz. Unlike Dorothy, I could never really go home again—at least not to the one I remembered. Since my first journey back in 1992, I manage to return annually to the "old stream," much like the Pacific steelhead salmon does every year. I return to regenerate, rebuild, and heal my past emotional trauma and calm my spirit.

My "journey into light" has been long and often very difficult and challeng-ing. Like that of Cambodia's once proud National Highway 6, the road I travel on has been full of many deep and often monstrous potholes. There was, as they say, little smooth-sailing weather during my journey. However, my journey is only a beginning as "life is a journey, not a destination." A great journey has its ups and downs. I intend to tackle life's great challenges and rewards, as they may come, one day at a time. I have already seen the worst of life under Angkar reign. Come what may, life can only get better, I truly believe.

I am always most hopeful because without hope, there is no journey. And without life's challenging and rewarding journey, there would be no life.

The journey shall continue, regardless.

Afterword

The Healing and Reconciling Process

DANIEL SAVIN, M.D.

It has been my good fortune to have worked with the Cambodian community since 1991, when I accepted my first job after training in psychiatry. My first position, as a volunteer psychiatrist at the Site II camp on the Thai-Cambodian border, opened my eyes to the plight of the Cambodian community. Though sometimes disturbing and stressful, this work taught me a lot about how people can survive, raise families, help others, and sometimes even thrive against all odds. During my time at Site II, I made some good friends among the refugees, some of whom I stay in touch with to this day.

Massive trauma, such as that experienced by the Cambodian community, can fracture an entire society as well as individuals. During the Khmer Rouge time, neighbors were rewarded for informing on neighbors, friends for informing on friends, and children for informing on parents. Trust was sometimes lost between members of the same communities and families. The feeling of safety within the community was damaged—by war, other human rights violations, and forced migration. But today we see signs, in this book as in other accounts of that time, that the Cambodian community is in the process of repair. How is this repair happening?

One necessary prerequisite for the restoration of trust and safety is a safe environment. A safe environment was not available for many Cambodians during the years following the Khmer Rouge regime. Cambodia itself was engaged in civil war until 1998, while the Cambodian Diaspora in the West struggled to cope with their memories and losses as they were building their new lives. The active presence of the Khmer Rouge during the civil war delayed healing in Cambodian society. After the death of Pol Pot in 1998, I saw a marked difference in Cambodian patients here in the United States as they began to feel safer talking more freely and openly about their bitter experiences during the Khmer Rouge years.

Still, even now, many former Khmer Rouge leaders live freely, with no requirement to reflect on their actions. Only when the past is fully examined, when leaders who commit atrocities are held responsible, can society begin to move forward with some assurance that the government and international community will not let such atrocities happen again. The U.N.-sponsored Khmer Rouge tribunal gives us a chance to move things forward.

Perhaps the journey of the Cambodian community will mirror that of the post–World War II Jewish experience. For several years after that genocide, Jewish survivors were not yet ready to tell their stories, and the community was not yet ready to listen. This attitude changed in 1961, during the trial in Israel of Adolf Eichmann, a man instrumental in the deportation of millions of Jews to their deaths. The trial caused a breakthrough, changing the attitude of Jewish society toward the Holocaust and toward Holocaust survivors. Jews became much more interested in learning what happened during that time, and survivors became more willing to tell their stories. The current trial of former Khmer Rouge leaders may have a similar effect in Cambodia.

Once in a safe environment, people find many ways to overcome their traumatic past so they can thrive again. Religious faith, traditional healers, positive family and social relationships, pleasurable activities, and Western mental health care all have their place. One thing that is common to all of these treatments is that people are helping people. In fact, what seems to me to be the most important part of healing is when individuals have positive relationships with others, either by helping or in being helped.

Ronnie Yimsut's story demonstrates this trend. Experiencing painful memories, Ronnie Yimsut decides to travel back to the source of his dreams and nightmares both, to assist with the historic 1993 elections in his homeland, Cambodia. He sacrifices time with his new family to aid the United Nations and Cambodia in their joint democratic effort. This shift of energy into helping others brings healing to Yimsut, just as it has done and will do for Cambodians everywhere. Through his volunteer efforts, Ronnie Yimsut found inner peace and reconciled his past in a way that no court of law and certainly no killing of the Khmer Rouge in revenge could ever do.

NOTES

CHAPTER 1   CHILDHOOD IDYLL

1. Like other children in town, I became virtually blind at night. The lack of sight was probably due to a vitamin A deficiency.
2. The Khmer word for "servant" is *kgnum*, which is also translated as "slave."
3. The five tower-shrines of Angkor Wat were believed to represent the five peaks of Mount Meru, the home of the gods and the center of the Hindu universe.

CHAPTER 2   BAMBOO IN THE WIND

1. During my high school and college days in America, I spoke to my teachers only when I had to.

CHAPTER 3   AN UNCIVIL WAR

1. The shells probably came from a 50-mm Vulcan cannon mounted on the famed "Puff, the Magic Dragon," a modified C-130 gunship.

CHAPTER 4   SHOCKS AND SURPRISES

1. The southeastern accent was known to come from Khmer Kampuchea Krom, an area in southern Vietnam where many Khmer lived. *Krom* means "low."
2. We would never see our house by the forest again. Later, a cluster of bombs from an American F-4 Phantom fighter-bomber destroyed it. Our neighbor Mak Ah Chhay was a little luckier; two sections of her house's concrete walls were left standing.

CHAPTER 5   A TIME OF PLENTY

1. Throughout the war, Cousin Khen was a voice of hope, bringing us traditional and contemporary Cambodian music as well as world news in Khmer from the Voice of America (VOA) in Washington, D.C.
2. Much later, the Khmer Rouge killed Uncle Khiev and his entire family except three: Ang Khen, who was in America, and Cousins Norica and Rasmi, who escaped on the last plane out of Cambodia. Only cousins Khen and Norica have returned to Cambodia. There's too much emotional pain to overcome in going there.
3. Lon Nol later died of a heart attack in the $4 million home in Hawaii that he shared with his wife and children. No doubt his family still has access to several bank accounts.

CHAPTER 6   AN ERA IS ENDED

1. Some Mith Chass later became powerful masters of the Mith Thmey, those who lived in the government-controlled areas.

CHAPTER 8   A GREAT LEAP BACKWARD

1. Much later, thousands of bodies were found in open mass graves a few miles from the processing centers.

CHAPTER 9   THE DEATH OF DOGS

1. Some of the Khmer Rouge who escaped Pol Pot's purge by crossing Vietnam's borders are now state leaders in Cambodia: Hun Sen, Chea Sim, and Heng Samrin, to name a few.

CHAPTER 10   MIRACLE AT THE TEMPLE

1. In 1999, I found this Angkar Leu cadre on a farm in Tapang, where he lives to this day.
2. My family had indeed been in Kralahn.

CHAPTER 11   DEAD WEIGHT

1. After childbirth, Khmer women traditionally take one to four weeks of bed rest over a fire. The smoke is believed to strengthen the new mother.
2. Later study of my injuries revealed that I'd been struck at least fifteen times.

CHAPTER 12   KILL OR BE KILLED

1. I still experience these severe headaches today.
2. Dorn Swar (a village name) is translated as "Grandma Monkey." Today this village is known as Prey Veng (Long Forest).
3. When I returned to Krobey Riel fourteen years later, Brother Som was shocked and very pleased to find out how wrong he was in thinking I would not make it.
4. Many years later in America, I'd be reminded of Caveman Club whenever I saw people swinging a baseball bat.
5. The Chinese deserve much credit for every single RPG fired and land mine exploded. Without Chinese support, my people would still be alive and I would never have killed my fellowmen for my own survival.
6. I continue to look for news of Wang's survival today.

CHAPTER 13   BAREFOOT ESCAPE

1. I believe in the potency of these verses. I still remember the chant today and I recite it in times of crisis.
2. So far, I've kept my promise to be good. As for becoming a monk, I'll consider that later.
3. Angkar killed anyone who spoke foreign languages.

CHAPTER 14   ALIEN WORLDS

1. I met Brian Ellis again ten years later. We remain dear friends to this day. I still have his business card.

2. Bob Fonda and Philippe Poulin are still friends.

CHAPTER 15   URBAN JUNGLE

1. Nek Chun would repeat this comment some twenty years later when I was an adult. I never learned my lesson in manners well, but I never forgot his comments.

2. I developed a blend of the Chens' spending habits, a balance of conscious frugality while buying only the best.

3. I still have my Cambodian accent now.

4. Post-Traumatic Stress Disorder (PTSD) was identified much later, so I dealt with my depression alone.

5. Today, the stickers are probably still in the Chens' basement room. They're hard to remove.

6. Perhaps Nek Chun wanted me to be tough like him. Perhaps he meant the best for me, but I was just too sensitive. I came to this realization fourteen years later when I was writing this book.

7. No one heard from Uncle Mao or Aunt Chea again until almost a decade later. Miraculously, they were still together and had gone on to adopt two orphans, who also ended up leaving them with hard feelings.

8. I still tell Thavy that she snatched me because of that cleaver, but she denies it.

CHAPTER 16   BACK TO THE PAST

1. Airport officials didn't dare extort money from foreign travelers, particularly Caucasians. They knew Khmer returnees would rather give in than fight a losing battle, so they got away with it. Later my relatives reminded me I could have gotten into deep trouble with these people by being so assertive.

2. In Phnom Penh's traffic hierarchy, a bicycle rider is next to the lowest on the chain, the pedestrian the lowest. The top dogs are the monstrous, old trucks that can and do get away with murder.

3. The tradition of eating dogs began under the Khmer Rouge regime. Today very few Khmer eat dogs.

4. The following year, I helped fund a well-digging project for their village.

5. A few years later, when I bought a piece of land, I asked Phan if he would be willing to take care of it. He and his family moved to my farm, and I sent them money and gifts and helped them out in other ways. After caring for our farm for four years, Phan decided to move to the Thai border and farm specialized crops.

CHAPTER 18   TURNING POINT

1. Fahrid never ceased to amaze me. He kept me sharp and focused with challenges. I wish him all the best, from one brother to another.

GLOSSARY

Khmer (Cambodian) terms unless otherwise specified

Ah: Little; can also mean contemptible

Ah khaoan: Little child (respectful title)

Ah la-eth: Puny one (disrespectful title)

Angkar: The ruling body of the Khmer Rouge; literally translated as "organization"

Angkar Leu: Higher rulers within the Khmer Rouge; literally translated as "high organization"

Angkar Youth Corps: Source of Angkar's spies; *see also* chhlob

Angkor: Site of Angkor Wat derived from the Sanskrit *nagara*, or "sacred city"

Apsara: Celestial maiden

"Assak kombang batt": "May I be invincible from my enemy"

B-40 RPGs: Rocket-propelled grenades widely available during and after the civil war

baht: Thai currency denomination; 2011 conversion rate is 32 bahts to 1 U.S. dollar

"Baht, tean": "Yes, sir" (spoken by males)

barang: Foreigners; originally meant Frenchmen (Thai: *farang* or *farangset*)

baray: Man-made body of water

baw-baw: Rice porridge

Bawng: Elder; for example, elder brother (*bawng pross*) or elder sister (*bawng srei*)

cadre: Communist political or military leader, rank, or file; also "comrade"

"Cha": "Yes" (spoken by females); *see also* "Baht, tean"

chau prey: Forest bandits; Khmer Rouge name for those in hiding

chhlob: Angkar's network of spies; can also refer to a single spy

chi: Gold measurement

chrach: Common water plant found in rice paddies

chun phearse khlourn: Refugee

"Dam doeum kor": "Plant a kapok tree," meaning "speak no evil."

Democratic Kampuchea: National name self-assigned by the Khmer Rouge

Devaraja: Angel in Sanskrit terminology

dipterocarp: One of twenty-two commercial lumber species in Cambodia; also known as *yieng*

Garuda: Large mythical birdlike creature that appears in both Hindu and Buddhist mythology

"Jumreap soeur": Formal Khmer greeting phrase reserved for addressing elders or higher classes

Kamaphibarl: High-ranking Khmer Rouge leader

kgnum: Servant or slave; also means "I"

khaoan: Child

khmang: Enemy; *see also* satrov

Khmen opah-youp: Khmer prisoner (Thai)

Khmer: Cambodian

Khmer American: Cambodian American or "Khmerican" (slang Khmer term)

Khmer Kampuchea Krom: Cambodian land annexed by Vietnam, and its native people

Khmer Krahom: Khmer Rouge; literally translated as "red Cambodians"

Khmer Leu (Surin): Cambodian land annexed by Thailand, and its native people

Khmer Rouge: Name coined by Prince Sihanouk for Cambodian communists (French)

Khmer Serei: Khmer freedom fighters based along the porous Thai border

"Kin mai": "Eat or not?" (Thai)

kmouy: Nephew or niece; gender-neutral term

kokoss: Hardwood tree highly prized for furniture making; also produces edible nuts

ko kup: Tropical fruit tree that produces delicately sweet fruit

"Kon euy kheng tuv": "Go to sleep, my child"; a motherly lullaby

Kong Top Pakdevat: The army led by the Khmer Rouge; literally translated as "Revolution Army"; *see also* Kong Top Romdoss

Kong Top Romdoss: The army led by the Khmer Rouge; literally translated as "Liberation Army"; *see also* Kong Top Pakdevat

krobey: Water buffalo

krom: A labor group of ten persons or fewer

kroma: Checkered cotton towel or long silk or cotton scarf; worn by Khmer Rouge

kru: Shaman; *see also* Lauk Kru

La-eth: Puny one

Lauk: Mister or sir

L'Bawng: *See* Lauk Bawng

Lauk Bawng (L'Bawng): Title reserved for a former Buddhist monk; literally translated as "Honorable Brother"

Lauk Kru: Respected teacher or master

Lauk Sastrajah: Professor, teacher, or master at higher level

"Leuk Dai Twaiy Preeah": "Lord Buddha is praised"

Mae: "Mother"; honorific used in the country

Mao Zedong: First chairman of the Communist Party of China highly regarded by Khmer Rouge cadres and soldiers, who often wore his style of cap

Ming: Aunt

Mith: Comrade

Mith Chass: "Old Comrade" (old people) who lived in Khmer Rouge–controlled areas when major cities were evacuated

Mith Thmey: "New Comrade" (new people) who lived in government-controlled areas when major cities were evacuated

moan: Hen

Mobile Brigade: A large labor group tasked with immense engineering projects, such as water reservoirs

m'they: Kindergarten

mui-Thai: Thai kick-boxing style, deeply rooted in the Khmer "Bokator" fighting style (Thai)

Nek: Respected in-law

Neyuk Rothmentrey Tie Muy: First Prime Minister (Cambodia had two at the same time, historic)

North Vietnamese Army (NVA): Communist army from North Vietnam led by Ho Chi Minh

Oan: Little one

oh bor: Fast boat with outboard motor

Oum: Older uncle or aunt

Pa: Father

"Pai": "Go" (Thai)

"Pai nai, khrap": "Where are you going?" (Thai)

Pa Vier: The children's father

phkak: Razor-sharp long knife; a traditional form of work or battle blade

pla thu: A low-grade version of mackerel fish (Thai)

Pou: Younger uncle

prahok: Fermented fish paste widely used in Khmer cooking as a flavor agent

prahok tek kreung: Fish paste slowly stirred with ground pork, bacon fat, tamarind, and herbs

Preah: Lord Buddha

Pret: Devil

pross: Male

riel: Cambodian currency

rieng: Mangrove tree that grows in flooded forests

romork: Siem Reap rickshaw, traditionally pedaled by local drivers

Sah-teeahronahtroth: Republic, as in "Khmer Republic"

sala: Roofed rest stop along the roadside, complete with a jar of water

Samdech: Honorific title similar to "sir"

Samlagne: Loved one

sampass: Khmer bow greeting, also used for begging

sangkom: Skinny

Sangkram: New Year

Sangkum Reastr Niyum: "Society Favored by the People"; a party founded by King Sihanouk

satrov: Enemy; *see also* khmang

"Sawady, Khun": "Greetings, sir or ma'am" (Thai)

smeth: Wild rice

"Soursdey": "Good day" or "Hi"; an informal greeting

Spean Thmor: Concrete bridge; serves as Siem Reap landmark

srei: Female

Srok Khmer: Cambodia; literally translated as "country of Cambodians."

Srok Siam: Thailand; literally translated as "country of Thais."

srov vear: A unique, quick-growing native rice variety (can grow a foot a day)

Surin (Khmer Leu): One of many former Khmer provinces annexed by Thailand

Tah: Grandfather

Tean: Sir

teuk: Water

teuk kroluk: Fruit shake

teuk tnout chu: Favorite local drink made of fermented sugar palm juice

Thai Daeng: Red Thai; Thai communists

trakourn: Morning glory, blackened water spinach

tro: A two-string Cambodian banjo made of coconut shells and wood

unkogne: Inedible large nut used for medicinal purposes and a traditional New Year game

viel smeth: Wild rice field

Vietcong: Communist guerrilla group in Vietnam that fought against South Vietnamese and U.S. soldiers

wat: Temple

Yeay: Grandmother

Youn: Vietnamese people and language

INDEX

Page numbers in *italics* refer to figures.

ABOUT THE AUTHOR

Born and reared near the famous Siem Reap "Angkor World Heritage Site," Ronnie Yimsut fled Cambodia after witnessing the massacre of nearly his entire family under the Khmer Rouge regime. He is a genocide survivor and an orphan, having become a "political" refugee at the age of fifteen. As a proud American of Khmer heritage today, he is a senior landscape architect for the USDA Forest Service and an activist involved in various national and international NGOs dealing with social and environmental justice issues, through which he has been working on the monumental Bakong Technical College (www.bakongtech-college.org) in his native Siem Reap.

Yimsut has been the subject of independent documentary films and news reports by *CBS News*, *NBC News*, *National Geographic Explorer*, PBS, Europe ARNTE TV, and others. His writing credits include *Journey to Freedom* (Documentation Center of Cambodia, 2006); *In the Shadow of Angkor* (*Manoa Journal*, University of Hawai'i Press, 2004); "Life Is a Poem" (earned an award from the Poetry Society of America, 2004); and "Tonle Sap Lake Massacre," in *Children of Cambodia's Killing Fields* (Yale University Press, 1997). In 2009 the *Milwaukee Business Journal* recognized Ronnie as one of "Milwaukee Area's Most Influential People."

David Chandler, Ph.D., is a professor emeritus of history at Monash University in Australia.

Daniel Savin, M.D., is an associate professor of psychiatry at the University of Colorado School of Medicine.

CPSIA information can be obtained at www.ICGtesting.com
Printed in the USA
BVOW030423070912

299692BV00001B/7/P